Rethinking Occupied Ireland

Irish Studies

James MacKillop, *Series Editor*

Rethinking Occupied Ireland

Gender and Incarceration
in Contemporary Irish Film

Jessica Scarlata

SYRACUSE UNIVERSITY PRESS

Lines from "Unfinished Revolution" by songwriter Peter Cadle are reprinted with permission.

∞ The paper used in this publication meets the minimum requirements
of the American National Standard for Information Sciences—Permanence
of Paper for Printed Library Materials, ANSI Z39.48-1992.

For a listing of books published and distributed by Syracuse University Press,
visit our website at www.SyracuseUniversityPress.syr.edu.

ISBN: 978-0-8156-3332-7 (cloth)   978-0-8156-5241-0 (e-book)

Library of Congress Cataloging-in-Publication Data

Scarlata, Jessica.
   Rethinking occupied Ireland : gender and incarceration in contemporary Irish film /
Jessica Scarlata. — First edition.
      pages cm. — (Irish studies)
   Includes bibliographical references and index.
   ISBN 978-0-8156-3332-7 (cloth : alk. paper) — ISBN 978-0-8156-5241-0 (e-book)
1. Motion pictures—Ireland.   2. Sex role in motion pictures.   3. Imprisonment in
motion pictures.   I. Title.
   PN1993.5.I85S33 2014
   791.4309415—dc23   2013043381

Manufactured in the United States of America

For my amazing parents, Betty and Richard,
with all my love and gratitude.

Jessica Scarlata is associate professor of Film and Media Studies in the Department of English at George Mason University. Her articles on Irish and Indian diasporic cinema have appeared in *Literature and Film: A Guide to the Theory and Practice of Film Adaptation* (2005) and the journal *South Asian Popular Culture* (2013). Her research addresses questions of exclusion, belonging, and national security as imagined in visual culture.

Contents

Illustrations

Acknowledgments

OVER THE COURSE OF WORKING ON THIS BOOK, I have been lucky enough to encounter many people who have freely given their support as friends, family, colleagues, and scholars. Without such generosity, this project would not have been possible. It has been a privilege to work with the outstanding people at Syracuse University Press. I am especially grateful to Irish series editor James MacKillop for his faith in this project. I would also like to thank acquisitions editor Jennika Baines for her patience and guidance through the publication process and Annalise Finnegan, who saw this project through its early phases. Finally, my thanks as well to Kelly Lynne Balenske, Lisa Renee Kuerbis, Fred Wellner, Mary Petrusewicz, Kay Steinmetz, and Marcia Hough for their many contributions to the production of this book.

This book emerged out of twin interests—Irish film and postcolonial theory—that were sparked early in my graduate career by dynamic scholars. My ideas took shape initially in the form of a dissertation for the cinema studies department at New York University, where the intellect of my advisor, Robert Stam, was matched only by his warmth and generosity. I am deeply indebted to him for his critical input and kindness and grateful for the privilege of having worked with him. Equally important to my time at NYU was Luke Gibbons, who managed to be present in New York as a source of feedback and ideas even while being thousands of miles away in Dublin. Like Bob, his warmth, humor, and encouragement made working on my dissertation feel more like a process of discovery and less like work. In addition, faculty at NYU and elsewhere provided valuable insight during the early stages of this project, especially David Lloyd, Anna McCarthy, and Chris Straayer, all of whom served on my dissertation committee.

The transformation of this project into a book would not have been possible without the tireless support, guidance, and critical feedback I received from four of my colleagues in the English department at George Mason University. Denise Albanese, Amal Amireh, Tamara Harvey, and Alok Yadav all generously made time in overburdened schedules to read and respond to my work. Their insights and questions pushed me to think beyond my own intellectual boundaries, and their encouragement gave me the energy to work whenever my own faith in this project began to diminish. Their mentoring and friendship have been and continue to be invaluable. Thank you, with all my heart.

I was fortunate to find a position in a warm and supportive department at GMU. I am grateful to Robert Matz for his savvy advice and encouraging feedback. I would also like to thank other members of the department faculty, especially Deborah Kaplan, Devon Hodges, Michael Malouf, and Cynthia Fuchs for their many and varied contributions. In addition to friends and colleagues at Mason, I've been lucky to know Matthew Fee, Roger Hallas, Carla Marcantonio, and Jeanette Roan, who all took the time to read and comment on different chapter drafts over the years. I thank them for their effort, their insights, and, most important, their friendship.

Much of the research for this book was done in Ireland, and I would like to acknowledge the people who made my work there possible. I thank the staff of the Irish Film Centre and the National Library in Dublin and the librarians at the Linen Hall Library in Belfast. I am deeply grateful to Margo Harkin for taking the time to answer my questions and discuss her work, and I would like to thank John Byrne for being equally accessible. My trips to Ireland would not have been possible without the generous hospitality of friends and their relatives who opened their homes to me (sometimes without even having met me before), shared stories, ideas, and insights, and pointed me in the direction of films I might have otherwise missed, given the unfortunate inaccessibility of much Irish cinema. Orla Ryan and Brian Hand have been amazing friends, and their impressive intellects have challenged me and helped to shape this project. I am also deeply and forever grateful to the Neary family on both sides of the Atlantic. Their important presence and boundless generosity in my life has been a blessing, and they have helped to make Ireland feel like a part of my own family history. In that vein, I would also like to acknowledge the Wiltons, the Quigleys, and the Murphys for their family stories, insights on Ireland, and many laughs they've given me over the years.

A book on visual culture is greatly enhanced by the inclusion of images. For their kind permission to reprint their work, I would like to thank the Derry Bogside Artists—Tom Kelly, William Kelly, and Kevin Hasson—John Byrne, and Bill Rolston, all of whom provided the photographs reprinted herein. I would also like to thank Maeve Murphy and Frances Higson for their generous permission to reprint images from *Silent Grace* and *The Magdalene Sisters*, and Alexander and Bonin Gallery for providing the image and permission for Willie Doherty's work.

Although writing is often a solitary experience, the conversations I have had outside of the specific framework of this book have been vital in stimulating ideas, and friendships that exist beyond the text have sustained me in the long journey of completing it. At the risk of this starting to sound like an Academy Award acceptance speech, I want to thank Deirdre O'Leary Cunningham, Dennis Mac Nulty, Mairéad McLean, Alev Adil, Nitin Govil, John MacMurria, Denise McKenna, Maxwell Leung, Lázaro Lima, Elena Gorfinkel, Shawn Shimpach, Keith Clark, Erika Lin, and Stefan Wheelock for conversations about gender, sexuality, race, violence, incarceration, national security, and of course cinema, that have helped to shape this project. Other friends have also provided much-needed support in many ways. They include Jennifer Egan, Abeer Saleh, Don Yates, halley harrisburg, and Michael Rosenfeld.

Finally, none of this would have been possible without the love and support of my family, especially my parents. My introduction to Irish politics came at the age of five through my father, when he explained the meaning of various Irish ballads to me. He and my mother are primarily responsible for my interests in art and film, and they have always encouraged my intellectual pursuits. I am deeply grateful to them for placing me, my sister, and our education above everything else in their lives. I am also thankful for my wonderful sister, Nancy Hood, her husband, Jeremy, and to Joe Goodin for keeping me grounded and laughing throughout this long and sometimes difficult process. I love you all.

Rethinking Occupied Ireland

Introduction

"But people in the North and the South have so much in common. . . . I mean we share so much . . . we share . . . we share a border."

—John Byrne, *From a South-Facing Family*

IN THE COLONIAL PRESENT, Derek Gregory adapts Giorgio Agamben's theorization of sovereignty and exclusion to the war in Afghanistan. Looking at the suspension of due process and the emergency legislation that legalizes the detention, internment, and rigorous interrogation of people accused of terrorist acts, Gregory makes a powerful case for the contemporary relevance to postcolonial theory of two of Agamben's concepts: the *homo sacer* and the space of the exception. As a status assigned to people who "could not be sacrificed according to ritual (because they were outside divine law: their deaths were of no value to the gods) but who could still be killed with impunity (because they were also outside juridical law: their lives were of no value to their contemporaries)," *homo sacer* reveals the importance of exclusion to the formation of political communities (Gregory 2004, 62).[1] People designated *homines sacri* exist in an in-between state, as the objects but not the subjects of a given power. The *homo sacer* inhabits a discursive space at the limits of legality, where the

---

1. The term "postcolonial" refers here to the theoretical framework Gregory uses to understand the dynamics of state power in these three contexts. Throughout his book, he accounts for the specificities of the history of each context and how each place has a different relationship to postcoloniality.

1

law "suspends itself" (62). This space is a threshold or border zone "not merely of exclusion but a zone of abandonment that Agamben called *the space of the exception. What matters is not only those who are marginalized but also, crucially, those who are placed beyond the margins*" (62). But this zone is not solely discursive; it materializes in certain kinds of carceral spaces, including the internment camps and detention centers used to hold "unlawful enemy combatants."[2]

The exceptional status denoted by the term *homo sacer* and the spatialization of power accompanying it are critical for an understanding of Irish films that engage with discourses of emergency, panic, and crisis in post-partition Ireland, and that therefore represent the physical spaces of incarceration designed to manage threatening populations. These spaces existed on both sides of the Irish border, and an analysis of their depiction on screen reveals the centrality of imprisonment to both the occupation of a territory and the construction of the postcolonial nation. *Rethinking Occupied Ireland* argues that concurrent on the island of Ireland are two states—each of which has at times disavowed the presence of the other—with a shared history of generating state-of-emergency discourses that in turn normalized the exclusion and incarceration of specific populations who, accidentally or deliberately, challenged the political, social, and religious systems that prevailed on either side of the Irish border. I draw attention to this shared history by focusing on ten films—*Maeve* (Pat Murphy, 1981), *Anne Devlin* (Pat Murphy, 1984), *Four Days in July* (Mike Leigh, 1984), *Hush-a-Bye Baby* (Margo Harkin, 1989), *Some Mother's Son* (Terry George, 1996), *H3* (Les Blair, 2001), *Silent Grace* (Maeve Murphy, 2001), *Sinners* (Aisling Walsh, 2002), *The Magdalene Sisters* (Peter Mullan, 2002), and *Hunger* (Steve McQueen, 2008)—that represent groups of Irish people who were barred from the benefits of citizenship under

---

2. For Agamben, the concentration camps of Nazi Germany exemplify the space of the exception, but other authors have extended his argument to include refugee and famine relief camps, colonies, and internment camps. See, for example, Edkins 2000, Kearns 2007, and Gal 2009.

both British and Irish rule.[3] Privileging a selection of films that reveal the dynamics of political and national exclusion as well as various tactics of resistance to such restrictions, I address the ways that internment and the sense of crisis that enables its existence reveal a crucial link between nationalism, state power, and the policing of gender and sexuality. A study of incarceration in Irish film facilitates a potent critique of state-of-emergency discourses and reveals the global relevance of Irish cinema and history to questions of terrorism, counter-insurgency strategies, and the inclusion of sexual and gender transgression in ever-lengthening lists of crimes against the nation.

In Gregory's analysis, the existence of exceptional spaces is a key part of the dynamics of invasion and occupation, but given the historical parameters of his work (the colonial *present*), he does not address what happens after the end of occupation. While all of Ireland was at one time colonized by Britain, the question of occupation becomes more complicated after the island's partition. The coming of the nation that anti-colonial nationalism establishes as the messianic end point of history was accompanied by the installation of a border that left Ireland's six northeastern counties under British rule. Northern nationalists found themselves on the wrong side of this new border, caught in a unionist state that began curtailing their civil rights. A non-sectarian civil rights movement emerged in the 1960s but was met with brutality by the Royal Ulster Constabulary (RUC), which, after Derry's Battle of the Bogside in Derry, led to the deployment of the British Army to the province, initially to protect the Catholic population. However, the army soon became part of the vast security apparatus in Northern Ireland, which posited nationalists as alien. In the republic, Irish nationalist culture lamented the loss of these counties, even as the government set about building a new state and distancing itself from

3. Three of these directors are not from Ireland. Mullan grew up near Glasgow, and McQueen and Leigh are both British. However, all three films are set in Ireland and address specifically Irish concerns. I include them under the term "Irish film" because "films about Ireland" is too awkward to use repeatedly as a critical term.

northern nationalism.[4] The nascent republic, reeling from the violent shocks of British colonialism that had permanently altered Irish culture, defined itself against British national identity, which in turn meant affording the Catholic Church a privileged position in the life of the nation (see Kiberd 1995). The special role of the Church—codified in Article 44.1.2 of the 1937 Bunreacht na hÉireann (Irish Constitution) until its amendment in 1973—combined with the constitution's recognition of the family "as a moral institution possessing inalienable and imprescriptible rights, antecedent and superior to all positive law" (Article 41.1.1), left numerous Irish citizens, particularly women, unprotected by the law, which in effect refused to intervene in Church or family affairs.

Thus, while violence and martial law in the North became the most overt way that Ireland was occupied, the rest of the island was occupied by a conservative form of Irish nationalism that colluded with the Catholic Church in policing the borders of gender and sexuality. In the North, internment without trial, the restructuring of the judicial system to secure guilty verdicts for those accused of terrorism, the division of neighborhoods along religious and political lines, and the impunity granted to state security officers who killed or injured civilians or collaborated with paramilitary groups all helped to exclude Northern Irish nationalists from British citizenship. Confinement within the borders of Northern Ireland also meant that they were excluded from the benefits of Irish citizenship, even though the constitution claimed them as members of the nation. That same document, while declaring men and women equal before the law, also asserted that the state, recognizing "that by her life within the home, woman gives to the State a support without which the good of the nation cannot be achieved," promised to ensure that "mothers shall not be obliged by economic necessity to engage in labour to the neglect of their duties in the home" (Bunreacht 41.2.1, quoted in Conrad 2004, 72).[5] This rhetorical

---

4. See for example the Offences against the State Act, passed in 1939. Office of the Attorney General, *Irish Statute Book*, http://www.irishstatutebook.ie/1939/en/act /pub/0013/sec0022.html (accessed March 1, 2011).

5. Crediting Ruth Riddick with the initial observation, Katherine Conrad notes that for the constitution, the terms "woman" and "mother" are synonyms (72–73).

location of women in the domestic realm, consistent with middle-class and Catholic views about gender and the family, was not simply an ideal. It had material repercussions for women ranging from employment discrimination to physical internment within Magdalene laundries run by Catholic clergy in the postcolonial republic.[6] Ostensibly homes for unwed mothers and other "first fall" cases, the laundries functioned as prisons for women tried and convicted of certain crimes as well as for women accused by the family or Church of sexual transgression. Bearing the burden of national chastity, both groups of women were interned indefinitely, sentenced to indeterminate terms of unpaid hard labor, and left vulnerable to the arbitrary rule of individual priests and nuns.

The films I cover explore Irish history from the perspective of those marginalized within or ejected from Irish and British national narratives, thus providing an ideal occasion to interrogate the legacy of Irish nationalism for constructions of gender as well as representations of heroism, vulnerability, and violence. In their exploration of Ireland's past and present, these films become a mode of postcolonial historiography, which, Gregory claims, is as much an act of resistance as it is of recall. For Gregory, the task of postcolonial historiography is to resist the amnesia of colonialist history, and it must also "stage 'a return of the repressed' to resist the seductions of nostalgic histories of colonialism" (Gregory 2004, 9). Irish nationalism excels at this type of history, particularly in popular cultural forms such as ballads and murals (see for example Rolston 1992 and Davies 2001). However, the danger with recalling and retrieving the brutalities of a colonial history is that such an act sets the stage for amnesiac and nostalgic *nationalist* histories, which, in recounting the violence of colonialism, establish the innocence of the colonized (in their existence as the objects but never the subjects of brutality and discrimination) and place the postcolonial nation beyond reproach. By including the Irish Republic in my analyses of cinematic zones of abandonment, I demonstrate the need for postcolonial historiography to guard against the amnesia and nostalgic appeal

6. In a column titled "Golden Balls," Nell McCafferty points out the hypocrisy of firing pregnant, unmarried Irish women—whose bodies show evidence of "transgression"—while doing nothing to the men who impregnated them (McCafferty 1984, 65).

of nationalism as well as colonialism. In Ireland, a key part of this task involves addressing the symbolic and actual role incarceration has played throughout the island's history.

Imprisonment is a central trope of Irish nationalism. As tour guides explain at Dublin's former prison turned heritage site, when Kilmainham Gaol was initially built in 1796, it was primarily intended to house criminals, but the failure of the United Irishmen rebellion of 1798 quickly filled it with political prisoners as well. This tension between the British-imposed label "criminal" and an Irish insistence that offenses against the state were justified political acts is repeated throughout the history of the incarceration of Irish people by British agents. In ballads, murals, stories, and souvenirs, Irish nationalist culture celebrates a history of men and women who challenged British rule, transforming incarceration into a virtue and a triumph. However, as I argue throughout this book, the potent visual language generated to represent national heroes—which relies on an external invader as a foil and turns to Christian iconography to express suffering—facilitates a narrow conceptualization of the terms "political prisoner" and "resistance," which in turn obstructs a more complicated understanding of the dynamics of nationalism on both sides of the Irish border. These omissions in Irish nationalist history do not concern merely the exclusion of women from heroic national narratives. Women are celebrated (even if marginally) for their involvement in Irish nationalism. However, their admittance into the epic struggle for Irish freedom entails a separation of women's issues from national issues, which sets the stage for the victory of a patriarchal and traditionalist nationalism to take root after colonialism is over. The inability of Irish nationalism to account for the possibility not simply of female political prisoners but also of "woman" as a political identity that plays a role in every aspect of the incarceration of nationalists may be one reason for the ambivalence that Megan Sullivan demonstrates characterized feminist responses to the issue of political prisoners (Sullivan 1999, 2–10).[7]

---

7. Of course, as Sullivan notes, disagreements over the ideologies and tactics of republicanism remained the primary reason. Sullivan also writes that whereas incarceration in

Films that represent carceral spaces—actual prisons, neighborhoods under surveillance, or institutions confining women who failed to observe the protocols of a gender-sexuality regime—provide an opportunity to re-evaluate what constitutes political resistance in Ireland. Just as important, though, they compel a discussion of the politics of film form, one that has particular relevance for Irish film, which has often taken a critical view of Irish history but, despite moments of dynamic experimentation, does not have a strong tradition of radically independent political filmmaking akin to that of Cuba or Brazil, for example. While scholars and supporters of political film may wince at the two-dimensional heroism of commercial cinema, we sometimes establish our own politics of heroics concerning cinema's struggle against audio-visual and narrative continuity, which in turn valorizes experimentation as an inherently more political mode of address. In Ireland, where the most experimental films flourished under government funding that dried up in the early 1990s, this perspective risks placing Irish cinema on a downward trajectory toward increasing political irrelevance. The films I cover vary in style; some deploy the aesthetic frag-mentation, narrative disjunction, and national-popular orientation often associated with Third Cinema (discussed below), while others revel in the audio-visual perfection, emotional catharsis, and individualism of com-mercial film. Most pick and choose from each mode of filmmaking, blend-ing the conventional with the avant-garde in ways that challenge existing views about the political efficacy of each. *Rethinking Occupied Ireland* brings films from this earlier moment into contact with later films in order to examine the dialogue between experimental and commercial cinema. Delineating the shape of political filmmaking in Ireland, I am interested in how, given film's complexity as a medium, its form and narrative both

---

feminist discourse becomes "a figurative example of women's imprisonment by patriar-chal forces, whether those forces [are] nationalist, Republican, or British," and "as a literal representation of the material needs of women who were themselves imprisoned or who had spent years visiting male relatives in jail," the issue of women prisoners' rights and conditions remained a point of contention in northern feminism even after the protests in the H-Blocks and Armagh ended (2).

facilitate and obstruct resistance to hegemonic national narratives—often within the same movie.

Locating "Occupied Ireland"

As the line where what is the nation (or state) encounters what it is not, the border delimits the space of the exception, and the border between Northern Ireland and the Irish Republic has thrown Irish national identity into permanent crisis. Visually, the Irish border is imperceptible; it does not follow any physical features of the landscape, and no signs indicate its presence. However, despite its geographical invisibility, the border, as Deirdre O'Leary argues, remains "a fundamental feature of the Irish political landscape," affecting "the nature of the political regimes North and South of it," and exploited by both "for symbolic and practical effect" (O'Leary 2004, 14). One function of the border that fills both a symbolic and practical role concerns the question of state security. Through its militarization, the border was in fact rendered visible. The British Army watchtowers that dotted the Irish landscape a mile into Northern Ireland served as a visual reference point for the border in ways that evoked immanent violence and implied a need for security. Constructed to enable surveillance of the surrounding countryside, the presence of the watchtowers (the last of which came down in 2006) suggested the possible danger of cross-border collusion among Irish nationalists and of the movement of criminal bodies across states. As *British* Army installations, they also served as a distraction from the *Irish* government's vested interest in maintaining the border, either as a way of distancing itself from the militant nationalism of the north (Cleary 2002, 101) or as a way to protect its traditional Catholic values (Conrad 2004, 71).

In recent years, Irish visual culture has exploited the border's degrees of invisibility, sometimes using it to emphasize the seamlessness of an Irish nation that transcends state lines and sometimes to question the efficacy of surveillance and thus undermine the authority of vision and faith in visual technology. The border often factors into Irish film and photography, revealing an area of Irish culture that resists what Cleary has called the "discursive invisibility" of the Irish border—the reluctance in Irish and British discourse to directly address or represent the border (Cleary 2002, 98). Films such as *Hush-a-Bye Baby* (Margo Harkin, 1989), *After 68* (Stephen Burke, 1994), *Bogwoman* (Tom Collins, 1997), *Omagh* (Paul Greengrass, 2004), and *Breakfast on Pluto* (Neil Jordan, 2005) all feature moments when characters cross the border, whereas Joe Comerford's *High Boot Benny* (1994) is set entirely on the border.[8] More recently, the Irish visual and performance artist John Byrne seems to have built his career on the border and its symbolic and practical ramifications. Much of Byrne's work explores the contradictions within Irish and British or unionist nationalism from the vantage point of a Catholic raised in the North and obsessed with the border. For Byrne, the border "dilutes the Irishness of people from the North," qualifying them as *Northern* Irish once they travel south (O'Leary 2006, 198). This claim—based on his own experiences living in Belfast, London, and then Dublin—undermines the nationalist tenet that the island of Ireland is one nation, one culture, and one people. Likewise, Byrne's photographic, performance, and video work gleefully violate the doctrines of Irish nationalism, while also acknowledging the painful realities for nationalists north of the border.

In *From a South-Facing Family* (1997) (fig. 1), Byrne alters a family photograph, placing his adult head on the body of himself as a child. His family looks out at the camera from against a wall patterned with multiple images of a saint. The child-man body is comic in its incongruity, and, as Sean Kelly notes, it suggests an unresolved past. Kelly writes that while the "spooky" image is clearly funny, "at the same time there is a certain note of pathos as one identifies with the 'child man' and the strange cultural conundrum that he inhabits" (Kelly 2005). That cultural conundrum, expressed visually in the photo, is reinforced through the text that Byrne lays over it:

8. Cleary offers cogent critiques of *Cal* and *The Crying Game*, particularly in their refusal to recognize the border and thereby risk granting any political legitimacy to the actions of the republican characters they portray. Many of the films I list here were made after the publication of Cleary's article, but some do pre-date it. My pointing out the border's presence in these other films is not an attempt to refute Cleary's overall argument, but only to make a case for the willingness of Irish *visual* culture to engage with this invisible entity.

1. *From a South-Facing Family* by artist John Byrne. Photograph from performance commissioned for the 1997 Dublin Theatre Festival. Courtesy of the artist.

We were a fairly typical northern Catholic family at the time. You'll notice we're all facing south. . . . But we couldn't get RTÉ [Radio Telefís Éireann]. Yeah, we were a south facing family, which was nice, 'cause we got the sun. . . . But we didn't worship it, we weren't stupid, we weren't primitives, we were natives apparently. . . . We were sophisticated. We had the fashionable St. Martin de Porres wallpaper. He was a family favourite, 5'3" and an animal lover . . . and of course, we had the eye level holy water troughs. Do you remember that craze? . . . eye level holy water troughs? . . . no? But people in the North and the South have so much in common. . . . I mean we share so much . . . we share . . . we share a border.

Byrne's photograph problematizes notions of national and religious belonging while also acknowledging the material effects of cultural and political identities. The rambling text, like the self-portrait child-man, is comically disjointed and resists a sense of organic wholeness. Like the St. Martin de Porres wallpaper visible behind the family, the text subverts the seriousness bestowed on religion in the context of Ireland by a multitude of forces. Catholicism, deeply intertwined with twentieth-century Irish nationalism and routinely articulated to Irish history as a central component of Irish identity throughout the island, is here reduced to a surface effect. The photograph's mise-en-scène hyperbolically signifies "Catholic" through the multiple tiny images of the diminutive saint. Byrne's text presents this decor as part of the family's typicality, a move that mocks not only the place of Catholicism in Irish culture but also the perception and fear of Irish Catholic devotion by those outside the fold. But any notion of the family's being typical or of the speaker (Byrne) and the audience belonging to the same community is thrown into question when Byrne's imagined interlocutor does not in fact remember the eye-level holy water decorating "craze" that supposedly swept through the homes of Northern Catholic families. Is the person Byrne addresses Protestant? From the South? Not Irish? Not typical? Or is the Byrne family the anomaly? The work refuses to clarify these ambiguities, just as it resists resolving the child-man's past.

If the photograph destabilizes the idea of Catholic typicality, it also poignantly addresses the fragmentation of an Irish national identity, thus offering a glimpse of what the child-man's unresolved past may be. The vaguely 1960s style of clothing and Byrne's approximate age as an adult suggest that the photo was taken on the eve of the troubles. Facing south toward the overwhelmingly Catholic Irish Republic, but unable to get the signal for RTÉ (its national broadcast company) and therefore cut off from the imagined community that television promotes, the members of Byrne's family are both native and alien: native to the island of Ireland and, as Irish Catholics, made alien in the unionist or Protestant British province of Northern Ireland. However, the text suggests they might be just as out of place in the republic when Byrne names the border as the "so much" that people in the North and people in the South share. His sardonic observation casually brushes aside the genuine feelings of shared culture, history, and geography that often cut across the border, but it also chips at the illusion that a transcendent Irish nation exists independently of political boundaries. In naming the border—and by implication, the partition it signifies—as the primary commonality among Irish people,

Byrne undermines the notion that the border slices through—and therefore unnaturally disturbs—a continuous culture, and he bluntly confronts his viewer with the exceptional status of Ireland, revealing that national identity can be just as contingent as state boundaries. Irish people are, paradoxically, united by their divisions.

Byrne's most public act as a professional "border worrier" (a term he self-applies) was the inauguration in 2000 of his Border Interpretative Centre in County Louth on the main road between Dublin and Belfast, at the precise spot where the border lies. A satirical celebration of the border as "Ireland's most significant inland feature," the Centre offered a wry critique of national pride by gleefully embracing the very thing that has helped to confound easy definitions of "Ireland" and "Irish" and that stands as a 338-mile-long monument to the failure of Irish nationalism to achieve its central goal. As O'Leary observes, in a post-Agreement era of cross-border cooperation, Byrne's performance and installation also discarded "the usual language of rapprochement and politics to question assumptions about . . . the burgeoning heritage industry and its consequences on the island, the divided Ireland of republican mythology, the porous notion of Irish identity, and the abiding existence of this amorphous, meandering line" (2004, 198). Among the many souvenirs that the Centre sold during its weeklong lifespan were do-it-yourself border kits, encouraging visitors to grow their own borders at home. An absurdist comment on heritage tourism and its attendant commodification of the nation (O'Leary 2004, 195–98), the border kits also evoke internal divisions within Ireland: the physical and social partitions within an already partitioned nation. Such homegrown borders along class, gender, religious, and ideological lines are both informal and formalized; they are self-imposed as well as imposed from outside. Internal divisions within Ireland, North and South, often correspond to physical spaces of confinement—the home, Magdalene laundries, prisons, northern working-class neighborhoods bounded by barbed-wire walls and army checkpoints, and low-income housing estates in the republic, like Dublin's Ballyfermot or the now-demolished Ballymun towers—so that while the Irish border contradicts the easy movement through space promised by tourism, internal borders point to the limited mobility of certain segments of the population in both states on the island. Dedicated to confining and controlling the bodies of people construed as threats to society, the state, and national security, these spaces reproduce zones of abandonment, turning Ireland into an echo chamber of exceptionality, exclusion, and alienation.

Byrne's celebration of the border as a central part of national heritage thwarts the messianic logic of Irish nationalism as laid out in Article 2 of the 1937 constitution (but amended in 1998 as part of the Belfast or Good Friday Agreement), which asserted, "The national territory consists of the whole island of Ireland, its islands and the territorial seas," and which explained that the constitution would be limited to Saorstát Éireann (the Irish Free State), "pending the re-integration of the national territory" (Bunreacht). At the same time that the Irish Republic imagined Northern Ireland as a violation of the laws of nature, the unionist government north of the border sought to delegitimize Irish nationalism by refusing to acknowledge *any* connection with the twenty-six county republic— ignoring the Irish language, fostering a rigid British nationalism rarely reciprocated across the Irish Sea, and imagining the statelet as "Ulster," despite the fact that the historical province of Ulster includes the "southern" counties of Donegal, Monaghan, and Cavan (Cleary 2002, 68–72). Following the logic of Irish nationalism to its extreme, the existence of Northern Ireland is both an affront to the ordained order of things and an indeterminate delay before the inevitable coming of the (Catholic) nation. Taking unionism to its (il)logical conclusion, the six northeastern counties of Ireland are under constant threat of attack by a mass of nationalists, a threat against which not even a militarized border is sufficient protection.

This is a south-facing book. I echo Byrne's artistic practice in that my vantage point is Northern Ireland, which means I look at films set in the republic through analytical lenses that might at first seem more obviously relevant to the North, given Northern Ireland's cinematic association with a state of siege. In doing so, I reverse the proportions of most books on Irish cinema, which devote considerably more space to films set in the Irish Republic and look at films set in the North in relation to a wider Irish nation.[9] Their position is consistent with a national cinema approach that must address the peculiarities of Irish history (including colonialism, partition, and a near-constant stream of emigration since the mid-nineteenth century) as well as those of Irish film history (weak state support, tax incentives for foreign production companies, and the presence of non-Irish funding and talent from the silent era to the present). But a southern-based view can also present the chronic state of emergency that dominates the history of Northern Ireland as the exception to governmentality. Making the shift north enables my analyses to follow Walter Benjamin's insight that "the condition of the oppressed teaches us that the current 'state of emergency' in which we live is not the exception but the rule" (Benjamin 1969, 257).

Over the following chapters, I trace a cinematic historiography of what Lauren Berlant has termed "hygienic governmentality" and the various tactics used to resist it in Ireland. Deriving the concept from Foucault's "Governmentality" and Benjamin's "Theses on the Philosophy of History," Berlant defines hygienic governmentality as a form of government whereby the ruling bloc guards its political, economic, and social hegemony by constructing specific populations as threats to "the common good," which therefore "must be rigorously governed and monitored by all sectors of society" (Berlant 1997, 175). Berlant's concept is a helpful addition to Agamben's state of exception because hygienic governmentality seizes hold of the means of visual and literary representation to garner support for state repression and exclusion, relying on media to repeat the same images, ideas, and talking points in order to build what Gramsci would call spontaneous consensus (Berlant 1997, 175). By setting up parallels between the republic's use of hygienic governmentality against men and women whose sexuality was imagined as a threat to a Catholic, heteronormative state and Britain's use of similar strategies against populations suspected of anti-state violence, I argue against teleological histories

---

9. The most thorough books on Ireland and film include: Gibbons, Rockett, John Hill 1988; Pettitt 2000; McLoone 2000; and Barton 2004. For books specifically on cinema and Northern Ireland, see McIlroy 2001 and Hill 2006.

that see the republic as postcolonial, postnational, and also postmodern. In this way, I also avoid the potential trap of uncritically supporting Irish nationalism in the context of Northern Ireland. When viewed alongside representations of the North, films set in the Irish Republic function as a stark reminder that the politics of the body cannot be separated from the politics of the state.

My focus on categories of occupation facilitates a comparison of various institutions of power—state, religious, and familial—in ways that illuminate the embodied modes of domination and resistance within these institutions and the difficulty that cinema has in holding onto the materiality of the body, particularly in a culture steeped in allegory and national-religious discourses of transcendence. Filmmakers interested in using the bodies of their characters to represent the dynamics of power and resistance must grapple with two centuries of images, ballads, poems, and plays in which Ireland is embodied as a woman. Complicating this iconographic legacy is a particular fusion of Catholicism and nationalism that heroicizes the male nationalist, whose body is able to bear insurmountable pain and degradation. Spanning the years 1981 to 2008, the films I examine use bodies as points where nationalist history, state/church/army power, notions of home and motherhood, religious identity, and heroic republicanism converge. They share an interest in moments and people marginalized within or omitted from normative conceptions of Irish and British citizenship. Each of the films in this book reveals a history of subjugation enacted on the physical bodies of specific groups of people that vary from film to film and context to context. Because the films I study focus on moments of crisis and emergency discourses, together they offer new definitions of the terms "political prisoner" and "resistance," and they generate new meanings for the nationalist slogan "Ireland unfree will never be at peace."

Politics and Irish Film

The conflict in Northern Ireland dominates cinematic conceptions of "politics" and "violence." Fictional film borrows its representations of the troubles from journalism, but it also influences those representations, providing ready-made structures for narrating current events. Images and descriptions of the troubles have circulated internationally on television and radio and in journals and newspapers, but such coverage has not ensured a depth of analysis of the history and politics pertaining to the conflict. In non-fiction media, the one-dimensionality of coverage of Northern Ireland stems in part from the analytical blind spots produced by an approach that, Cleary argues, locates the root causes of the conflict in a religious bigotry that it portrays as intrinsic to the political culture of Northern Ireland, "and hence looks largely to internal solutions as well" (Cleary 2002, 106). Fiction follows a similar approach and adds the obscuring trope of the fanatic IRA man caught up in ritualized violence against an alternately colonialist or civilizing British state and army (Hill 1988, 147–93). John Hill and Martin McLoone have extensively addressed the ways that this version of the conflict frequently assimilates national struggles to the gangster genre and thereby mobilizes the genre's fatalism and ethnic determinism to dramatize the affective allure of violence. Hill, McLoone, and others analyzing IRA films work off a consensus that films about militant nationalists share four basic and highly problematic narrative components that obstruct a complex cinematic engagement with Irish history. These films: (1) repeatedly substitute personal motives for political ones, (2) represent violence as a tragic flaw in the national character, (3) imagine the agents of violence only as men, and in so doing, (4) posit a clean split between a public culture of men, nations, and guns and a private one of women, homes, and heterosexual romance (Hill 1988, 147–94).[10] Even a film like *The Crying Game*, which promises a queering of nationalism but uses the state (in the form of Fergus's imprisonment) to safely contain homoerotic desire, offers merely a postmodern twist on the standard troubles film, where a heteronormative and feminine domestic space stands in opposition to an irrational commitment to republicanism (understood primarily as anti-social violence), giving the repentant IRA

---

10. Hill's essay is the first to map out these arguments, but see also Martin McLoone, *Irish Film: The Emergence of a Contemporary Cinema* (London: British Film Institute, 2000).

man a light to guide him as he navigates his way out of the depths of nationalist fanaticism (Lloyd 1999, 53–72; Cleary 2002, 97–143). It is this domestic space "upon which governmentality relies" (Lloyd 1993, 72) that holds the promise of the ex-republican's assimilation into normative citizenship, an assimilation that requires submission to the laws of the state and a paradoxical acceptance of his partial citizenship.[11]

These arguments have shaped the primary analytical approach to films that engage with the national question. As core arguments in Irish film studies, they provide salient critiques of dominant cinematic images of warfare in the North. Accepting them, this book shifts the focus of the discussion on violence in Irish cinema (a unifying concern of the chapters here) by asking a different set of questions that demand a closer look at how cinematic representation shapes gender and nationalism in relation to one another. The films often overlooked when Irish cinema is viewed through the spectacular lens of IRA violence are the ones that begin to answer David Lloyd's request that cinema tell stories of the North "against the grain of historiographical and cinematic verisimilitude" (Lloyd 1999, 53–72). In doing so, they offer a wider range of possibilities for what might count as political subject matter and what might comprise "political film."

Writing on *The Battle of Algiers* (Gillo Pontecorvo, 1966) as political cinema, Michael Chanan argues that there is no single concise definition of what constitutes political film; "on the contrary, there are so many different ways of being political and so many different types of political film as to defy definition" (Chanan 2007, 38). Chanan points out some of the pitfalls in thinking through the category of political film, which include the assumption that "political" is synonymous with "propagandistic" as well as the argument that "all films are essentially political because they express one ideology or another" (39). He concludes that what is at stake in the concept of political film is "the politics of cinema; the gulf between

11. In *Cal*, Cal assists in an IRA doorstep killing, becomes increasingly involved with the dead man's widow, and in penance ultimately allows himself to be arrested at the widow's farm. *The Crying Game* ends with Fergus's acceptance of a romantic relationship with Dil (albeit one safely contained by a glass partition) and his willing submission to imprisonment.

a film that mobilises the viewer's intelligence and the duplicitous idea that cinema is nothing but entertainment" (39). In a similar vein, Mike Wayne recognizes that the question of what constitutes "political cinema" is itself "a political question," and he offers the criterion that political film address the "unequal access to and distribution of material and cultural resources" as well as the ways that such access or lack thereof has helped to construct and maintain "hierarchies of legitimacy and status" (Wayne 2001, 1).

Central to both Chanan's and Wayne's formulation of political cinema is the question of Third Cinema, a provocative and influential idea first expressed by the Argentinian filmmakers Fernando Solanas and Octavio Getino in their 1969 essay "Towards a Third Cinema," and further developed across a large body of writing by authors including Chanan and Wayne, as well as Julio García Espinosa, Teshome Gabriel, Paul Willemen, Robert Stam, Ella Shohat, and Julianne Barton.[12] In *Irish Film*, Martin McLoone devotes considerable time to the relationship between Third Cinema and Irish national cinema, questioning to what extent Irish film may be considered Third Cinema. Offering a cogent summary based on Solanas and Getino's essay, McLoone defines Third Cinema as "a revolutionary form of oppositional filmmaking, anti-imperialist and decolonizing in its politics, artisanal and collective in its working methods and geared towards raising political questions in its audience, rather than merely offering ideology marketed as entertainment" (McLoone 2000, 122). He then traces the growth of this notion, explaining that while Willemen argues that the strength of the concept lies in its mutability and flexibility, Chanan asserts that Third Cinema was founded "on militant mass political movements of a kind which in many places no longer exist and upon ideologies which have taken a decisive historical beating" (quoted in McLoone 2000, 123). Given the battered state of Third Cinema's foundational movements and ideologies, Chanan argues that Third Cinema requires a new terrain in order to survive, and McLoone

---

12. Robert Stam points out that before Solanas and Getino wrote the essay, the Brazilian filmmaker Glauber Rocha had begun to outline a cinema along similar lines with his concept of the "aesthetics of hunger" (Stam 2000, 153–58).

questions whether the contested relationship between national cinemas and Hollywood might be this new ground (McLoone 2000, 123).

McLoone suggests that what he identifies as a three-tiered structure for funding filmmaking in Ireland might correspond to the First, Second, and Third Cinemas mapped out by Solanas and Getino,[13] where big-budget films shot in Ireland by international studios correspond to First Cinema, medium-sized co-productions that offer indigenous Irish talent a greater deal of artistic control would be akin to Second Cinema, and low-budget films made and funded entirely by Irish people would be the closest Irish film comes to Third Cinema. Through this analogy, McLoone foregrounds the effect funding has on cinematic conceptions of Ireland. He argues, convincingly, that films made in Ireland by non-Irish filmmakers with substantial funding tend to exploit Ireland for its cinematic potential as a mystical, mythical land, a space inhabited by quirky Celtic characters, a timeless space of simple rural values—in short, all "the hoary old myths about Ireland and the Irish" (McLoone 2000, 126). By contrast, Ireland's "third cinema" (he deliberately uses lowercase letters to separate this form of filmmaking from Third Cinema) and some medium-budget cinema with non-Irish funding are more concerned with issues specific to Ireland and Irish national identity. These films (by Jordan, Thaddeus O'Sullivan, Murphy, Bob Quinn, Comerford, and Black, among others) constitute Ireland's national cinema, defined "not by an essentialist

13. Put very simply: First Cinema is big-budget commercial cinema; it offers emotional catharsis, individualistic narratives reflective of capitalist ideology's emphasis on the individual and audio-visual perfection, and is produced for profit. Second Cinema, epitomized by European *auteur* cinema, challenges the production and aesthetic strategies of First Cinema but is still individualistic in that the director—or author—is imagined to be the artist without whose singular genius the film would not exist. Second Cinema may challenge capitalist hegemony, but it is still rooted in a bourgeois liberalism. For histories of and debates about Third Cinema, see Paul Willemen 1994; Jim Pines and Willemen 1994; Wayne 2001; and Anthony Guneratne and Wimal Dissanayake 2003. See also the following essays by Teshome Gabriel: "Towards a Critical Theory of Third World Films" and "Third Cinema as a Guardian of Popular Memory: Towards a Third Aesthetics," both in Pines and Willemen 1994.

conception of Irishness, but by a desire to explore the contradictions and complexities of Irish identity" (McLoone 2000, 128).

The value of McLoone's discussion of Third Cinema in an Irish context is that it accounts for the relational aspects of Third Cinema. Like Wayne, McLoone sees Third Cinema in a dialectical relationship to First and Second Cinemas. While I find the concept of Third Cinema compelling and invaluable for understanding the politics of film form, and while I agree with Third Cinema theorists that this mode of filmmaking is not limited to the so-called third world, I am not convinced of its usefulness for this particular book. One reason for my skepticism concerns the particular stance Third Cinema takes toward history. As Gabriel, Stam, and Wayne have argued, Third Cinema directors reveal the urgent connection between history, historiography, and present power structures. For Third Cinema films, history is "an open site of conflict and change" (Wayne 2001, 3). While the films in this book grapple with contested histories, they are—with the exception of Harkin's and Murphy's films—less concerned with history itself as a *current* site of struggle. Instead, many of these films offer heroic histories. This heroism stems in part from the fact that they tend to end on a moment that the films themselves establish as a historical threshold for Irish history, after which things changed for the better. The promise of change then retroactively heroicizes the actions of the characters and installs a border between past and present that some films try to trouble and some try to stabilize.

The Politics of Home

Set in Northern Ireland, Mike Leigh's *Four Days in July* (1984) illustrates the difficulty in sealing off temporal, spatial, and analytical borders. Sympathetic to its republican characters, the film demonstrates why an analysis of gender and nationalism in the North has implications for the republic as well. It frames the conflict in Northern Ireland not as the ritualistic violence mindlessly enacted between two pre-modern communities—in fact, we never directly *see* any acts of violence, we only hear characters recall them—but as a response to a state that has structured inequality into all aspects and phases of its governance so that the word "citizen" has radically different meanings on either side of the peace line. In moving away from the trope of the IRA gunman, *Four Days in July* allows us to imagine anti-state violence as a protest against the exceptional status conferred upon northern nationalists within what republicans see as their occupied home.

The idea expressed by a character in *Cal* that "there's bad bastards on both sides" of the conflict is qualified by Leigh's choice to set his story during an official holiday when one side, with the support of the state, commemorates and celebrates subjugating the other. The film cuts between the two communities in an editing pattern that imitates a wish to transcend the sectarian divide by focusing on similarities between two sets of characters, repeating the journalistic practice of reducing the conflict to strife between two opposing sides and claiming impartiality by representing each. But it subverts this TV news structure by allowing the striking imbalance of power between the two communities to surface in mundane details.[14] Following two couples who are each awaiting the birth of their first child—Protestants Billy and Lorraine and Catholics Eugene and Colette—the film reveals the profoundly different relationship Protestants and Catholics have to the state through a depiction of the day-to-day lives of the couples, which are thoroughly suffused with the politics of loyalism and republicanism, conveyed through dialogue and mise-en-scène. Paradoxically, these incommensurate levels of citizenship emerge through the similarities that saturate the narrative. For example, both wives stay at home, but Colette's husband is unemployed, while Lorraine's is a soldier in the Ulster Defence Regiment (UDR).[15] Both couples have their own

14. Stephen Burke's short film *81* (1996) does something similar. In the film, a fictional French TV crew arrives in West Belfast to interview a Catholic family (the Friels) and a Protestant family (the Campbells) about the hunger strike. The film exaggerates similarities between the families for comic effect, but these similarities also highlight economic, political, and social differences through which sympathy for the Friels emerges.

15. Allen Feldman explains: "This locally recruited reserve unit of the British army, akin to the American National Guard, supposedly replaced the infamous B Specials, a Protestant militia that functioned as a police reserve and was known for its anti-Catholic bigotry and indiscriminate anti-Catholic violence. The UDR was formed in 1970 and,

house, but Colette and Eugene are squatting in a tiny "two up, two down," attached house marked for demolition that sits across from a vacant lot littered with the rubble of burned and bombed buildings. On the other hand, Billy and Lorraine live in a roomier home on a tidy street lined with quintessentially British brick Georgian houses.

The couples' lives are also linked temporally as the film depicts their ordinary routines, cutting between the two families as they make breakfast, visit with friends, prepare for the baby's arrival, settle into bed, and pack for the hospital. But the upcoming holiday disrupts these activities, and the couples' attitudes toward the Twelfth further mark the disparity between Catholics and Protestants in relation to the state. Eugene and Colette's friends Brendan and Carmel take their children to the republic to avoid the holiday's annual riots and police brutality. On the other hand, Billy, excited about the upcoming celebrations, grumbles over government regulations for bonfire safety that restrict the size of a fire to a fifteen-foot radius and forbid the burning of tires and foam mattresses: "A person should be allowed to burn what he wants on the Twelfth." Remarking on the stark change in the relationship between Catholics and Protestants after 1968, Eugene recalls helping Protestants find wood for their bonfires as a child, and Colette responds, "You can't see kids doing that ever again, can you?" But Brendan reminds them that relationships between the two communities were never idyllic when he states, "God, if they'd known you kick with the other foot, they'd have put *you* on the bonfire."

The film emphasizes the geographical and ideological rift between the two communities by keeping the two couples physically separate until they end up in the same maternity ward, which is notably devoid of political markers, and Eugene and Billy are brought together to pace nervously in the waiting room. When Colette and Lorraine go into labor, the film cuts between the two women as each realizes her water has broken,

---

despite its official nonsectarian recruitment policy, is mainly comprised of Protestant volunteers. Many of its members have been exposed as holding dual membership in Loyalist paramilitary organizations [such as the Ulster Volunteer Force, or UVF] and have been involved in sectarian murders" (Feldman 1991, 278).

arranges to go to the hospital, and screams in agony as she delivers her baby. They finally meet when they are placed in adjacent hospital beds with their newborns. The two women begin a friendly conversation, but this spatial and experiential unity offers no ideological reconciliation. The film self-consciously references the idea that birth is a universal aspect of humanity, and that motherhood, with all its pain, excitement, and serenity is something both sides of the peace line share. But any promise of solidarity that might emerge between the two women based on their common experience of being first-time mothers is frozen when they tell each other their babies' names. Lorraine mentions that her son's name is Billy, after his father, and Colette's body tenses at the mention of this loyalist heritage, Billy (for King Billy) being as stereotypical of Protestant loyalists as the name "Paddy" is of Irish Catholics. When Colette tells Lorraine that her daughter is named Mairéad, the Irish for her mother's name, Margaret, Lorraine's face hardens and she asks, "Why Mairéad, then? Why not Margaret?" But her body language suggests that she has already associated the choice of an Irish name with republican politics. In the final shot, the two women sit in their beds, in tense silence, looking down at their babies, and the curtain that had been pulled back between them cuts the frame in two and is rendered by the shot as solid and alienating as the peace lines.

While the film's editing style mimics impartiality, the narrative and audio-visual details reveal a clear sympathy for its Catholic characters, which it achieves in part by gendering each side of the divide. Protestantism and loyalism are male, aligned with mobility through public space and presented as forceful, militant, and oppressive, while Catholicism and the nationalist community are constructed as female, associated with and confined to the home, and presented as wounded and oppressed but resilient through strong community ties that come out of that shared oppression. The Protestant realm is a patriarchal one, dominated by Billy, who dismisses his wife's fear for her safety when left alone, stating, "Well you won't be alone much longer," implying that the arriving infant will be sufficient company to keep her mind occupied and allay her fears. In the matriarchal Catholic home, Colette interjects into the men's banter, correcting them and solving riddles that none of them can figure out. Because Eugene is on crutches, Colette is also the more mobile of the couple, while Eugene leaves the house only once, to accompany Colette to the hospital.

Before its title sequence, *Four Days in July* opens with an establishing shot that conveys the ordinariness of the state of emergency. As a group of children playfully run and bicycle through the sunlit back roads of the Falls, their movements are repeatedly halted at street corners by patrolling British Army Land Rovers snaking their way through the neighborhood. This shot places the narrative geographically and temporally—West Belfast in the 1980s—and it synecdochally characterizes the Catholic community as one under surveillance, restricted in its movements, and subject to invasion by the state. By contrast, the shot that follows the credits introduces the Protestant side through a medium close-up of Billy in sunglasses, whistling "The Sash My Father Wore"[16] and driving to a checkpoint in a Saracen tank with other UDR soldiers. At the checkpoint, Billy and the other UDR men—Big Billy and Little Billy—stop and search a loyalist who rants at them about their heritage, explaining that as Ulster men, they are descended from a race of Ulster people who inhabited Ireland first, even before the Irish, but departed for Scotland for a while and then returned to settle the plantations of Ulster. This parody of loyalist hagiography, claiming both native and settler status simultaneously, is strengthened by the fact that *all three* UDR men are named Billy, as if that were the only name loyalist families could think up, creatively stunted as they are by a fervor for the triumphalist trappings of a distant past.

But the humor ends abruptly when Billy and Big Billy return to the UDR base and discuss "cleaning out" the Falls. Billy likens the North to Vietnam, explaining that the British cannot tell the difference between loyalists and republicans, just as US marines couldn't tell "one gook from another." He worries that in ten years Catholics will outnumber Protestants, and the North will be (re)united with the republic through a referendum.

16. "The Sash" is a song in praise of the military history of the sash worn by members of the Orange Order, the principal organizers of the Twelfth marches: "It is old but it is beautiful and the colors they are fine/It was worn at Derry, Aughrim, Enniskillen, and the Boyne/Oh my father wore it as a youth in the bygone days of yore/And it's on the Twelfth I love to wear the sash my father wore."

His solution is to let the UDR handle the whole situation alone because, as (loyalist) natives of the North, they can tell the two populations apart. Billy relates a recent conversation, "'Give us a 48-hour blackout,' says I, '48 hours, no press, no television, you know we just go in there and root them out and that'll be it, no problem.'" Big Billy goes a step further in his ideas for securing Ulster from republicanism when he suggests building "a proper defensive border against the Fenian [Irish republican] state." Billy agrees, "Oh, aye, like the Berlin Wall or a mile-wide moat," and Big Billy excitedly interjects, "Right, and the first prick who sticks his head over the top of it, zap him!"

The discussion between Billy and Big Billy establishes the profound sectarian bias within the unionist government of Northern Ireland, which sees itself as defending Ulster from the onslaught of republicanism, much like King Billy squelched the Catholic threat in the 1690s. Imagining themselves shooting phantom nationalists who rise up from the republic to claim Ulster, Billy and Big Billy reflect the siege mentality of unionism—the Ulster Defence Regiment defends Ulster from the imagined threat across the border and from its agents who have "infiltrated" Ulster in the form of northern nationalists. Like the ranting Ulster man, the two Billys deny the native status of Irish republicans. Significantly, the UDR is a branch of the British Army, and in their wish to guard the sanctity of the border and kill the residents of the Falls, the sectarian Billys implicate the British government. It is not only Stormont Castle that takes a defensive stance against roughly 45 percent of the citizens of Northern Ireland, but Westminster Abbey as well, as is apparent in Britain's Prevention of Terrorism Act, emergency legislation that in theory could have been applied to both unionist and nationalist communities, but in practice targeted an overwhelming number of working-class nationalists.

After Billy and Big Billy dream aloud of shooting republicans, Catholics, nationalists (they do not distinguish among the three), the film cuts to a shot of Eugene at home in the morning. His metal crutches clink as he descends the stairs, passing a picture of the Pope on his way. In cutting from the muscular Billys, whose flak jackets, army boots, weapons, and Saracen add bulk and protection to their bodies, to an image of Eugene laboriously performing a simple daily task, the film not only contrasts a hard Protestant body with a wounded Catholic one, but also implicates the former in the condition of the latter. Eugene's fragility is consistent with cinematic aesthetics of Irish Catholic masculinity in the North,[17] but he is also a victim of state violence. The film solidifies this implication in a later sequence, when Eugene traces a history of the troubles through his body, moving backward in time and down his body as he points to places where he was injured on three separate occasions: in 1979 he was hit by a stray bullet that a British soldier fired at joy riders careening through a checkpoint; in 1976 he was injured when a UVF bomb went off in a bar in the Falls; and in 1973 he was walking home from Mass on the Antrim Road (known as Murder Mile) when he was hit in a drive-by shooting by loyalists randomly targeting Catholics.

Eugene's disabled body becomes a physical record of the exceptional status of residents of the Falls. A working-class Catholic neighborhood, the Falls Road area is criminalized by republican politics and frequently equated with violence. Therefore, the incarceration of Falls Road residents in their own neighborhood—through curfews, checkpoints, patrols, and other methods—is sanctioned by the label "terrorist" and legitimated through the primacy given to security. The film garners support for its Catholic characters by representing the state's monitoring of and hindrances to their movements. When Colette opens her curtains in the morning, three British soldiers on patrol appear in her window, their rifles cocked and ready for firing. "The Sash" wafts over the peace line and into Eugene and Colette's home, disrupting an amicable conversation among Eugene, Colette, Brendan, and their neighbor Dixie. A moment later, the chopping of a helicopter's blades cuts into their living room, and Colette grumbles, "They don't even want you to get your sleep at night." When Dixie and Brendan leave, they stop in front of a house whose windows and doors are sealed with cinderblocks. Their conversation competes offscreen with the noise of the helicopter as the film cuts to a shot of more soldiers

17. See for example, *Cal*, *Some Mother's Son* (Terry George, 1996), and *Nothing Personal* (Thaddeus O'Sullivan, 1996), all of which star the slender John Lynch, whose body is consistently burned, battered, starved, tortured, and blown up in his troubles films.

across the road. Dixie and Brendan exit the frame, but the film lingers on the sealed house in the evening summer light under the omnipresent sounds of surveillance.

Four Days in July walks a fine line between critiquing the effects of emergency legislation on the citizenship status of nationalists and slipping into a portrayal of oppression that is consistent with the more romantic traditions of Irish nationalism. The film presents the home as a space of confinement, but one that fosters a strong sense of community precisely through that confinement in ways similar to the sense of solidarity prevalent in films about political prisoners. Eugene and Colette often appear together in medium close-up shots, a motif that emphasizes the cramped nature of their small house and translates the closeness of this space into an emotional intimacy. As part of this confinement, the domestic spaces of living room, kitchen, bedroom, and bathroom become sites for critiquing the existing political order of things. In *Four Days in July*, as in republican communities of the North, the progression Foucault outlines in "Governmentality," whereby the family evolves from being the model for governmentality to becoming "an element internal to population and a fundamental instrument in its government" (1994, 216), breaks down. While house raids, internment, surveillance, and neighborhood curfews open houses to the prying eyes of the state, they do not succeed in producing state subjects. Instead, such restrictive governmentality often politicizes individuals against the state. But while Leigh's film subverts the function of the home in relation to the British state, it upholds its significance for the Irish nation. The home in Irish nationalism is the foundation of the community, the center of resistance to imperialism, and the cradle where the future of the nation is nurtured; and whereas Eugene and Collette's *house* may be run-down, their *home* is much stronger than Billy and Lorraine's.

For all its spontaneous dialogue, natural lighting, and handheld cinematography, *Four Days in July* ultimately slips into the metaphoric clichés of romantic Irish nationalism, which genders the nation female because it equates suffering with a feminine position, articulated primarily through portrayals of weeping, mourning, defenseless women in allegorical figures like Mother Ireland. Of the four central characters, only Billy, the male, Protestant, loyalist soldier, is able to move about freely. Lorraine and Colette are hindered by their pregnant bellies, Eugene by his wounded body, and Eugene and Colette by the state and the threat of violence. The film plays on notions of confinement, a word that signifies imprisonment and is also a polite synonym for pregnancy. In *Four Days in July*, the subordinate and victimized position is a feminine one, and in this, the film is consistent with anti-colonial nationalism that allegorizes the battered nation as a woman being raped, beaten, subdued. Such an allegory spills over into the separate but dialogically related discourses of colonialism and anti-colonial nationalism, both of which have, for different ideological reasons, declared the colonized male to be "feminized" because of his subordination.

This gendered metaphor of the nation maintains the hegemony of heteronormativity, precludes the possibility of a female liberator, obscures how occupying powers alter their violent tactics based on the gender or sex of the subjugated person, and hides the ways nationalism restricts and subordinates women, placing the onus for restoring the "purity" of the nation onto women and *only* women. Important for this book, the nation-as-subjugated-woman construction also cannot account for moments when suffering and vulnerability are a central performative aspect of masculinity, as is the case with Irish nationalist martyrdom. When films reiterate nationalism's gendered metaphors and use them to court sympathy for nationalist characters, nationalism, even when accepted as a valid political discourse—as in Leigh's film—remains a thing apart from feminism. Ultimately, by implicitly or explicitly accepting gendered national metaphors, films write actual women out of history, reinforce the romantic and mythic aspects of an uncritically nationalist history, and continue to restrict constructions of both femininity and masculinity.

Representing States of Emergency

Chapter 1 addresses the dialectic between feminism and Irish republicanism by exploring two important films from the 1980s: *Maeve* and *Hush-a-Bye Baby*. My analysis of these films engages the rest of Benjamin's thesis quoted above, wherein he sees the state of emergency as the rule rather than the exception. He then calls for a new vision of history appropriate to this insight, which will enable the historian to "clearly realize that it is our task to bring about a real state of emergency" (1969, 257). I argue that Murphy's and Harkin's films meet Benjamin's challenge in two significant ways. They contest state-of-emergency discourses within their narratives and they provoke crises in representation through the use of fragmentation and discontinuity on an audio-visual, editorial, and narrative level. Each film wrestles with traditional nationalist visions of Irish femininity and the Irish landscape while simultaneously addressing the omnipresence of the British Army in the streets of Belfast and Derry. Drawing out the contest that exists in the North between being seen—mostly through surveillance and journalism—and self-representation, I examine how the films trace continuities between the objectives of republicanism and feminism, even if Irish nationalist discourse is sometimes blind to such common goals.

Chapter 2 examines three films about the H-Blocks of Her Majesty's Prison the Maze (formerly Long Kesh internment camp): *Some Mother's Son*, *H3*, and *Hunger*, each of which must engage with the contradiction between the corporeality of the prison protests and the emphasis on transcendence that is central to how Catholicism and Irish nationalism frame martyrdom. I interrogate the films' use of Christian iconography and explore representations of vulnerability central to the constructions of masculinity that prisoners formed in response to the violence of the prison system. I also consider the extent to which the images and narratives of the three films can accommodate the hunger strikers' understanding of their own deaths, which, as Allen Feldman has argued, they saw as a necessary sacrifice for the resurrection of the republican movement (1991, 243). Ultimately, I argue that traditional cinematic conceptions of militant masculinity, which imagine a powerful, aggressive, imposing male body, are inadequate for understanding and representing the particular ways in which the Blanketmen used pain and suffering as a form of anti-state violence, embodying Terrence MacSwiney's declaration, "It is not those who can inflict the most, but those who can suffer the most, who will conquer" (Ellmann 1993, 60). I trace a contest between heroic and vulnerable masculinities, arguing that in the figure of the Blanketman

Irish republicanism found a new allegory for Ireland's subjugation and resistance, one that is clearly gendered male.

The mother-son dyad central to Catholicism and Irish nationalism gave the Blanketmen and their mothers a potent symbolic language that enabled them to link their struggle in the jails to the larger history of British colonialism and confront the current British government with an image of passive suffering that pulled focus from the prisoners' ties to a wider armed struggle. But this language obstructed representations of women political prisoners, specifically those in Armagh Gaol in the 1970s and 1980s. My third chapter addresses the discursive invisibility of Armagh prisoners, who were marginalized within republicanism as well as feminism, despite the relevance of their protests to both. In this chapter, I look at the few texts that do represent the women in Armagh, including republican pamphlets and murals, Maeve Murphy's film *Silent Grace*, and Pat Murphy's *Anne Devlin*, which, I argue, functions in part as an allegorical representation of the women in Armagh. Both *Silent Grace* and *Anne Devlin* turn on questions of silence, visibility, and agency. Like the play it was adapted from—*Now and at the Hour of Our Death*—*Silent Grace* alludes to the Virgin Mary in its very title: the apparition of the Virgin at Knock in 1879, as Luke Gibbons notes, was distinguished by her silence. Anne Devlin played an active role in Robert Emmett's 1803 rebellion, was arrested, tortured, and jailed, and is best remembered for her refusal to talk, a silence often celebrated as passive fidelity to Emmett rather than an active act of defiance on Devlin's part (Gibbons 1996, 108–9). In Murphy's film, Devlin's silence and her ability to "speak" through her body become forms of agency, yet the film resists essentialist notions of woman as body and a naïve celebration of silence as an inherently revolutionary state. In contrast, *Silent Grace* has trouble holding onto the materiality of the Armagh protests. While the film features an innovative attempt to appropriate nationalist iconography for the Armagh women, in its dependence on contemporary gender norms, *Silent Grace* also imprisons its characters within the symbolic language of patriarchal nationalism.

If silence could become a form of agency or a type of grace for republican women, for women in the republic it became a restrictive condition imposed on them by the Church and the family in order to protect a particular image of Irish identity. In chapter 4, I consider questions of exclusion and resistance in the context of the Irish Republic's Magdalene laundries run by Catholic nuns, where women who were sexually active, suspected of sexual activity, or the victims of sexual violence could find themselves incarcerated. In penance for their "sins," the women did laundry by hand six days a week for roughly ten hours a day. The chapter focuses on *The Magdalene Sisters* and *Sinners*, addressing how the nature of incarceration and the potential for resistance to penal inscription are altered when the penal institution is run by a religious order and is based on the "laws" of nationalism, sin, and sexuality. Both films take place in the 1960s, the mythical decade of modernization. Following Gibbons's argument that tradition is modernity's double rather than its opposite (1996, 82–93), I address the issues that arise from setting the film in such a nationally symbolic decade. I consider the ways that *The Magdalene Sisters* resists the lure of nostalgia while *Sinners* has a more ambivalent relationship to the past. I argue that by setting their narratives in the decade of national modernization, both films potentially imply that nationalist and Catholic restrictions on women's bodies and agency ended in the 1960s, which in turn creates the false impression that strictures on female sexuality are incompatible with modernity. *The Magdalene Sisters* complicates this relationship between past and present in part by deploying stylistic elements that are at odds with what initially seems to be the film's preference for realism. Furthermore, both films place extensive blame on the Catholic Church, eliding the ways that the modern, postcolonial Irish state colluded in this exploitation of Irish women.

1

Into the Quagmire

Feminism, Nationalism, Partition

IN *PICTURING DERRY* (Dave Fox, 1985), members of a photography collective recall that when they showed their work at an arts college in England, audience members complained that the photographs were too "heavy." While one of the photographers explains that the collective deliberately avoided politically weighty material, the film cuts to a series of the exhibited images—a woman standing on a hillside, a woman kneeling before an altar, a street scene of people going about their everyday tasks. All relatively mundane, these black-and-white photographs would be simple slices of life were they taken in London or Dublin, but when looking at images shot in Derry—a city whose very name is disputed—the audience perceives a political and emotional weight that oppresses and alienates them from the subject matter. The reception of these photographs in 1980s England reveals the way that meaning emerges through the circulation of images in a given field: decades of media coverage of the "troubles" have primed the English audience to see heaviness where the Derry collective sees everyday life.

Through surveillance, incidents of state and anti-state violence, and the accumulation of photojournalistic images of warfare, representations of space in Northern Ireland have become charged with a sense of menace. One result of the weight of that history has been a tendency in film and media to imagine political engagement as a burdensome trait of an essential Irish nature rather than as something that emerged in relation to a particular set of historical and political circumstances. Thus, for some of the audience members, the key to "lightening" the Derry collective's

32

photographs was to leave Irish people out of the image entirely. As one photographer explains:

> So they asked us why didn't we take photographs of scenery. . . . It was me that said, "Well, if we took photographs of scenery—if we go out and take a photograph of trees and bushes and a lovely green field, well, we don't know what's behind the trees and bushes." And little did I know that two years later my husband was to be shot dead by the British Army and the RUC—and they lay in wait for him . . . behind bushes and trees, and he was shot in a really scenic setting, by the Waterside. . . . So that's what scenery means to us; you don't know who's behind a bush or a tree. (*Picturing Derry* 1985)

For the arts-college audience, the countryside is the antidote to the oppressiveness of Northern urban life, but for the Derry photographer such binary oppositions ring false. A scenic setting seemingly empty of people offers no refuge from the politics of occupation. In fact, it only facilitates the violent actions of state security forces.

The imminent threat that the landscape conceals—in this case government assassins, but in other instances, paramilitary—is captured in Willie Doherty's work, which represents pervasive, invisible surveillance through alluring photographs of river embankments, hills, bushes, bridges, and streets that throb with a disconcerting silence as we realize every space is eerily devoid of people. But even when traces of human activity are present, they are hardly reassuring. In such photos, something has happened or is about to happen, and since the event itself always eludes the photographer and the viewer, we wonder what else is just beyond our grasp. The sense of recent or impending violence that saturates Doherty's landscapes is heightened by the stunning visual style of the photographs, especially in his later cibachrome prints. Vivid, glossy, and soaked with color, works like "Border Incident" and "Border Road (Diptych)" juxtapose the wild beauty of the Irish landscape with the charred remains of cars or the cement barricades installed by security forces to block traffic from crossing unapproved roads at the border.

In *The Outskirts* (fig. 2), deep-green shrubs backlit by a sumptuous, purple sunset compete for our attention with screeching tire tracks on a

2. Willie Doherty, *The Outskirts*, 1994, cibachrome print mounted on aluminum (48 x 72 in./122 x 183 cm), edition of 3. Courtesy of Alexander and Bonin Gallery.

road in the foreground. Severed from a historical or political sense of place, the photo might encourage us to focus on the picturesque landscape and muse over the juxtaposition of natural scenery with the industrial traces of modern life. But in the context of Derry's border roads, where a burned chassis could be the sign of a traffic accident, a car bomb, or a driver shot and killed by the army, every element in the frame resonates with evidentiary significance, even though the "evidence" itself gets us no closer to solving the mystery.

Doherty's photography—particularly his earlier, black-and-white work—has been characterized as photojournalistic in style, but his images reject the certainty of vision that both photojournalism and surveillance rely on. By infusing his work with an ill-defined threat, Doherty calls attention to the processes by which photographic images acquire meaning based not only on what is seen but also on what is unseen, what we can't see, what we wish we could see and know for certain. Leaving people out of the frame, Doherty denies the viewer the journalistic authority to narrate the lives of others or the sense of power through watching while remaining unseen that surveillance, and often cinema, entail. His photographs are heavy not because Irish people are overburdened with political conviction, but because the sense of being watched and the fear of an unseen presence press down on a given space, and like the pervading, silent fog prevalent in his early work, these vague threats haunt every corner of the frame. Evoking and undercutting the two modes of image making that dominate representations of the North—surveillance and media coverage—Doherty's work calls attention to the historical role of images in Northern Ireland as well as the urgent need for self-representation.

While Doherty's photographs and videos offer shrewd analyses of the politics of vision and the contestation of space in an occupied context, they are less concerned with understanding how each of these interacts with questions of gender. *Maeve* (Pat Murphy, 1981) and *Hush-a-Bye Baby* (Margo Harkin, 1989) approach the need for self-generated images of Northern Ireland through the audio-visual frameworks provided by feminist filmmaking of the 1970s and 1980s. As a result, they reveal the gendered politics of occupation and the ways that space is claimed, guarded, and placed under surveillance by a range of competing forces that often converge on the bodies of women. Northern Ireland is shaped by a "besieging cartography"—a term that Camille Mansour has used to characterize the militarization of space in Palestine's occupied territories (2001, 87)—of official and unofficial forces, which can make shooting a film on location difficult if not impossible. This occupation of space in the name of security takes the form of static installations—peace lines, police stations, army barracks, interrogation centers, and some checkpoints—but the moving bodies of soldiers and police officers on patrol also alter the map of cities as they move through them.[1] On the street, the relentless sense of a one-way

---

1. The "peace lines" are the walls of corrugated tin topped with razor or barbed wire separating Catholic and Protestant neighborhoods, particularly in Belfast. Using the term without irony, the British Army installed these barriers in the 1970s to replace the makeshift barricades of burned cars and debris that residents had built to mark the borders of neighborhoods that were increasingly all-Catholic or all-Protestant. More recent walls are made of concrete and razor wire and sometimes called "interfaces."

gaze during the thirty years of the troubles was manifest in the presence of security forces patrolling in flak jackets, combat boots, helmets, and tanks. They had the power to search, look, photograph, and shoot, but to stare at or photograph a tank or solider was (and is) to risk being stopped and questioned, at the least. For roughly three decades, Northern Ireland comprised numerous zones of abandonment, where exceptional status was conferred on women and men whose religious, class, and political affiliations marked them as threats to the British or Northern Irish state or to the political ideology that held local hegemony. These spaces were cordoned off and fell under heavy surveillance in the form of Royal Ulster Constabulary (RUC) stations and personnel, British Army soldiers and checkpoints, police and army cameras and microphones, and auxiliary security forces like the B-Specials and the Ulster Defence Regiment.[2] In loyalist and republican neighborhoods, outlawed paramilitary organizations including the Ulster Volunteer Force (UVF), Ulster Freedom Fighters (UFF), Provisional Irish Republican Army (PIRA, Provos),[3] and Irish Nationalist Liberation Army (INLA) helped to ensure that local areas would remain politically and religiously homogeneous, reclaiming space through their own unofficial checkpoints and border patrols.

The heavy presence of state security forces criminalized urban Catholic communities through a circular logic similar to that deployed against residents of South Central Los Angeles or the suburbs of Paris, where policing is justified by the assumed criminality of a population, while

2. Allen Feldman describes the B Specials as "a Protestant militia that functioned as a police reserve and was known for its anti-Catholic bigotry and indiscriminate anti-Catholic violence." They were replaced in 1970 by the UDR, a "locally recruited reserve unit of the British army, akin to the American National Guard" (Feldman 1991, 278).

3. The IRA split in the 1970s into the Provisional IRA, who advocated a sustained campaign of assassinations, bombings, and other forms of political violence, and the Official IRA, who were opposed to the use of force. Film and media texts rarely specify between an imagined, generic IRA and the Provisional IRA. However, actual members of the IRA do sometimes make this distinction, as do anthropologists and historians who have covered the history of the troubles. Throughout the book, I follow the lead of the text under discussion, usually referring to a cinematic "IRA" and an actual PIRA or Provos.

the criminality of a population is supposedly made evident by the constant presence of police or army personnel. This criminalization was also backed by emergency legislation that in effect suspended human rights for people under suspicion. In what is now a familiar governmental anti-terrorism strategy, Britain categorized republican violence against the state as crime, but treated it as an exceptional offense. As crime, it had no legitimate motivation, it stemmed from psychic and social pathology; however, because it was also non-crime, its perpetrators were not entitled to due process. And, because anti-state violence was also not war, republican combatants were not entitled to prisoner-of-war status. Furthermore, the invisibility of paramilitary members was used by the state to justify various policies that reconstituted republican neighborhoods as spaces of the exception, where the law was reordered to prove a pre-assumed guilt. Throughout the 1970s, under various policies, nationalists in Northern Ireland could be: interned indefinitely without charge; interned, tortured, released after seven days, and then charged; tried in special courts designed to secure convictions; convicted on the testimony of paid informers (known as supergrasses); arrested for setting foot on British soil; and randomly searched on the streets or at home.[4] High-rise apartment buildings like the Divis Flats were used as surveillance towers, while helicopters, tanks, foot patrols, and the sealing off of areas as no-go zones created an atmosphere of siege.

Doherty has stated his interest in the politics of vision, which in the context of Northern Ireland's troubles takes on an immediacy that has a direct connection to daily life. Media coverage has generally imagined the crushing presence of state security forces in nationalist areas as the unfortunate side effect of bringing law and order to protect the general population from a fanatic and unruly few. But members of republican communities—often preemptively silenced through the accusation of partisanship and fanaticism—have found other representational avenues to express the ways that a state of emergency becomes routine. For example,

---

4. I address the history of emergency legislation, special powers acts, and incarceration in the following chapters.

in his brief and cursory investigation into the events of Bloody Sunday, Lord Chief Justice Widgery preemptively silenced the anti-internment marchers through moralistic language that blamed those shot by paratroopers for their own deaths and injuries. Voices that contradicted the British Army's version of events were unheard, dismissed as biased, or marginalized. In response, the survivors of Bloody Sunday—relatives of the dead and wounded, civil rights activists, members of the nationalist community—have found multiple other ways to be heard, including anniversary marches, murals, posters, exhibitions, websites, and films. These venues served as unofficial archives until the exoneration of the victims came with the pronouncement of the Saville verdict in 2010, thirty-eight years after the event.[5] The security situation in the North resonates with Walter Benjamin's insight that the "tradition of the oppressed teaches us that the 'state of emergency' in which we live is not the exception but the rule. We must attain to a conception of history that is in keeping with this insight. Then we shall clearly realize that it is our task to bring about a real state of emergency" (1969, 257).[6] Benjamin connects recognizing the current state of emergency as the rule and not the exception to the need for a new conception of history. The revolutionary potential of this recognition lies in a new understanding not just of history but of historiography as well. Writing that Benjamin "demonstrated the need for a conception of history that could accommodate the spasmodic irruptions of multiple pasts into a condensed present," Derek Gregory sees postcolonial

5. The Saville Inquiry was established as part of the Good Friday Agreement. Its mandate was to reinvestigate the events of January 30, 1972, since the Widgery tribunal was a gross miscarriage of justice. Whereas Paul Greengrass's film *Bloody Sunday* (2002) is the most famous treatment of the events, other films with closer ties to Derry have also offered evidence and narratives ignored by Widgery. These include *Sunday* (Jimmy Mac-Govern, 2002) and *The Bloody Sunday Murders* (Margo Harkin and Eamonn McCann 1991). Exhibitions include the *Hidden Truths: Bloody Sunday 1972*, traveling exhibition curated by Trisha Ziff, 2000–2002. See also the Bloody Sunday Trust, http://www.bloody sundaytrust.org/index-02.html.

6. Lauren Berlant also cites this thesis in her explanation of hygienic governmentality (Berlant 1997, 175).

historiography as a possible model, given that numerous diverse histories converge in a postcolonial present (Gregory 2004, 7). As I noted in the introduction, in its role as a corrective to the domination of colonialist history, postcolonial historiography must challenge amnesiac and nostalgic histories of colonialism and/or occupation, but if postcolonial historiography is to truly engage with the past in order to "attain to a new conception of history" and bring about a real state of emergency, it must also resist the seductions of amnesiac and nostalgic nationalist histories. To truly aspire to a new form of history, postcolonial historiography must acknowledge the internal struggles and divisions that pre-dated colonialism as well as the deep rifts left in the postcolonial landscape by the colonizer and even the independence struggle. Because these struggles, like nationalism itself, are often gendered, feminist historiography has much to contribute to this project.

In Northern Ireland, the severity of censorship facilitated an amnesiac history of colonialism that immediately rewrote the present even as it unfolded. Access to power requires access not only to historical memory but also to its circulation. This circulation of memory is partly the function that mural painting serves in northern republican neighborhoods. Along with hand-painted road signs in the Irish language, and graffiti crossing out the "London" on highway signs leading to "Londonderry," murals on gable walls mark national(ist) territory and disseminate an oppositional history, one that rejects the legitimacy of the British or unionist state. Republican murals are adept at resisting colonialist nostalgia and amnesia. Depictions of the death of Ulster warrior Cúchulainn, the famine of 1847, the executed leaders of 1916, Che Guevara, Palestinian flags and Irish tricolors, dead hunger striker Bobby Sands, and victims of the SAS's shoot-to-kill policy recall the brutality of colonialism, link Ireland's colonial past to Northern Ireland's occupied present, and situate Irish republicanism within global liberation struggles. However, in doing so, they risk mobilizing the nostalgic and amnesiac nationalist histories that tend to dominate postcolonial cultures. In Ireland, a real state of emergency would be one in which the conceptions of history that lend legitimacy to structures of oppression along national and religious lines and preemptively dismiss republican voices as fanatic, hysterical, or divisive are challenged alongside those that exist along gender lines and dismiss feminist voices as alien, divisive, and even traitorous. Such modes of historiography must be thrown into crisis together so that communities silenced by occupation have a space to be heard without being explained away by Britain or co-opted by nationalism for poetic rewriting.

Maeve and *Hush-a-Bye Baby* strive toward the conception of history that Benjamin advocates. Set and shot in Belfast and Derry, respectively, at a time when most film shot in the North was news footage and fiction films set in Northern Ireland were often shot in Britain or the Irish Republic, both films shift the focal point of representation from the alternately romanticized and demonized figure of the IRA gunman in his urban gangster milieu onto the ordinary lives of women and teenage girls in Catholic, republican neighborhoods. In training their cameras on the mundane, Murphy and Harkin radically alter the very terms on which Northern Ireland is represented, discussed, and debated. In each of these films, the North is neither a space apart from the Republic of Ireland or the United Kingdom, nor is it comfortably attached to either state. It is a relational space, readable only in the context of these two other states, a tumultuous space where the government inscribes its presence on the bodies, homes, and streets of people who are only nominally citizens. Made by feminist filmmakers from the North whose work is often sympathetic to the politics of Irish republicanism, *Maeve* and *Hush-a-Bye Baby* provoke a crisis in cinematic histories of the North by representing a state of emergency from feminist *and* republican perspectives. In redefining the time and space of the troubles, both films rethink the spatial and temporal boundaries of "occupied Ireland."

Each film is set during the first half of the 1980s, an agitated moment in Irish history during which the extreme forms of state restriction and control over the bodies of citizens on both sides of the border became more visible than in earlier decades. In the North, the 1981 hunger strike brought a media victory to the republican movement. Protests staged by male and female political prisoners and their relatives—begun in 1976—culminated in the death of ten men during the hunger strike and spotlighted the chokehold that the British and Northern Irish governments

had secured over the nationalist community during the years leading up
to it. The 1981 protest was the second hunger strike in two years, and
although women prisoners were unsuccessful in lobbying to participate
in it, three women had joined the first, in 1980. For republican women,
participation in all prison protests was important for their visibility as both
women and Irish republicans. While male prisoners relied on a performance of martyrdom for publicity, Irish feminists focused on the right
to bodily integrity to garner support for the women. *Maeve* addresses this
overlap between feminist and republican concerns and tactics when its
main character tells her boyfriend, "When you're denied power, when
it's frequently co-opted, the only thing you have left to fight with is your
body." But whereas republicans in the North found ways to turn their bodies into politically motivating spectacles of disempowerment, on the other
side of the border, the symbolic use of women's bodies deployed in Ireland's various past independence struggles often served the restrictions
the postcolonial Irish Republic placed on the bodies and freedoms of real
Irish women by effacing the contributions women had made to the political life of Ireland.

That state's vise grip on women's bodies became woefully apparent
with the 1983 referendum approving a constitutional ban on abortion (the
eighth amendment), the illegal status of which had not changed since
the 1861 "Offenses against the Person" Act, but was now constitution-
ally protected (Conrad 2004, 72). The politicians and priests who shrieked
about the disastrous threat women's subjectivity posed to the good of the
Irish nation reached their shrillest pitch in Bishop Joseph Cassidy's cry
that "the most dangerous place to be [in Ireland] at the moment is in the
mother's womb" (Gibbons 1992, 13). Such hyperbole and hysteria imagines the uterus of a pregnant woman as a contested space, not unlike the
North of Ireland. In this configuration, women are the potential enemies
of nationalism; like the British colonizers of the past and the British Army
of the present, they occupy the national womb, threatening the innocent
Irish life that tries to grow in a hostile environment. This construction
of uterus as national space masks the actual dynamics of a patriarchal,
borderline-theocratic postcolonial state that not only regulated women's

access to birth control and abortion, but also sanctioned the incarceration of women in Magdalene laundries.[7]

The amendment was vehemently contested, and in the months before and after the referendum passed, several incidents occurred in Ireland that seemed to heighten the urgency and intensity of the abortion debates. Among these were reports that statues of Mary were moving in grottos and churches throughout the country, symptomatic of Ireland's feminism-induced moral illness. It was Mary, the Virgin Mother, who was moving and not Jesus or any of Catholicism's numerous saints. That the Holy Mother would choose to exercise her kinetic autonomy at the moment when the country was debating the issue of restricting the control real women had over their own bodies, including the right to leave Ireland to seek abortion in England, reveals the difficulty in representing the physical bodies of real women without the intrusion of the metaphysical and allegorical bodies that have traditionally served as representations of feminine virtue in Catholicism and Irish nationalism. *Maeve* and *Hush-a-Bye Baby* explore the historical relationship between feminism—scorned during the War of Independence by conservative nationalists as an English import—and Irish nationalism.

Martin McLoone has referred to the "interface" between feminism and republicanism as "a dialectical quagmire," implying the impossibility of resolving tensions between the two (McLoone 2000, 149). But the questions that arise from a feminist critique of Irish republicanism and a republican critique of feminism do not necessarily need definitive resolutions in order to warrant investigation. *Maeve* and *Hush-a-Bye Baby* plunge into this dialectical quagmire, and both films address feminism's triangulated relationship to the repressive Northern Irish state on the one hand and Irish nationalism (North and South) on the other. They do this by depicting the constant governmental state of emergency in the North, while also confronting the tradition in Irish nationalism of imagining

7. Citing Laury Oaks, Conrad writes of the abortion debates, "At stake at the time was not only women's agency over their own bodies, but also the permeability of the borders between the Republic of Ireland and the rest of Europe" (Conrad 2004, 71).

Ireland as a woman, a tradition that sets itself up in defensive opposition to female autonomy. In *Maeve*, this sense of state crisis is manifest in the British and UDR soldiers who threaten women's bodies as well as in the menacing presence of unionists who antagonize Maeve's family. In *Hush-a-Bye Baby*, the RUC and army frequently emerge from the margins of the frame to disrupt the narrative and to hinder the movements of Goretti and her boyfriend Ciaran every time they come close to experiencing something like a normal teenage life.

State surveillance is omnipresent in both films, but the Church and local community are also always watching, and the films each address this internal monitoring, although in different ways. *Maeve* critiques the heroicism of Irish republican historiography, while *Hush-a-Bye Baby* also crosses the border into the republic to address the status of women in the postcolonial state. Critiquing nationalist patriarchy from within, both films recognize that although Catholic men in northern, republican neighborhoods are subjugated by the British and unionist governments, they are also capable of repeating the structures of oppression within their own communities along gender lines. Both films advance an argument for the end of British occupation and unionist segregation, but they do so with an eye toward what happens after liberation, especially for women. In *Maeve*, this historical awareness is conveyed through debates, stories, and arguments among the characters, while in *Hush-a-Bye Baby*, Goretti's trip to the Irish Republic offers a glimpse into the future of nationalism when women's liberation is neglected as a connected and equally important issue. As part of their acknowledgement of the oppression of men and women under British occupation, neither *Maeve* nor *Hush-a-Bye Baby* imagines Irish men as brutal. Violence against women is enacted by the state, not the men of their community, who are at worst sexist and oblivious to women's subjectivity. Thus, both films address degrees of oppression rather than construct a blanket patriarchy. Often, women respond to the sexism of the men in their own communities with a sense of solidarity and humor that the films tie to all-female spaces, whereas their interactions with state power are often terrifying and leave characters deprived of agency. Through humor as well as polemics, Murphy and Harkin achieve what troubles films usually fail to: they separate sexism and patriarchy from essentialist constructions of Irish masculinity, and they divorce maternity and gentleness (imagined as political naïveté) from essentialist images of Irish femininity.

Maeve is sympathetic to its eponymous character's attempts to raise the consciousness of her sister and others within the republican community, but the film also implies that Maeve's conception of patriarchy as a monolithic mode of domination at times blinds her to how the men in her community are themselves vulnerable to state violence and to the possibility that women have a vested interest in republicanism. In *Hush-a-Bye Baby*, the adolescence of the characters limits their overt political activity, but the film represents Goretti's emerging sense of self through a feminist perspective that accounts for the complexity of Irish nationalism as a discourse and as a power structure. Nationalist patriarchy in the North of Ireland does not enjoy the same level of power as its southern counterpart, and it does not hold the same hegemonic position in the North as unionist patriarchy does. At the same time, nationalist patriarchy has achieved ascendancy in Northern Catholic communities, and expectations of heterosexuality and motherhood within a Catholic marriage still hold sway over the choices and self-images of women in *Maeve* and *Hush-a-Bye Baby*. In Belfast, Maeve must constantly defend her feminist position against accusations that her politics will weaken the nationalist cause, the undertone being that a feminist agenda is un-Irish and unpatriotic unless it remains subordinate to the national question, while in Derry, Goretti contends not only with the social expectations of her own community but also with the entrenched patriarchy of the republic when she crosses the border into Donegal.

On the level of content, *Maeve* and *Hush-a-Bye Baby* narrate new histories that challenge hegemonic ones, but in representing various states of emergency, the films aspire to a new mode of historiography, one suggested by Benjamin's writing. A motif of fragmentation recurs in the *Theses*, in how they are written and in the metaphors Benjamin uses to express the fragility of memory as it faces ideological and governmental appropriation. This motif also suggests a new conception of *historiography*, where the release of disruptive fragments of memory can shatter the historical "truths" undergirding hegemony. *Maeve* and *Hush-a-Bye Baby* attempt to bring about the "real state of emergency" that Benjamin calls for by addressing questions of history in their narratives and questions of historiography in their form, through audio-visual, editorial, and narrative discontinuity. The films use narrative and stylistic fragmentation as a motif to resist a sense of organic wholeness and to question patriarchal nationalism as well as the legitimacy of the Irish and British states' claims of ownership over the bodies of their citizens. In *Maeve*, memories appear as personal flashbacks that are not overtly marked as such, so that their placement in time becomes disorienting. Murphy also breaks the film's continuity through a series of debates between Maeve and her republican boyfriend Liam that seem to occur outside of time. During these discussions, which concern nationalist historiography and its marginalization of women, "the realist conception of character within the narrative is abandoned and they come to represent elements within an intellectual argument" between the two discourses (Johnston 1981a, 58). *Hush-a-Bye Baby* constructs a critical, self-reflexive history using jarring fragments such as flashes of the Virgin Mary's image, allusions to the horrifying events surrounding the abortion debates, and a representation of how the presence of the British Army disrupts the ordinary lives of the film's teenage characters.

States of Emergency

Maeve explores the dialectic between feminism and republicanism through the director's own view that "in Ireland, their revolutionary potential is in relationship to each other" (Fox 1984, 31). The title character, Maeve Sweeney, returns from a self-imposed exile in London to visit her family in the republican Falls Road area of West Belfast. Maeve's return to Belfast stirs up memories—portrayed through flashbacks—of childhood and adolescence, and through the flashbacks, the film offers glimpses into the ideological confrontations that led her to seek refuge in London. The film flows in and out of three timeframes: Maeve in the present as a dedicated feminist, Maeve as a teenager looking for a way out of republican culture, and Maeve as a young girl driving through the countryside, a captive audience for her father's stories. The same actress plays teenage and adult Maeve, so that the adult character's closely cropped, feminist-chic haircut is often the only marker orienting the spectator in the present. Like John Sayles's *Lone Star* (1996), *Maeve* often transitions between past and present within a single shot, panning from one time period to the next without the clear break of a cut to mark the shift in time. Through Murphy's approach to temporality, the film crosses the border between past and present, and history is bound up with personal memory. The film offers a subjective and intimate history that contrasts with the official history of the state as well as the heroic histories of Irish nationalism. By setting its narrative in the Falls, among women who have varying degrees of investment in feminist and republican politics, *Maeve* deploys a feminist critique of Irish nationalism and British imperialism, but just as important, the film offers a republican critique of imperialism and, a little more gently, feminism.

As a filmmaker, Murphy has dedicated her career to protecting women's stories from historical exclusion. *Nora* (2000) rescued Nora Barnacle from the shadow of James Joyce, and *Anne Devlin* (1984) portrayed the woman who acted as Robert Emmett's housekeeper during the 1803 uprising as having her own stake in Irish liberation. But in an unfortunate irony, Murphy herself has been all but forgotten within feminist film studies outside of Ireland. Although Claire Johnston wrote about Murphy and *Maeve* for *Screen* in the 1980s, scholarship on Murphy outside of the realm of Irish film studies stops there. This oversight is unfortunate, especially given Murphy's contributions to feminist filmmaking, and despite the slightness of her filmography, her work deserves to be placed alongside that of Margarethe Von Trotta, Lizzie Borden, Chantal Ackerman, and other directors celebrated for formulating a new language of cinema to tell women's stories. Murphy's first feature-length film, *Maeve* takes representation to task alongside British and Irish historiography. The film mimics the structure of personal memory, including fragments of images that have no obvious narrative purpose—such as a shot of men unloading blank TVs from a van and piling them on the street—in order to deconstruct what Murphy has criticized as "heroic memory," an amalgam of Celtic folklore, Irish history, and Catholic martyrdom. It is this memory, according to Murphy, that leaves Irish nationalism frozen in a glorious, mythical past and unable to engage with the realities of the present. The film aligns this stagnation with male characters, primarily Maeve's father, Martin, who tells folkloric stories that seem to grow out of the green landscape, and her boyfriend, Liam, who "moves from an alienation from the kind of [republican ideology] which had sustained his father, to a conviction that those beliefs can be mobilised in the service of a more progressive politics" (Johnston 1981b, 66). Although Liam is willing to make concessions to feminism (once the nation is whole again), from Maeve's perspective, his position remains problematic in part because the myths that nationalism rests on prevent women from being portrayed as the agents of history.

Throughout *Maeve*, Murphy empties the mythical, allegorical, and heroic content of names, places, and representational forms in order to make room for the everyday. The names of Maeve and her sister Roisín resonate with national significance: Maeve is the Warrior Queen of Connacht who invades Ulster in the *Táin Bó Cuailgne* (*The Cattle Raid at Coole*) and is ultimately defeated by Cúchulainn, the hero of the Ulster Cycle claimed as a cultural symbol by both loyalist and republican communities, while Roisín Dubh (Dark Rosaleen) is a female allegorical representation of Ireland, spoken of and to in *aisling* (visionary) poetry. But these names lose their poetic overtones and become important primarily as cultural signifiers of the sisters' Irish identity as the film engages with the mythology of Irish nationalist history, which displaced women's struggle for equality with women who functioned as virtuous heroines or national allegories.[8] Likewise, the film opens with a critique of film genre through a simple juxtaposition between cinematic representation and the everyday when it opens with a close-up of Martin Sweeney's face illuminated by the changing colors of light flickering off the TV, which is accompanied by the blaring sounds and triumphant music of a war film. The film-within-a-film's

---

8. Comparing Maeve Sweeney's return to Belfast with Queen Maeve's raid on Ulster, Luke Gibbons explains that when the *Táin* was adapted for late nineteenth-century culture during the Irish Literary Revival, the sexual power and physical prowess of Queen Maeve was cut from the text to bring her more in line with Victorian femininity. Thus, in the feminist context of Murphy's film, he argues, "It is hardly surprising . . . that . . . the return of another Maeve to Ulster should bring about a direct confrontation with this mythic version of the past" (Gibbons 1996, 118–19).

heroic rendition of war is undercut when Martin pulls back the curtain in the front room window and watches the British Army hustle his neighbors out of their homes and down the dark street in what at first appears to be a sweep of arrests, but turns out to be a bomb scare evacuation. Rather than go outside, Martin retreats to the kitchen and sits down to write a letter. As he begins the letter aloud, "My dear Maeve, I thought I'd take this opportunity to write to you," the film cuts to a shot of Maeve at a party in London, and then to an aerial shot from her point of view of a stone ring set into the Irish landscape as her plane approaches Belfast. A man sitting next to her comments on the megalithic ruin, explaining that he is in Ireland to do research for an article on stone rings for the *Journal of Lost Knowledge*. As they pass through a security checkpoint, the man offers Maeve a lift, but when he learns that she's heading into the city center, he tells her, "Oh, I'm afraid I won't be going anywhere *near* Belfast."

These early sequences offer examples of the tension between Maeve's experience and what Gibbons calls "history inscribed with a male authorial voice" (1996, 118–19). Murphy does not take it for granted that Maeve can simply tell her own story. Instead, the character must immediately compete with not one but two male versions of what knowledge should be communicated and how. The film offers different national forms of patriarchy, which are positioned at varying points of power. Irish and British historiographies may share a tendency to marginalize women, but English epistemology remains tied to the central colonialist article of faith that an objective point of view exists, and it is that of the detached Englishman. Martin's letter, set against the cinematic simulacrum of war and its real-life double, sets Maeve's story into motion, motivating the cut to Maeve in London. But this patriarchal summoning is rebuffed by Maeve's point-of-view shot from the airplane—a vantage point that is all encompassing yet also detached. Maeve's perspective resembles aerial surveillance, a modern form of knowledge that contrasts with Martin's old-fashioned epistolary voice-over. But her own view is then co-opted by the Englishman next to her, descending on rural, romantic Ireland to seek and collect lost knowledge for his journal. Tellingly, the Seeker of Lost Knowledge (as the film's credits call him) pursues archival knowledge for its own sake and avoids the contested geography of modern Belfast, where knowledge is inextricably bound up with positions of power. His presence implicitly raises the question of how Irish knowledge came to be lost, and from whose perspective such knowledge is lost.[9] Like the landscape painters of the American West, whose romantic depictions of American Indians as a vanished "race" obscured both the fact of living Native Americans and also the processes by which previous generations were killed and dislocated, the Seeker of Lost Knowledge has no interest in going anywhere near the Irish people of the present. The view of Ireland Maeve sees from the plane is the view he prefers—a glorious green landscape of ancient white-gray ruins and no people.

The stone ring is the first of several ruins in the film, most of which are connected to Martin Sweeney as he drives a young Maeve through the countryside. *Maeve*, Gibbons argues, references the stasis of mythological nationalist history through shots of ruins in the lush countryside, which serve as the backdrop for Martin's stories. Embedded in the landscape, ruins resonate with heroic and folkloric memories, naturalizing history precisely through their intimate ties to the earth (Gibbons 1996, 118–19). Here, national history grows out of the ground; it is essentially linked to the matter of the nation. In *Maeve*, the landscape is "one of the primary means of arresting the flow of events, becoming . . . a form of congealed memory" (Gibbons 1996, 119). But *Maeve* doesn't celebrate the mystical connection between land (which, in Irish nationalism, is *always* linked with woman) and time; rather, the film proposes "a history divested of myth and (self-) deception," a history free of "the cycle of myth and violence in which it has traditionally been encased" (Gibbons 1996, 119–21). As Murphy explains, Martin's stories "interpret the landscape for [Maeve] and prevent her from experiencing it for herself" (Johnston 1981b, 64). His memory interferes with her experience of the landscape, also affecting her relationship to history—Irish history, women's history, and her

9. The Seeker of Lost Knowledge is an interesting concept for a character, triggering associations to Lady Gregory, who collected Irish folklore during the literary revival, while her husband, as an agent of the crown, aided the death and displacement of the people whose "disappearing" traditions she collected.

own personal history. This is echoed in her arguments about history with Liam, which take place outdoors, as Liam attempts to convince Maeve to subordinate her own interpretation of history, her own memories, and her own experiences to the primacy of the national struggle.

Maeve yanks history out of a romantic republican ether and back down to earth by rooting it in the everyday experiences of women in Belfast. In so doing, the film reveals the inner workings of historiography, the process by which stories and people are included or omitted. Whereas Sullivan observes that the deletion of women's experiences and needs from the stories of republican men motivates Maeve's voluntary exile from Belfast (1999, 81–83), Claire Johnston argues that women successfully displace colonialist and nationalist female allegories. Maeve's own feminist discourse ultimately obtains a central space in the narrative and in the frame, and the arguments between Liam and Maeve are crucial to this project (Johnston 1981a, 59). Johnston observes that Maeve progresses from being an off-screen voice at the beginning of the first debate about nationalist history between her and Liam to occupying the center of the frame by the end of the film (Johnston 1981a, 58). But this success is hard won; it does not simply evolve. Throughout the film, Maeve articulates a sense of urgency where history is concerned. When the republican men around her recall nationalist histories yet urge her to "forget the past," Maeve is irate; she is all too aware that forgetting is impossible because "the past comprises the present" (Sullivan 1999, 82). Like Third Cinema, which sees history as a current site of struggle, *Maeve* routinely reminds its spectator that the past is contested terrain, occupied by competing nationalisms. It achieves this visually and on a narrative level, especially in an argument Maeve has with Liam on Cave Hill. Pointing out the power the past holds when wielded in the present, Maeve expresses the need for women to seize the means of historical production for themselves:

Maeve: The past is more powerful than you think. You can't just go back and organize real events that had their *own* reality and their *own* time and arrange them into some pattern that suits you.

Liam: But the work is to take hold of the myth and move forward. To appropriate it and not be used by it like our fathers were.

Maeve: You're *wrong*. The past has its *own* power. It feeds off people believing in it. The more you focus on it, the more reality it gains. The past is a way of reading the present, but it's only liberating if it. . . .
Liam (cutting her off): Then there's no argument.
Maeve: What you're talking about is a *false memory*! The way *you* remember, the way you *want* to remember excludes *me*!

After the Cave Hill argument, Maeve turns away from Liam and walks down through the hill's thick brush while he follows. All on-screen sound is cut off, and Maeve narrates the legend of the formation of the river Boyne in voice-over: "There was once a well, into which it was forbidden to look, but a woman looked in it, and the water rose up out of the well and pursued the woman and drowned her, giving birth to a stream that fertilized the country." At first, the story seems disconnected from the image, as if it were an incongruous intrusion on the soundtrack. But its placement over the footage of Maeve descending the hill and the shot's occurrence immediately after her argument with Liam draws a parallel between Maeve and the woman pursued by water, as if Maeve herself were fleeing from the forbidden well in order to escape being drowned by the poetics of Irish folklore. The story interjected illustrates her point: There is *no* room for her in a heroic, mythic memory. As a woman, her only value is as a national symbolic figure. In the violent imagery of the story, the water chases the woman because of her transgressive assertion of subjectivity, her choice to look, while also signifying her intellectual curiosity (thirst for knowledge). The water pursues her and drowns her for this transgression, but the story justifies the water's brutality through the creation of a fertilizing river. Maeve runs not only from Liam but also from the punishing and sacrificial mythological appropriation of women that the story represents, a story where an act of violence against a woman—one with biblical overtones—is recuperated as a necessary sacrifice for the greater good.[10]

10. Maeve's anger at the rewriting of history and her subsequent departure here resonate with a scene that Sullivan argues is about retelling the past in a way that trivializes

The rural landscape and Celtic history—the space and time of "Ireland"—form the mythical dyad of Irish nationalism. Both have become exclusionary sites of discovery for Irish cultural nationalism in which the presence of material women is obscured by the invention of their allegorical counterparts. Throughout *Maeve*, the countryside, its sites of national significance, and its ossified stone ruins resonate with memories of the dead generations whose failed rebellions form heroic links in the chain of republican history, which is steeped in the poetics of failure rewritten as sacrifice. The rebellions of 1798 and 1803 and the Easter Rising of 1916, while militarily unsuccessful, are nonetheless celebrated for the national martyrs and symbols they generated. Like Christ's sacrifice for humanity, the Irish republican martyr gives his own blood to the inevitable rebirth and eternal life of the nation. Paul Willemen points out that Cave Hill resonates with nationalist historical significance as "the site where [Theobald] Wolfe Tone and the Society of United Irishmen took their famous oath in 1795 to rid Ireland of the English" (Willemen 1994 141). He argues that the presence of Cave Hill adds an additional dimension to Murphy's film, further pulling it away from the conventions of seamless realism. Willemen notes the non-sectarian politics of the United Irishmen, who nevertheless, he states, were shortsighted in their consideration of class and gender. Through the convergence of Maeve's socialist feminism, Liam's socialist republicanism, and Tone's secular, middle-class republicanism, the sequence on Cave Hill functions as what Benjamin has called a "dialectical image, consisting of 'the numbered groups of threads that represent the weft of the past as it feeds into the present'" (Willemen 1994 142).

---

women's participation. As a teenager, Maeve runs into her uncle in a pub and must endure his recounting of her father's incarceration. When Maeve points out that her mother kept the family together while her father was in prison, her uncle dismisses that contribution. This confrontation, Sullivan points out, wherein a group of republican men silence Maeve's defense of her mother as a humorless intrusion on their storytelling, is what immediately precipitates Maeve's expression of her desire to leave Belfast (80–83). See Sullivan 1999, 77–85 for a compelling reading of this scene in relation to surveillance and gender, and as a means to critique psychoanalytic feminist film theory.

Willemen uses *Maeve* as a point of departure to discuss a new avant-garde in cinema, but the questions he raises about the extra-diegetic significance of location are compelling for the rest of the film. Maeve's discussions with Liam shape a feminist critique of republicanism over the course of the film, from her realization that nationalism's heroic memory excludes women to the couple's final argument in Clifton Street cemetery, when Maeve explains that a nationalist project that sees the political demands of women's liberation as extrinsic to the cause of national liberation is an incomplete one, or perhaps, given the setting, a moribund one. Many of the same United Irishmen who took their oath in 1795 and fought in the 1798 rebellion were subsequently buried in the Clifton Street graveyard—some had been executed for treason, others died later in an Ireland bound more tightly to England through the 1800 Act of Union. In their final argument, Liam accuses Maeve of creating her own woman's nationalism and speaking as if women were a separate nation, "a nation within a nation." Maeve responds, "Nationalism is a response to an attack, to imperialism. We *are* like a nation within a nation. Men's relationship to women is *just* like England's relationship to Ireland. You're in possession of us. You occupy us like an army." This statement turns the traditional relationship between colonialism and femininity on its head. Instead of using a feminine allegory to describe the nation under colonization, Maeve uses an imperialist metaphor to explain women's subjugation under patriarchy. Her analogy offers a reason for women's commitment to both feminism and republicanism, and it opens another way into nationalism for women, a way that lets them participate in history and the national struggle as embodied women, outside of the parameters of reproductive heteronormativity and maternal allegories. Although Maeve herself has chosen to leave her republican community, her statement opens up a route of exchange between feminism and republicanism.

The historical significance of the landscape is one concern of *Maeve*, but the film is also very much an urban one. If for Gibbons and Johnston *Maeve* is about finding a way for women to experience and interpret the land and history of the nation without the interference of a patriarchal authority, how does Belfast function in this project? What importance does the city have to the film's feminist intervention? Significantly, Maeve is aligned with two cities—London and Belfast—and their different forms of modernity. London, represented in the single shot at the film's beginning, is a space of bright, airy apartments, wine, and the gathering of intellectuals. But London also has a deeper significance for Irish history. Not only is it the center of the empire and the destination of numerous Irish emigrants, but its association with the women's suffrage movement in the 1910s has also prompted traditionalist Irish nationalism to discredit feminist politics (along with homosexuality) as an English import alien to Irish nature. Belfast, on the other hand, offers the nightmare of modernity seen in warfare and occupation. The Seeker of Lost Knowledge avoids Maeve and Belfast because of their associations with the immediate materiality of the present. Maeve is no mythological Warrior Queen, and there is no *lost* knowledge to discover in Belfast—Ireland's historical relationship to England is legible in the weighty presence of soldiers in flak jackets. Marked by checkpoints, surveillance technology, rubble from bombings, and the moving agents of the state, Belfast, like Derry in *Hush-a-Bye Baby*, is a site of the current and ever-shifting production of knowledge. The same body that is a natural part of the city on one street is a hostile, threatening, and threatened presence on another.

The film uses Belfast as a site of collision between heroic memory and the physical realities of daily life under an occupation. In one flashback, Maeve comes sharply up against the disparity between nationalism's vision of Irish womanhood and the realities of women's lives in Northern Ireland when her class recites Pádraig Pearse's poem "The Mother:"

> I do not grudge them: Lord, I do not grudge
> My two strong sons that I have seen go out
> To break their strength and die, they and a few,
> In bloody protest for a glorious thing,
> They shall be spoken of among their people,
> The generations shall remember them,
> And call them blessed;
> But I will speak their names to my own heart
> In the long nights;
> The little names that were familiar once

Round my dead hearth.
Lord, thou art hard on mothers:
We suffer in their coming and their going;
And tho' I grudge them not, I weary, weary
Of the long sorrow—And yet I have my joy:
My sons were faithful, and they fought.

Written by Pearse while he was awaiting execution for his role in the 1916 Easter Rising, the poem offers an ideal, emblematic mother who resigns herself to her sons' sacrifice for the nation and in doing so becomes not just the individual mother of two sons but also, through *their* blood, mother to the nation. Like the Virgin Mother, the Irish mother suffers a personal loss in order to become mother to something eternal and greater than herself. In Murphy's mind, the poem expresses Pearse's belief that his own imminent death for the Irish nation is necessary and will give retroactive meaning not only to his own life but also to that of his mother. For Pearse, if sons were born to die for Ireland, mothers were born to contribute to the Irish nation by bearing the cross of their sons' sacrifice. In addition to "projecting himself forward into his mother's grief," Murphy explains, Pearse "offers her as comfort the notion that his *action* transforms him into the role of hero, so her *reaction* links her (through him) to the role of a hero's mother, an archetypal image of suffering. In Ireland, all the complexities of Pearce's [sic] personality are reduced to a mythic image—the Catholic ideal of manhood, complete sexlessness—and a repudiation of femaleness apart from tragic images of a Pietà-like mother and Caitlin ni Houlihan" (Johnston 1981b, 67).

While Maeve sits daydreaming, the girls in her class take turns reciting lines, and each speaks her part with mechanical boredom, completely alienated from the meaning and sentiment of the poem and focused mainly on getting through the rote recitation and avoiding the wrath of the dour nun who sits at the head of the classroom in front of a map of Ireland, the nation that failed to materialize despite Pearse's martyrdom. By contrast, in the next sequence within this flashback, Maeve sits in a hospital bed wounded from a clash with police during her participation in a protest turned riot. The riots were broadcast on the news, revealing the reason for Maeve's absence from school that day and provoking a visit from three of the nuns who run her school. When they enter her hospital room, Maeve shrinks down under the blanket, and rather than check on her condition, the nuns lash into her—physically and verbally—castigating her for participating in the riots, for her direct, rather than poetic, participation in politics. The same nuns who feed girls with glorious images of martyrdom, nationalist sentiment, and vague notions of Irish freedom punish them for making political spectacles of themselves.

The occupation of the Falls as depicted in the film reinforces the analogy Maeve made to Liam establishing both feminism and nationalism as a response to an attack. Her direct experience of violence at the hands of the state, violence against her own body, not against the feminized body of the community or the nation, is consistent with the film's overall treatment of state violence against a specifically female body. Murphy's film undertakes the daunting task of representing the physicality of gendered violence despite centuries of allegorizing Ireland as a subjugated woman. The film forces open a space for women to act as agents of history. Maeve's arguments with Liam are a key part of this process, but just as important is Murphy's use of the representational strategies advanced by political film and the interventions of feminist filmmaking in this project. Murphy's film achieves what Teresa de Lauretis has argued is a key aspect in distinguishing feminist cinema: addressing the "spectator as a woman regardless of the gender of the viewers . . . the film defines all points of identification (with character, image, camera) as female, feminine, or feminist" (de Lauretis 1985, 161). As part of its project of bringing the female body back down to earth, when the film does visualize violent and/or sexual encounters between the British Army and women in Belfast, it does so in specifically anti-spectacular ways. There are four main encounters between the women in the film and the armed agents of the state, three of which are visually depicted, and all of them take place in the city. While the Irish countryside is leaden with the heroic and exclusionary memory of patriarchal nationalism, the city of Belfast is clearly an occupied one, where women negotiate the gendered violence of the British Army and the Northern Irish or British state.

Through scenes where its female characters must interact with British troops, *Maeve* represents Britain's declared state of emergency, and it reveals the urgent need for a resistance that recognizes the specific oppression of women. At one point in the film, two British soldiers on patrol stop Maeve and her sister Roisín in a playground. As two young girls play on nearby swings, the soldiers point their guns at the two women and command them to jump. The ridiculous nature of their demand is heightened by the fact that one of the girls bobs her head to follow Maeve and Roisín's movement. But while the soldiers' orders seem utterly pointless, this moment is hardly a comment on the absurdity of military occupation. The soldiers target Maeve and Roisín as members of a republican community, but they order the women to jump at gunpoint in order to leer at their breasts. In this brief sequence, Murphy's film visualizes what Gregory notes in the context of Palestine, "Occupation *is* violence" (2004, 104). There is no security value in the soldiers' command; its usefulness (from the perspective of the occupier) lies in its power to humiliate and degrade. Here, *Maeve* neatly summarizes the state security forces' regular harassment of northern nationalists and how that harassment took different forms according to the gender of the person harassed. Equally important within the mise-en-scène is the cliché of a universal "childhood innocence" evoked by the presence of little girls on swings.[11] Like the children whose play is disrupted by patrolling army vehicles in *Four Days in July*, the girls in this sequence are denied a politically neutral space in which to play, just as their two adult-women counterparts cannot simply walk and talk in a cinematic idealization of sisterly bonding without a reminder of their doubly occupied status: as women, but more specifically as women who appear at home in a working-class, republican neighborhood.

If the daytime presence of British soldiers can turn ordinary strolls into scenes of sexual and national degradation, nighttime excursions in the film become particularly dangerous for women. In a scene where Roisín

---

11. My thanks to Margaret Yocum for pointing out the notion of carefree (or "trouble"-free) innocence evoked by the swings.

is accosted by soldiers late at night, Murphy appropriates the cinematic signifiers of a woman alone and vulnerable on the empty city streets. In doing so, she challenges nationalist female metaphors, but also the ways that crime films use women as a stand-in for the spectator and exploit impending violence against women for cinematic thrills.[12] The scene opens with a shot of a van pulling up to a dark and deserted area of the Falls. Roisín gets out and begins to walk home through the wet, dimly lit streets. The camera tracks alongside her as she walks stiffly and briskly with her hands in her pockets and her eyes straight ahead. She picks up her pace and other footsteps make themselves heard offscreen. Roisín nervously looks around her and walks even more briskly as the extra footsteps speed up to match hers. Finally, Roisín breaks into a sprint, and the other footsteps clatter behind her. She looks over her shoulder as a man barks an order to stop, and one soldier suddenly appears from a darkened area at the edge of the frame and grabs her, while another catches up with her from behind, and a third rushes up to his comrades.

Her stalker, the soldier, demands her name and address. As he calls it in to headquarters, the soldier who had been lurking in the darkness stands right up next to her, and bulked up by his equipment and supported by his rifle, he towers over her and asks what she's doing out so late at night. When Roisín replies that she was working, the soldier sneers, suggesting that Roisín is a prostitute and therefore fair game for sexual harassment. Understanding his assumptions, Roisín corrects him, saying, "I work in a bar." Circling around her, he asks her for identification, and when Roisín replies, "I don't need it. I know who I am," he snatches her purse from her hands and begins rifling through it. The other soldier, who mistakenly called in the wrong address, informs Roisín that she does not live where she claims to. She corrects him, and as he calls in her correct address, the first soldier circles back behind her and asks what "Roisín" is

12. Alfred Hitchcock's famous dictum "torture the women" neatly sums up the way that violence against defenseless female characters becomes a means to give spectators the cinematic pleasure of being terrified but physically safe in their seats. See Clover 1992, 53.

Irish for. When she replies, "It's not Irish *for* anything, it's just *Irish*," the soldier goes to put his arm around her, and like a lecherous drunk at a bar, begins to ask why she's acting so aloof when he's just trying to be friendly. The soldiers' actions are doubly terrifying—as a woman, Roisín is vulnerable to sexual harassment or assault by armed agents of the state against whom she will have no legal recourse, but as a republican woman, she is also at risk for being treated as a terror suspect. Emergency legislation granted the state the right to detain suspects for seven days without charge without notifying family of their whereabouts and without allowing them access to a lawyer. Women who were detained reported invasive gynecological exams, humiliating strip searches, and verbal threats of rape during interrogation (Women against Imperialism 1980). Roisín shoves him away, the soldier stumbles, and Roisín stands on the corner laughing as all the soldiers regain composure. She continues to laugh defiantly as they grab her and drag her home, before throwing her through her family's front door, containing at least the threat she poses to femininity by returning this unruly woman to the domestic realm.

Roisín's defiance is strengthened by her willingness to make a spectacle of herself, but she and Maeve are limited in their power against armed men. One night, Maeve and Roisín pass through a checkpoint, and as they round the corner, they witness a scene fraught with the potential for an allegorical reading, as a British soldier, pants around his knees, thrusts his body into a woman who stares blankly ahead. This moment echoes an earlier story Roisín has told Maeve about an incident that occurred at a party in a friend's house. Roisín and her friend went up to bed, and a soldier entered the house, climbed the stairs, removed his boots and crawled into bed between them and said, "Right. I haven't seen my wife for six months, and I'm dying for a fuck, so youse decide which one of you it's going to be." Roisín recalls how the soldier had his rifle in the bed and kept clicking the safety catch on and off. She and her friend started screaming, and the soldier grabbed his boots and ran out of the house. Although the woman at the checkpoint is made up to suggest a prostitute, Róisín's vivid recollection of the clicking of the safety catch raises the question as to whether sex for any reason can be considered consensual when one of the people involved is an armed member of the state security forces. The drabness of the scene plays off a canon of visual representations of the bleak anonymity of urban life, where the loneliness and distance inherent in looking is heightened by both the architectural structures imitating the picture frame (windows, doorways). However, this shot is focalized through feminist Maeve, who might read the encounter in a particularly political way, possibly in terms of women's economic oppression. The film then cuts to a shot of Maeve and Roisín from the prostitute/rape victim's point of view, as they look almost blankly back at her, demonstrating a level of disempowerment among all three women that makes explicit the connection between gender and state oppression, illustrating the need for feminist, nationalist, and working-class resistance to the British state. The selective silence of the soundtrack also helps ground the encounter in the material world: the only sounds are the soldier's grunts and the clanking of the door against which the two lean, making audible and palpable the violence of the soldier's act.

In her interview with Johnston for *Screen*, Murphy states that one of the criticisms republican women made of her film concerned what they saw as the lack of a strong female republican voice. While accepting their criticism as a weakness of the film, Murphy explains that she had intended for Roisín to fulfill that role, although not verbally: "[Roisín's] strength is such that she doesn't have to articulate herself in the way that Maeve does. She doesn't experience that kind of alienation" (Johnston 1981b, 70). Although not explicitly connected to a specific republican organization, Roisín seems to offer a strong female republican presence. Furthermore, Roisín and her mother do "live a feminism," even if it diverges from Maeve's (Sullivan 1999, 76). But rather than articulate these political positions verbally in extended debates with Maeve, Roisín expresses them through her body—in her frequent position as a potential victim of sexualized state violence and in the tactics she fiercely uses to defend herself. In her encounters with the state security forces—except for when she is with Maeve—Roisín successfully defends herself through non-linguistic means and at the same time disrupts the state's projects of surveillance and intelligence gathering. When stopped by the soldiers late at night, Roisín's refusal to translate her name into English establishes a barricade (however small) that stalls the state project of gathering information in order to "read" a particular community and therefore police them more effectively. By shoving the British soldier, she seizes hold of the state's own violent methods, which are often unacknowledged as such, having been sanctioned by the declaration of a state of emergency. Her subsequent laughter further confounds the soldiers, who can no longer read her as either clearly innocuous or potentially lethal. Possibly assuming she's drunk or daft, they physically throw her back to her own family. Finally, Roisín's willingness to make a spectacle of herself protects her from the army a second time, when she and her friend scare away the would-be rapist with their screams. Although it is Maeve who exclaims to Liam that the repeated loss of power leads to the need for embodied protest, Roisín lives this statement. She is much more corporeal than Maeve, screaming loudly, laughing heartily, running, and even bathing, none of which Maeve is shown doing to any great extent. But with Roisín's political embodiment comes a level of double vulnerability that marks her as both a nationalist and a woman—while Maeve finds independence in London, Roisín remains the daughter tied to her parents' house and her community's home.

At the heart of *Maeve*, then, seems to be a split between the corporeal and the discursive, where Roisín is the embodied sister and Maeve is associated with the potential aloofness of the feminist intellectual. This dichotomy operates on several levels. It can be seen as a problem or contradiction in the film, where republicanism is once again placed in the realm of the physical at the expense of the intellectual. It could also imply that in order to understand how gender oppression operates in northern republican communities, women have to leave, as if a higher level of consciousness were available outside of Ireland. In the *Screen* interview, Murphy recounts that after seeing *Maeve* in 1980, Irish feminists questioned her on the film's possible linking of exile and feminist consciousness. She explains that the contradictions in *Maeve* were intended to be productive, and that she did not want to risk shutting down debate by imposing resolutions on them: "The film provokes both identification with and criticism of the main character. It doesn't demand unequivocal support . . . [Your response as a spectator] is dependent on how you see Maeve as a character. If you see her as an unproblematic heroine, a model for women's behaviour, then there is an implication that you have to leave Ireland to become a feminist" (Johnston 1981b, 70). Identification with Maeve along the lines of classical narrative cinema traps the spectator. The title character's perspective is not necessarily the only one endorsed by the film. Murphy thus refuses to simply replace a nationalist heroic memory with a feminist one.

Because the spectator's reading of the film's political sympathies stems from how Maeve is understood as a character, it is significant that Murphy cast the stronger actress, Bríd Brennan, for the part of Roisín and not Maeve. Roisín's emotional accessibility contrasts with Maeve's alienation from her home and family, tilting the film's sympathy slightly toward Roisín. Unlike her sister, Maeve is clearly out of place in West Belfast even before she leaves for London. But her discursiveness is necessary for her polemical function as a character and should not be mistaken for a cold detachment favored by the film. Rather, Maeve's value comes through her exile. Maeve guides a non-Northern Ireland audience through the spaces of Belfast, but she's not of the place in the same way that Liam, Roisín, and the rest of her family are. Excluded from the republican fold for her feminist critiques even before her exile, Maeve is able to provide a conceptual framework for what happens to the bodies of the women in the film in part because she is no longer preoccupied with survival. Although she is alienated from her friends and family in Belfast, she brings home a sharp clarity through which to articulate the importance of feminism to a national struggle. While the film depicts the specific ways in which women suffer and resist the brutality of the army, Maeve's feminist analysis of the situation repeatedly puts women into the center of the debate, not as an appendage to the nation or as a supplementary national identity, but as integral and vital members of a nation who share a stake in its future. In a sense, Maeve functions as a feminist historian, observing and interpreting the actions of the women and men around her. Her function is just as vital to the future of Irish women as Roisín's.

The film offers no narrative resolution to the contradictions and conflicts it presents; such a solution would repeat the narrative structure of the official history it problematizes. But as Murphy has stated, it does offer a visual resolution of the tensions among the three Sweeney women toward the end. In a sequence filmed at Giant's Causeway, Maeve, Roisín, and their mother, Eileen, appear together in the frame for the first time. They walk toward the ocean over the geological formation's smooth, odd-shaped stones. Maeve breaks away from the group and settles down behind a rock to watch the sea. A man in a dark peacoat wanders over, sits next to her, and states with theatrical grandiosity, "Nothing between you and the North Pole." Maeve ignores him, and he crosses behind her and squats down very close to her, so that he is both leaning over her and speaking into her face. He announces, "78,000 stones and only one that's octagonal." Maeve asks which is the octagonal one, without a trace of interest in her voice. The man stares at the sea and states with performed poetic significance, "I've forgotten now . . . I put a mark on it so's I'd remember . . . but the ocean washed the mark away." The peacoated stranger's performative grandeur, implying the futility of marking and claiming space in the face of (mother) nature, becomes somewhat ironic when moments later his unionist sympathies are revealed. Through him, the film offers one final patriarchal system that sees itself as the rightful possessor of the female land and refuses to relinquish even one inch to Irish nationalism.

As her father did when she was a child, the man disturbs Maeve's experience of the landscape. He reads it for and to her, with geographical facts, statistical data, in a failed attempt to chart the land for his own knowledge, like the Seeker of Lost Knowledge. Just as Maeve as a child walked away from her father's final story, annoyed or bored with this man's attempt to appropriate her experience, Maeve gets up and climbs back onto the rock. Filmed with a wide-angle lens, the man's head and shoulders fill the right half of the screen, pressing uncomfortably close to the frame, while Maeve stands above him, seemingly far away. With the wind lashing his face, the man stares wildly into the ocean, while Maeve studies him from above. The man begins to rail against the wind, shouting the "rhetoric of the Ulster covenant" (Gibbons 1996, 125), as Maeve joins her mother and sister in their retreat from him. The mad Ulsterman's cries compete with the roar of the wind and sea, and fade as the women walk farther away, finding shelter behind a rock and taking turns swigging from a bottle of whiskey. Roisín grumbles that she thought they came up to Giant's Causeway to get away from "that shite," and this time, Maeve makes a joke, "Hey Roisín, three to one, c'mon let's throw him in the sea." The sequence ends with Roisín and Maeve helping their mother to climb back up onto the 78,000 stones, and the three women walk away from the ranting Ulsterman.

In *Maeve* the focus on the body works against the Cartesian mind-body split favored by patriarchy and colonialism, where women and the colonized are imagined as bodies useful for labor, in need of discipline, and existing beyond the boundaries of discourse. Instead, through the articulation of the female characters' bodies with feminist arguments, violent experiences, and city spaces in addition to the traditional rural ones, *Maeve* renders the materiality of the body as an important part of thought, speech, and representation, as it has been throughout Ireland's struggle against colonialism and as it often is in feminist movements. Significantly, the discourse drowned by the wind and water toward the film's end is not only patriarchal but also unionist. In this penultimate sequence, the body aligned with state and gender hegemony is the one mystified and rendered as excessive and irrational, "full of sound and fury, signifying nothing." The Ulsterman's presence on screen enacts a reversal of unionist and patriarchal power structures and a subversion of the typical cinematic alignment of romantic discourse with republican and feminine irrationality. But, as Sullivan notes, although the image of the three Sweeney women is an expression of female solidarity suggestive of strength, *they* are still the ones who have to leave, not the ranting patriarchal figure (76). Thus, even within its moment of visual resolution, *Maeve* suggests that this solidarity is a beginning rather than a final victory.

Unfinished Revolutions

The image of family that closes *Maeve*—a shot of a mother and her two daughters—is repeated at various points in *Hush-a-Bye Baby*, which also explores the dialectic between republicanism and feminism, but does so more explicitly through notions of motherhood and pregnancy. Kathryn Conrad begins her analysis of the ways that reproductive rights are bound up with communal and national identities in Ireland with a quote from the civil rights activist Bernadette Devlin McAliskey: "Unionists must ensure that the nationalists don't outnumber them. On the other side, what are we confined to—outbreeding them? What are our choices? Either we shoot them or we outbreed them. There's no politics here. It's a numbers game" (Cahill 1995, 57; cited in Conrad 2004, 70). McAliskey puts the options facing nationalists in stark, if also exaggerated, terms— produce more babies on "our" side or more corpses on "theirs"—revealing the national stake in sex and pregnancy.[13] But her assertion that "there's no politics here" is misleading. As Conrad notes, feminist analyses of gender and nationalism have revealed the many ways that women's bodies become national and political zones, making sex anything but a private or non-political realm (2004, 12–14). Furthermore, McAliskey herself notes the political aspects of motherhood in *Mother Ireland* when she explains that the fact that the lives of working-class mothers have always involved making do with minimal resources meant that women in the Catholic ghettos of the North had a strong community support system in place to share resources and information when the British government began removing Catholic men from their homes with the introduction of internment in 1971.

In the North, women's identities as mothers have often provided not only motivation for participation in the national struggle but also inroads into political activism and a potent symbolic language with which to confront British oppression. Examples include demonstrations staged by the Relatives Action Committee (discussed in the following chapters), who protested the revocation of political status for republican prisoners by publicly embodying the role of suffering mother, as well as women's resistance to the Lower Falls Curfew of 1970, when the British Army placed residents

13. This issue is not limited to Northern Ireland. As Amal Amireh writes, "In the sixties and seventies, fertility became an actual weapon for the Palestinians who remained inside Israel." Citing Golda Meir's famous claim that she could not sleep at night for fear of the number of Palestinian births and conceptions and Shimon Peres's assertion that "politics is a matter of demography not geography," Amireh explains, "Palestinian poets responded to the call to arms with a vengeance. In a poem entitled 'Here We Shall Stay,' Tawfiq Zayyad threatened that the Palestinians in Israel will 'keep on making children/ One revolutionary generation/After another'" (Amireh 2003, 755).

of Belfast's Lower Falls area under house arrest. During the curfew, three thousand women from the Upper Falls, some with children in tow, broke through the army cordon to bring food and milk to the residents of the Lower Falls. Begoña Aretxaga, who interviewed women in the Falls, notes that many of the women carried the food in prams, thus using the universally harmless image of a mother pushing a baby carriage as a means to confront the army of one of the world's strongest signifiers of imperialism.[14] The Falls activists revealed the way that occupation politicizes all aspects of life, undermining an idealization of generic innocence as the opposite of political knowledge. Like the swing set in *Maeve*, not even a baby carriage is a politically neutral space.

Hush-a-Bye Baby tells the story of fifteen-year-old Goretti Friel, who lives in the largely republican and Catholic Creggan housing estates in Derry. She meets and falls in love with Ciaran McGuigan, a Derry teen from a similar background, who lives with his mother and brothers in the Bogside (also a predominantly Catholic area). Goretti and Ciaran start dating, and through their outings together—walks through Derry city, evenings babysitting Goretti's two young nieces, events at the local community center—the film portrays both the oppressiveness of British Army occupation and the close-knit community that emerges in opposition to it. Eventually, Goretti and Ciaran have sex, and the next day Ciaran is lifted in a British Army raid on the Bogside and taken to Castlereagh Interrogation Centre, a notorious site of police brutality.[15] While Ciaran is incarcerated, Goretti learns she is pregnant, and slowly, a sense of isolation invades the narrative. As Goretti's pregnancy develops, so does her fear of exclusion from this community. She becomes increasingly separated from her family and friends, trapped in her own body, and plagued by nightmares

14. In the case of the curfew, food also became a central concern. Many of the women from the Upper Falls were worried about the danger of mothers not having enough food to feed their children, especially milk. As Begoña Aretxaga writes, "The lack of milk became, in women's consciousness, the epitome of British depravity" (Aretxaga 1997, 59).

15. See, for example, Ian Cobain, "Inside Castlereagh: We Got Confessions by Torture," *The Guardian*, October 11, 2010, http://www.guardian.co.uk/uk/2010/oct/11/inside-castlereagh-confessions-torture (accessed March 2011).

of the Virgin Mary. The film ends with a freeze-frame of Goretti's face after her parents have burst into her bedroom in response to her screams of pain and terror as she either miscarries or goes into premature labor.

Like *Maeve, Hush-a-Bye Baby* links its exploration of the dialectic between republicanism and feminism to an interrogation of visual representation, but analyses of the film often treat its innovative formal elements as secondary to its thematic content. Set and shot in Derry (Northern Ireland) and Donegal (the Republic of Ireland), the film exists in dialogue with media-generated preconceptions of both Northern Ireland and the Irish Republic. It both refuses to portray the North as a war zone populated by fanatics and destabilizes visual clichés of the South as quaintly pastoral and blissfully disconnected from the violence of modernity. Harkin takes aspects of the teen film—adolescent characters, first loves, curiosity and ignorance about sexuality, pop music, domestic spaces, public spaces segregated by sex, and a problem that isolates the main character from her parents—and places them within the specific context of a Catholic, nationalist, working-class community close to the Irish border, revealing the intricate ways the state of emergency in the North is woven into daily life. While the subject matter of *Hush-a-Bye Baby*—women's rights and the occupation of Northern Ireland—is overtly political, the film is also political cinema in its production and aesthetics. Disrupting its narrative with sounds and flashes of images that at times seem almost extra-diegetic, the film becomes an open text that allows for moments of incongruity, disorientation, and meandering.

Made in 1989, the film takes place in 1984, roughly a year after the abortion referendum passed by a narrow margin in the Irish Republic and the same year that Stormont Castle voted against extending Great Britain's 1967 Abortion Act (which had decriminalized abortion under specific circumstances) to Northern Ireland. Although the film's main characters live in Derry city, where most of the film is set, they cross the border into the Irish Republic, which enables the film to engage directly with the passage of the eighth amendment as well as several poignant events that happened in the republic at the time of the abortion debates. Because of the film's treatment of the South, analyses of *Hush-a-Bye Baby* tend to concentrate on the film's exploration of the relationship between women's reproductive rights and the place of Catholicism in Irish nationalism. But they do so in a manner that seems to take for granted as commonsense a continuity between northern and southern nationalism.[16] The film does portray positive and negative cultural continuities across the Irish border, but it also spotlights that border explicitly, visually marking it as a fortified division between two distinct states. By crossing and thus calling attention to the border, *Hush-a-Bye Baby* alludes to how Northern Ireland is connected to and also positioned between Irish and British nationalisms.

Analyses of *Hush-a-Bye Baby* that read the film exclusively in terms of Irish cinema miss an opportunity to position the film in relation to political cinema in the United Kingdom. This move is important for understanding Ireland's connection to a British nationalist state of emergency within the wider United Kingdom, one with strong overtones of post-imperial crisis. The Derry Film and Video Collective was created under the auspices of the 1982 ACTT Workshop Declaration, a cross-organization initiative in the United Kingdom that helped to foster the development of independent and non-commercial cinema. Together with the newly formed Channel 4, the Workshop Declaration opened British media up to previously under-represented groups. This same legislation facilitated the founding of Sankofa, Ceddo, Black Audio Collective, and Retake Film and Video Collective, all in Britain. These collectives were organized in the face of the increased racial violence and white English-British nationalism of the Thatcher years. They became sites of opposition to an increasingly militarized British police force, racism, and amnesiac and nostalgic histories of colonialism. As Manthia Diawara points out, members of the Black British collectives saw their films as a continuation of resistance from the streets into the cinema (or TV) (Diawara 2006,

---

16. For example, Ruth Barton has characterized the film as "a swingeing critique of a culture embedded in a regressive, male-dominated nationalism," although she does not specify whether this culture is understood as northern, southern, or both (Barton 2004, 119). In a similar vein, Sullivan discusses the film in relation to the 1992 "X Case" in the republic (explained in chapter 4), which, as she acknowledges, happened after Harkin's film was released but nonetheless resonates with the concerns of the movie (Sullivan 1999, 113–14).

127). But like the members of Derry Film and Video, these filmmakers also set out to combat amnesiac nationalist histories. Derry Film and Video shares with Sankofa and Retake in particular an interest in addressing the intersection of nationalisms, gender, sexuality, and representation. While discussions of Derry Film and Video rarely locate the collective within the UK workshop movement, histories of the UK workshops almost never even mention Derry Film and Video. Like the erasure of Pat Murphy from film histories outside of Ireland, the omission of Derry Film and Video reveals significant blind spots in the realm of political and feminist film studies—Northern Ireland, explicitly tied to violent, patriarchal nationalism through British and US media, simply ceases to exist as a site for cinematic, nonviolent struggle. But Harkin and Crilly felt a strong connection to this movement; they enthusiastically followed the work of the other collectives, met members of Sankofa and Black Audio at Channel 4 events, and had particularly close ties with Sheffield Film and Video, an Asian British collective. According to Harkin, "politically we strode an Irish/British corridor—we proclaimed our Irishness but our contest was with Britain and Ireland and we did see ourselves as being in a battle for the right to speak."[17]

Within an Irish framework, the border's visibility in Harkin's film is also critical for understanding the ways that the film's characters are caught up in two states of emergency on the island—an imagined crisis in the national family of the republic and the construction in the North of all republicans as terrorists-in-waiting—that spill across the border in both directions. This focus on a double state of emergency enables the film to have a firm feminist perspective without indicting the whole of Irish nationalism or portraying female characters who support nationalism and are part of a Catholic community as the docile followers of patriarchy. At the heart of *Hush-a-Bye Baby* is a positive ambivalence that respects the complexities of women's and girls' relationships to their own bodies, nationalism, the Church, and their communities. Much of this ambivalence is achieved through the focus on teenage characters rather

17. E-mail with Margo Harkin, March 29, 2011.

than adults. Bound by the politics and morality of the adults in their community but possessing a nascent autonomy over their own bodies, the teens in the film experience the intrusion of the state, the Church, and the nationalist community in profoundly corporeal ways that shake this fragile independence. Examining occupied, national, and gendered locations, the film opens up a space to draw parallels between the besieging cartography of Derry city and the incarceration of women and girls within a metaphorical prison of national feminine virtue that extends across the Irish border and echoes with similar restrictions on women in Britain too. The effects of Britain's emergency legislation in the North—checkpoints, foot patrols, helicopters, arrests, paid informers—coexist with a sense in the republic that the national family was in a state of severe crisis, and the film's characters seem to be equally limited in their ability to resist both sets of emergency discourses.

But while Goretti, Ciaran, and other characters find themselves almost powerless against the forces that oppress them, the film itself succeeds in bringing about a real state of emergency by provoking a crisis in cinematic representation. *Hush-a-Bye Baby* deploys an aesthetic of fragmentation that carefully resists definitive answers to the problems it explores. Refusing to resolve Goretti's predicament—whether she miscarried or went into labor, how her parents and the community reacted, whether Ciaran was released from prison and shouldered his parental responsibility—the film avoids the narrative trap of closure and mirrors the lack of resolution to women's struggle for reproductive freedom as well as to the status of Northern Ireland. By moving back and forth across the border, the film makes clear that the Irish "Free State,"[18] like "Free Derry," promises a freedom from British rule that is ultimately compromised by Irish patriarchal occupation. In doing so, *Hush-a-Bye Baby*, while deeply sympathetic toward its northern nationalist characters, suggests that the border is not

18. I use this term colloquially, as I have heard friends use it, as a way of contrasting the occupied North with the unoccupied Irish Republic. I do not intend to imply a refusal to recognize the legitimacy of either state on the island of Ireland.

the only partition in Ireland; the nation is just as divided by the politics of gender and sexuality. Bringing the abortion debates to bear on women and girls in *Northern* Ireland, who are already living under a state power that denies them access to representation, *Hush-a-Bye Baby* offers new interpretations for the nationalist slogan "Ireland unfree will never be at peace" that see nationalist and feminist resistance to state censorship and oppression as a continuous struggle.

After a subtitle conveying not only the place and time of the story but also its nationalist politics—"Derry, North of Ireland, 1984"—the film opens with an audio-visual play on pregnancy and the notion of the uterus as a space rather than a body part. In slow motion, a small fist and chubby arm drift toward and away from the camera, evoking the visual tropes of fetal photography (Cullingford 1994, 51). But the camera's shot of this cute baby fist is obstructed by something long and willowy, like seaweed swaying with the tide (Cullingford 1994, 51), thus evoking the infant's corpse that washed ashore in Cahirciveen, triggering what became known as the Kerry Babies case (discussed below). Uterus and ocean are also conflated on the soundtrack as the rhythmic swoosh of water is interlaced with a gentle thumping and a faint but constant unearthly moan similar to a person mourning or a ship's foghorn.[19] A female scream disrupts these sounds, and the film cuts to a shot of a toddler dunking a Barbie doll in the bathtub, slopping water onto the floor as her babysitter and aunt, fifteen-year-old Goretti, screams in frustration. The comically simple explanation for the preceding mystifying image of Woman as water—recalling the aquatic imagery of Celtic mythology in *Maeve*'s story of the well—establishes the humor that the film uses to undermine the seriousness imposed on women's virtue and sexuality by a patriarchal traditionalism, a stance conveyed

19. Elizabeth Butler Cullingford writes that these audiovisual allusions deliberately evoke the Seamus Heaney poem "Limbo," which deals with infanticide, and which Goretti and her classmates discuss in a later scene (Cullingford 1994, 51). Cullingford offers a powerful reading of the film's use of this poem, concluding, "In appropriating Heaney's art for cultural politics, Harkin inserts it into the sphere of community activism" (55). See Cullingford 1994, 45–56.

on the soundtrack in the next sequence, which features Cyndi Lauper's 1980s teen-girl anthem, "Girls Just Wanna Have Fun."[20]

Giddiness and a utopian rendering of teen culture dominate the first half of the film. The girls' boisterous behavior is matched by the raucous and playfully flirtatious interaction between girls and boys. After her scream of exasperation, Goretti appears in the following shot dressed to the hilt in 1980s aerobics gear—an electric blue leotard, an off-the shoulder gray shirt, bright tights and legwarmers, complete with a big pink bow in her hair. She and the other girls on the disco dancing team—all in similar outfits—practice their moves to the Lauper song. The film cuts between the girls dancing in one of the Derry community center's gymnasiums and a group of boys playing soccer in a gym on the upper level. When the boys finish their game, they strut down the hallway to the showers, passing the girl's gym on the way. Two of them, Ciaran and Lenny, stop and bang on the glass partition for the girls' attention. Ciaran stands in the background surveying the scene of Goretti, Majella, and Sinéad, while Lenny presses against the glass and gyrates his hips for the girls, who ignore him and continue dancing in poses that mimic images of sex appeal circulated in women's magazines and in the posters of models that adorn the girls' bedroom walls. The film continues to cut between the boys and girls as they dress in their respective locker rooms. In the girls' space, Goretti asks Majella about Ciaran, and she and Majella tease each other about their crushes, clutching each other in mock passion and pretending to kiss. When they accidentally touch tongues, the girls shriek with laughter, hurling themselves across the locker room, tearing down a changing room curtain, and embarrassing the bashful Sinéad. In the boys' locker room, Ciaran and Lenny tell dirty jokes, falsely boast of sexual prowess, and size up the sexual availability of girls. When Ciaran expresses an interest in Goretti to Lenny, Lenny advises him that he'd have better

---

20. In a US context, the visual play on fetus-doll-corpse also recalls the gruesome posters waved by anti-choice protesters at women's health clinics, in which what seems to be the hands and feet of dolls are used as "evidence" of the supposed fetal butchering practiced by so-called abortionists.

luck with Majella, "Now, she's a nice wee girl; she takes her own knickers down." In addition to Goretti's sexual reputation (or lack thereof), Lenny also divulges the Friel family's republican credential, "Staunch as fuck they are, the whole family. Their uncle was stiffed [killed or incarcerated] by the Brits."

The all-girl spaces of the locker room and the single-sex classroom give the girls in the film a sense of strength and community, enabling their mild subversion of sexual and gender expectations. In a scene that opens with a shot of a porcelain sculpture of the Virgin adorned with flowers, Goretti, Sinéad, Majella, and their friend Deirdre use the awkwardness of being taught the lessons of adult relationships by a Catholic priest to their advantage. The young, attractive, and sympathetic, if also slightly oblivious, priest—the appropriately named Father Devine—speaks haltingly about the sacrament of marriage, which, "no doubt most of you girls will be entering in the near future." He is distracted by what at first seems to be a downward gaze of embarrassment coming from the classroom full of girls—a stereotypical image of Catholic reticence about sexuality even when "sex" education is safely confined within the respectable boundaries of marriage. But when the film cuts to their point of view, we discover that they are actually staring at the space *under* the priest's desk, at his crotch. The film cuts back to the girls, barely containing their giggles under fixed smiles, and then back to the priest's wide-open legs. In the series of alternating shots that follow, the film cuts between medium close-ups of Father Devine and Majella, whose flirtatious facial expressions become increasingly exaggerated until she suggestively pushes her tongue through her chewing gum and ogles the priest through half-closed eyes. Now made self-conscious by the girls' steady and clearly sexualized gaze, Father Devine clears his throat and presses his knees together in what is usually a woman's defensive gesture against a male gaze.

Interior spaces—bedrooms, classrooms, locker rooms, dance halls, and even churches—are tied to a sense of home and community, but public space is fraught with a greater sense of occupation. *Hush-a-Bye Baby* depicts the many physical borders in a complex constellation of social and political institutions and identities. The borders installed by the state in Derry take architectural and human form; there are immobile watchtowers and checkpoints, but the ambient body of an armed agent of the state is also enough to mark a border. As soldiers move through the city stopping and searching civilians, they become the ever-shifting thresholds between communal and state spaces, changing the map of Derry for its inhabitants. The film uses the relationship between on-screen and offscreen space to convey this instability. After his first kiss with Goretti, Ciaran struts down the street. On the soundtrack, a playful flute version of Sinéad O'Connor's "Three Babies" gives an extra bounce to his step. But the crackle of army radios soon announces the presence of British soldiers, who suddenly step into the frame as the non-diegetic music abruptly stops. One soldier stands in front of Ciaran and another behind him, while the offscreen revving of an engine implies the presence of more army personnel. The soldier in front of Ciaran wordlessly pats him down before allowing him to continue on his way. As Ciaran walks away from the impromptu checkpoint, he mutters angrily in Irish, "And good night to you too!" The silence of their interaction conveys the routine aspect of this kind of stop and search on the street; each party knows his role and can perform it without verbal direction. Aside from the hope of discovering possible arms or explosives hidden on Ciaran's body, the soldier has no interest in him. Ciaran's sarcastic "good night to you too" resonates with anger not only about being searched but also about being objectified. The soldier's refusal to engage verbally becomes a way of denying his subjectivity. Powerless to resist this negation and invasion, Ciaran can only mutter to himself, at a safe distance from the soldier, and in the "native" language he must attend classes to learn.

The state has the power to turn ordinary streets into repressive spaces, but the borders between republican and non-republican areas do not mean the same thing for women as they do for men. After Goretti becomes pregnant, she walks past a gable wall that reads, "YOU ARE NOW ENTERING FREE DERRY," in a shot that functions like the Cave Hill sequence from *Maeve*. As Patsy Murphy observes, the notification on the wall functions ironically to emphasize Goretti's entrapment because of her unwanted pregnancy (Murphy 1990, 10). But the gable wall, known as Free Derry Corner, memorializes the Battle of the Bogside in August 1969, when residents of the Catholic neighborhood erected barricades to prevent the RUC from entering the area. After several days of rioting and police violence, the British Army was called in to restore order. They did not leave until 2007. The gable wall is all that remains from the original Bogside houses, which were torn down to make way for new housing estates and apartment buildings. When Goretti walks past it, the wall is evidence of how an embattled history is woven into the fabric of everyday life in the present and remains unresolved. The wall also evokes histories obscured by the national question. Sullivan notes that the irony in the shot recalls McAliskey's recollection in *Mother Ireland* that even after the barricades were built between the nationalist Bogside (Free Derry) and the rest of the city, "Derry wasn't that free this side of the wall either. All the internal contradictions that went on before the barricades went up went on afterwards. The women in Derry were still producing three square meals a day, and the men in Derry were still eating them" (Sullivan 1999, 112). As Maeve tries to impress on Liam at Cave Hill, nationalist memory celebrates its glorious past but remains blind to shortcomings and contradictions in its present.

If *Maeve* liberated the female body from the stagnation of heroic national memory, *Hush-a-Bye Baby* does something similar with Irish culture. Although by film's end Irish has failed Goretti and Ciaran as a means of effective communication, and the Virgin Mary has become at best indifferent to Goretti's predicament, initially, Catholicism and traditional Irish culture offer a sense of belonging and protection, and the film infuses them with vibrancy and beauty. In one sequence, Goretti and her sister Fidelma attend mass with Fidelma's two daughters. Sinéad O'Connor's crystalline voice introduces the sequence with "The Bells of the Angelus," the chorus of which is "Ave, ave, ave Maria," pushing out the diegetic sound. Goretti and Fidelma each carry a child as they light candles at the feet of a statue of the Virgin, and shots of the flickering white candles—prayers and petitions to Catholicism's main intercessor—dissolve into close-ups of the sisters' faces. This tender moment rich in audio-visual appeal ends abruptly with a cut to the exterior of the church. As Goretti and Fidelma step outside, O'Connor's voice gives way to the chopping of helicopter blades—the sound of omniscient surveillance and a contrast to the serenity inside. Later, as part of its treatment of Catholicism as an everyday aspect of the characters' lives, the film affectionately mocks the sacredness of Mary's image through Sinéad (played by Sinéad O'Connor), who, in one sequence, sits at a vanity table in her bedroom in a shot typical of cinematic depictions of girl culture. But instead of making herself up in front of the mirror, she wraps a tea towel around her head to resemble Mary's veil, holds rosary beads between her fingers, tilts her head back in holy serenity, and closes her eyes, but then opens them again and screws up her face in a squint, trying to see how she looks as the Virgin Mother.

Harkin uses laughter and playful sexuality to undercut the solemn magnitude that postcolonial nationalism in the republic bestowed on the Irish language with the ineffective policy of compulsory and rote language education. Irish is a living language in the film, one that does more than promote mythic nationalist sentiment. The film's characters carnivalize Irish, giving it a new vibrancy and relevance for everyday life. In one of the Irish classes Deirdre and Goretti attend at the community center, Ciaran enters the room and Deirdre says half in Irish, half in working-class Derry English (but entirely subtitled), "*Dia dhuit* [God]! I wouldn't mind doing a lying week with him!" After being introduced, Ciaran says to the class (in Irish), "I assume you're all fluent Irish speakers, *gaelgores?*" When Goretti asks Deirdre to translate, she answers, "I think he just said we're all Gael *whores!*" The two girls giggle, and the lesson begins with the students using a "Do you like . . . /I prefer . . ." construction as a chance to joke and flirt. When the teacher asks a student if he likes tea, he replies, "I prefer whiskey [*uisce beatha*], the water of life." The lesson continues around the room, with the instructor building on the previous answer, asking Goretti if she likes whiskey. Goretti answers, "No, I have enough life [*beatha*] in me already, I prefer milk," and, returning her pen to her mouth, glances in Ciaran's direction. When the students take over the questioning, Deirdre turns to Goretti and asks, "Goretti, *a chara*, do you like boys?" and Goretti replies, "I prefer men," prompting Deirdre to nudge her and joke, "Gael whore!" much to Goretti's delight. After class, Ciaran bumps into Goretti (literally), and asks in Irish if she'd like to go for a Coke with him. As Goretti leaves with Ciaran, Deirdre teases her again, yelling in English, "I thought you prefer milk with men!"

Once Ciaran and Goretti start dating, Irish becomes the foundation of a joke in which the film gently mocks Ciaran's political posturing. The scene also dislodges the Irish language from essentialist notions of Irishness, thereby re-imagining culture as a fluid thing. On one of their many walks through Derry, Goretti and Ciaran pass a checkpoint. As in the earlier checkpoint sequence, a British soldier suddenly steps into the frame and stops them. He asks Ciaran for his name. When Ciaran answers, the soldier asks him to spell it. Like Roisín in *Maeve*, Ciaran attempts to obstruct the army's intelligence-gathering mission by refusing to comply. Instead he speaks firmly to the soldier in Irish: "Bord Fáilte! Agus Sinn Fein! Agus Aer Lingus! Agus Bord na Móna! Agus tiocfaidh ár lá!" But the film undermines his bold protest by translating this defiant speech in subtitles: "Irish Tourist Board! Sinn Fein! Irish Airlines! Irish Peat Board! Our day will come!" In Ciaran's outburst at the solider, Sinn Fein is lumped in with various national industries in the republic, and, significantly, his tirade ends with *tiocfaidh ár lá*. Here, the eschatological slogan that adorns republican murals throughout the North, promising the inevitable liberation of Irish nationalists through the (re?)unification of Ireland, becomes an empty phrase, divested of all agency.[21] In response to Ciaran, the soldier smiles and states in Irish, "Well then, tell me what impact the troubles have had on Irish social, political, and economic life." After they leave the checkpoint, Goretti asks Ciaran what the soldier said. Ciaran responds that the soldier was bluffing, which is all part of "the game" between occupier and occupied. He also explains, "The thing you need to understand

21. Conrad has noted Ciaran's inability to understand the soldier's question, which, she argues, is due to his proximity to the conflict in Northern Ireland, "the quotidian nature of the Troubles has made it impossible for him to think about their impact in a more than personal way" (Conrad 2004, 94). But I disagree with the idea that proximity hinders analysis, since its corollary is that distance is necessary for critical thought. Sullivan sees this moment as a total defeat for nationalism, consistent with her emphasis on what she sees as the uselessness of Irish throughout the film (Sullivan 1999, 114). But this analysis cannot account for the teenagers' exuberant play with Irish as a living language in the first half of the movie.

about the Irish language, Goretti, is that not *everything* can be translated. You better stick to asking for cups of tea!" concealing his own ignorance beneath a patronizing tone.

The Irish that facilitated Ciaran and Goretti's relationship but leaves Ciaran powerless before British soldiers also breaks down as a mode of communication between them when, the day after they have sex for the first time, Ciaran is lifted in a raid of the Bogside and jailed. During his incarceration, Goretti learns she is pregnant. She cannot tell him in person because his mother and the rest of his large family get priority for the few visits he is allowed, so she writes him a letter in Irish, using an English-Irish dictionary. As Goretti sits at her desk, her halting voice-over conveys the letter's contents. She struggles to write in the national language, looking up words and phrases in a dictionary and sounding them out as she transcribes them. The delight she took in learning Irish is gone, and the language reverts to its role as somber guardian of Irish faith and tradition when Goretti looks up the word for pregnant, finding only the idiomatic translation *acompur clannagh,* "to carry the family."[22] This translation recalls censorship of the word "pregnant" in film and television on the grounds that it was too carnal for public utterance, and it also goes a step beyond elevating the status of the fetus to child by conflating it with the entire family. Because the family is the foundational unit for the nation, Goretti suddenly has the full burden of patriarchal nationalism thrust on her. In the space of a sentence, she has gone from being a fifteen-year-old girl to being the bearer of the nation. Conrad writes that this moment "marks her entry into the larger politics of reproduction: as an Irish Catholic woman, the burden of carrying—maintaining, reproducing—the family is indeed upon her" (2004, 95), and Sullivan argues that "while the Irish language is assumed to connote a specific Irish identity, a pregnant woman is only identified in terms of her status as a mother"

22. Speakers of Irish who read drafts of this chapter or were in the audience when I presented on the film have pointed out that this translation is inaccurate and grammatically incorrect. But my analysis proceeds from it because this one is the one given by the film in a shot of Goretti's Irish-English dictionary. This translation, like the shot that lets us see it, conveys Goretti's perspective.

(Sullivan 1999, 115). But Goretti is a woman only in reproductive terms; legally (and in many ways emotionally) she is still a child. Her position between childhood and adulthood adds to her burden: Goretti is biologically old enough to be pregnant, but still subject to her parents' authority and dependent on them for survival. Furthermore, the isolation and secrecy usually accompanying pregnancy in teen movies is compounded by the presence of the British Army in Northern Ireland. Because Goretti's letter is in Irish, the prison authorities confiscate it; their censorship prevents Ciaran from knowing Goretti is pregnant.

Goretti's Irish translation of "pregnant" ushers in a confinement of women through their bodies that the film's characters had successfully held at bay with their laughter and their attempts to claim Irish for their own purposes. The film cuts from a shot of Goretti writing the phrase "I am carrying the family" to one of her sitting on a bus as her letter continues in voice-over, wishing that Ciaran were going with her to the Gaeltacht (the Irish-speaking area of Donegal) to learn Irish as they had planned. As the bus she and Deirdre ride crosses through the fortified border into the republic, the film introduces a somber and monotonous violin-and-cello motif that signifies Goretti's increasing isolation from the world around her. Harkin reverses the North-South relationship common to troubles films, where Northern characters escape South toward freedom. In *Hush-a-Bye Baby*, Goretti is even more confined once she enters the Irish Republic, and the romantic Irish landscape itself seems to collude with the patriarchal Catholicism of southern nationalism, tormenting her with the return of repressed historical memories. During her time in the republic, Goretti's pregnancy grows in significance, confining her through ever-increasing levels of fear and loneliness. When the film moves into the Gaeltacht, the historical shards of events surrounding the abortion debates flash up with increasing frequency, disrupting the narrative and troubling the cultural ideology embedded in representations of the West of Ireland and the Gaeltacht—a mythic conception of Ireland as a picturesque land beyond time, not so much pre-modern as external to modernity. In this heroic, noble, idealized Ireland, the virtues of housework, Catholic devotion, feminine purity, and the primacy of the patriarchal family are forever maintained. It is a space where such modern "problems" as the women's movement and the "threat" feminism poses to family values do not disturb the glimmering national character reflected in sparkling seas and vibrant green fields. Although references to abortion traumatize Goretti in the context of the narrative, the film uses allusions to moving statues, infanticide, the concealment of pregnancies, and the death of Ann Lovett in order to unsettle precisely this regressive national image, prying open a space for the representation of Irish girls and women as earthly beings whose sexuality is neither volatile nor sinful.

One of the strongest critiques the film makes is against the Republic of Ireland and the conservative assumption that the erasure of women from the public sphere will "restore" the well-being of a nation that had never adequately addressed its postcolonial social and economic problems in the first place. The film achieves this partly through its treatment of the Virgin Mary, the initial image from which Harkin constructed her film. In an interview, she explains that *Hush-a-Bye Baby* began in her mind with a series of images, the first of which "was a shocking one, very over the top. It was of the pregnant Virgin Mary. I would have recurring and grotesque images of this. She would be in a glass case and be so pregnant that she would shatter the glass" (Murphy 1990, 9). Mary hovers over the entire film, initially as an inanimate and benign presence manifest in the statue adorned with yellow flowers in the classroom, the painted statue in the school's hallway, and the devotional statues in the church and in the characters' homes. However, as Goretti endures "the unremitting nightmare of an unwanted pregnancy" (Murphy 1990, 9), the statues of Mary become uncanny, her presence increasingly frightening, and this menace begins in the Gaeltacht. The first of these references opens with a dissolve from a close-up of Goretti's face on the bus to a close-up of the face of a small statue of Mary encased in glass in a grotto.[23] Goretti and Deirdre stop in front of it, cross themselves and have a conversation about the moving statues, wondering whether in Donegal they're safe from the phenomenon.

23. Conrad shrewdly observes that the film is full of "virgins under glass," and by the end of the film, Goretti, frozen on the viewer's TV screen, has become yet another one (2004, 98).

In the next sequence, Goretti stands in the kitchen helping the *Bean A Tí* (the woman hosting their homestay) make a cake as Irish music plays on a portable radio. When the woman leaves to fetch eggs, the music ends and a female voice announces, "and we return to the very sensitive and controversial subject of abortion." Goretti picks up the radio to hear the discussion more clearly, and the woman comes back in to get her bowl, startling Goretti, who fidgets with the dial pretending to look for a station, as if merely listening to a debate on abortion—even one broadcast on RTE—were so shameful it could only be done in secret. When the woman leaves again, Goretti turns back to the station only to hear a woman claim that abortion is "plain and simple murder" and repeat Bishop Cassidy's statement that "the most dangerous place in Ireland was the mother's womb." A pro-choice female voice retorts that fifteen-year-old Ann Lovett had the benefit of such "wisdom" as she lay dying in childbirth, alone at a grotto of the Virgin Mary. Goretti stands in the back corner of the kitchen, in a wide-angle shot that exaggerates the size of the room, making her seem all the more young, small, and helpless. The film cuts to a close-up of Goretti's face as the pro-choice voice points out that anti-abortion legislation is more effective in isolating women than it is in magically removing abortion as an option. The musical motif signifying Goretti's isolation introduced in the border sequence returns as the camera closes in on her face. The film cuts between close-ups of Goretti's face and her hands working in the bowl of flour, as she digs a cradle in the flour and breaks an egg over the bowl. The egg falls into the bowl in slow motion, landing with a thud while the membrane continues to drip slowly from the shell. The yolk, protected by the amniotic sac of the egg white, slithers back and forth in the flour, possibly a manifestation of Goretti's wish for an abortion.

The music continues into the next sequence, in which flashes of the statue that the girls had passed earlier disturb Goretti's sleep, as if to punish her for the wish not to be pregnant. Her nightmare persists as the statue's belly swells, filling the small space of the grotto and pressing against the glass, the clay now turned to flesh and cloth. Goretti cries out for Deirdre, who sleeps next to her, undisturbed. The music's crushing isolation, briefly suspended when she calls out for Deirdre, resumes in the following sequence, which opens with a shot of a blue plastic bag twisting in the ocean. Goretti sits up on the stony beach, dwarfed by its scale, watching the ocean, and the film cuts between shots of the ocean and its rocky shore and slow tracking shots moving toward Goretti. The repeating dragging sound of rocks advancing and receding as waves break on the shore echoes the mesmerizing repetition of the music and the hypnotic visual repetition of the shot sequences. The ocean, perpetually crashing on the shore, is indifferent to Goretti's situation, and possibly even seductive in offering her a way out through drowning.[24] Rather than offering her relief from her thoughts, the gray-blue vastness of the beach and ocean bear down on Goretti, underscoring her powerlessness and the effectiveness of shame in paralyzing and silencing women and girls, who, through their social isolation, become erased from the image of the Irish nation. Despite what Bishop Cassidy believes, when the "mother's womb" and the "mother" herself are reduced to an environment, a public space for the breeding of the nation, when sex education and reproductive freedoms are lacking, when pregnancy is offered as proof of moral weakness, and when there is religious, social, and legislative pressure to carry a pregnancy to term regardless of the health, age, and general well-being of the "mother," the most confining place for a woman or a teenage girl to be is in her own pregnant body.

While Goretti's pose on the beach may be reminiscent of self-discovery in "the time-honored romantic fashion, through communion with nature," Gibbons points out that the blue plastic bag that opens the sequence serves as a metonym for what became known as the Kerry Babies case (Gibbons 1992, 13). In 1984, a jogger on a beach in Cahirciveen, County Kerry, found the corpse of an infant who had been stabbed to death, wrapped in a blue plastic fertilizer bag, and thrown into the ocean. After a cursory investigation into recent pregnancies and births in the area, the *gardaí* (police) settled on Joanne Hayes, an unmarried woman

---

24. Conrad writes, "That Goretti, while pondering the waves upon the shore of egg-like stones sits visibly below the high-water mark suggests that she sees the ocean as a means to a permanent escape from the containment enforced by her condition" (2004, 95).

living with her family, as their primary suspect. Hayes had been having an affair with her employer, Jeremiah Locke, who was married. They discovered that Hayes had recently given birth on her family's farm, and that the baby had been buried on the property after being choked to death by the umbilical cord, Hayes, or a member of her family. Upon exhuming the second baby and performing DNA tests on both, the *gardaí* discovered that the two babies had different DNA. In a world where women's reproductive freedom is not perceived as a constant threat to the good of the nation, such a finding would have thrown sufficient doubt onto whether Hayes was the mother of the Cahirciveen baby as to acquit her of those infanticide charges. Instead, in what became a naked display of state-sponsored misogyny and discrimination (Locke was never accused of anything), the prosecutor came up with the theory of superfecundation, proposing that Hayes had been having sex with two men and had become pregnant by both, which is how the babies could have different DNA and the same mother. Despite the biological and geological (the flow of the tide in relation to where the Hayes family lived and where the baby was found) evidence exonerating Hayes, her body became both a public forum and an untamed space.[25]

Superfecundation is fairly common in cats, but the chances of its happening in human women are infinitesimal. The doctor who testified about this theory stated that it was *virtually* impossible, which the prosecutor took to mean that it was not outside the bounds of possibility. Hayes's body thus became a perversion of the miraculous body of the Virgin Mary, whose hymen (in some versions of the story) remained intact after birth—if a virgin birth is physically possible in human history, why not superfecundation?[26] The theory bestowed on Hayes's body a magical level of fertility, which became evidence of her unbounded sexual desire. In this theory, a woman's agency as a whole person becomes secondary

25. See McCafferty 1985 for an excellent analysis and history of the Kerry Babies case.

26. This connection is strengthened by the color of the fertilizer bag in the ocean. Unlike the gray bag that the Cahirciveen baby was found in, Harkins's bag is blue, the color of the Virgin Mary (Cullingford 1994, 48).

to or subsumed by the awesome force of her unbridled sexuality. When babies out of wedlock are offered as proof of immorality,[27] a woman's having two babies outside the bonds of marriage is proof of a transgression so far beyond the boundaries of propriety that she ceases to be human and becomes animalistic, feline. The astounding ability of Hayes's body to create multiple babies with different genetic components also obscures the fact of paternity, making Locke's part in conception incidental, just as Ciaran, through his incarceration, is rendered defunct as a father.[28]

Silence and secrecy close in on Goretti, depriving her of agency and freedom. This silence is not only her own reticence about her pregnancy, but the erasure of women from the public sphere as well except as nurturing environments for the nation or as terroristic threats to its future citizens. In the context of the North of Ireland, where (at least in the 1980s) safe havens for nationalists were few and far between, the need for nationalist babies may offer more social acceptance and freedom for unwed *mothers*, but it may also further confine women and girls who wish to terminate a pregnancy. When Goretti does break her silence for the first time, it is to Deirdre, who throughout the film provides Goretti with a modicum of protection from social, national, and religious condemnation. Deirdre's laughter, her swagger, and her protective confidence recall Roisín's confident corporeal resistance to the British Army in *Maeve*, and her autonomy is never undermined or restricted by broader social and political structures. On the way back to Derry, the girls pass the statue of the Virgin again, only

27. In an essay on the practice of firing unmarried pregnant women from teaching jobs in Catholic schools because of their breach of Catholic morality, Nell McCafferty notes that the Church usually offers a baby as evidence and points out that since only women can have babies, the policy is inherently gender-biased, protecting men at the expense of women (1984, 55).

28. But the presence of a virgin mother at the heart of Catholicism is too limiting and essentialist an answer for how Hayes was imagined in the media. Ireland in the 1980s was merely one of many nations to imagine a national crisis of morality, as evidenced by Ronald Reagan's terror of imagined "welfare queens" whose raced and classed bodies in his construction also seemed to breed infinite, fatherless children.

this time, rather than respect Mary's role as intercessor to God, Deirdre addresses her directly, "Don't you fuckin' move, I'm warnin' ye!" allaying her own fears about the power of the Virgin Mother and making Goretti laugh in the process. Deirdre's carnivalesquely profane speech opens up an earthly space wherein the two girls are briefly relieved of the strictures placed on them by an ideal of purity, chastity, and silent sacrifice. Her statement elicits laughter in its violation of the sacred, and it echoes one made by the republican prisoner Mairéad Farrell that while on a no-wash protest in Armagh Gaol, the women used to joke, "Mother Ireland, get off our backs," explaining this figure of passive national motherhood had no relevance to their filthy bodies and prison cells or to their active participation in militant Irish nationalism (*Mother Ireland*). The idea that the paragons of virtue embodied by the Virgin Mary and Mother Ireland imprison women within a patriarchal appropriation of their bodies and a denial of agency is suggested in the dissolve that closes this sequence, from a close-up of Mary's face to Crumlin Road Jail where Ciaran is being held.

Goretti and Ciaran are both stuck, caught up by forces far more powerful than they are. Ciaran's confinement, although physically and psychologically arduous, will also bring him closer to his community, while Goretti's carries the risk of her being ostracized. Republican prisoners have been adept at forming solidarity in jail and thus resisting the prison's function of isolation and individualization. The camaraderie fostered by political incarceration is evident in a "comm" (communiqué) from Ciaran, smuggled out of the prison to Goretti. In the scene where Goretti reads the letter, she and Deirdre are on a beach in Derry, a visual echo of the earlier scene of Goretti contemplating the ocean—and possibly its associations with suicide or escape—in Donegal. Ciaran's voice comes onto the soundtrack, apologizing and explaining, "We talk a lot about how things should be in here to make things better for everyone." His voice cuts out, and Goretti tells Deirdre that Ciaran wants to marry her, implying that for Ciaran, acceptance of his responsibility through marriage is part of building a future nation. *Goretti's* needs and desires are subordinate to *his* sense of duty to her and to the nation. But for Goretti, the offer of marriage is too late. No longer sure she wants to marry Ciaran and raise a family, Goretti seems suddenly aware of alternatives. She throws the letter down and runs off, yelling, "I'm only fifteen you know!" But, as Conrad points out, rejecting "the heteronormative model insisted upon by the Church . . . she is left few other choices" (Conrad 2004, 97).

Conrad argues that the film's characters are subject to multiple gazes to the point where *Hush-a-Bye Baby* "suggests throughout that personal agency is profoundly affected by the surveillance to which those in Northern Ireland are subjected on a daily basis—by the state, by the Church, and ultimately by each person who internalizes the gaze of these powerful institutions and begins to regulate herself" (Conrad 2004, 98). But there is a final, extra-diegetic gaze that the film not only addresses but also refuses to internalize: the censoring eyes of the state toward Irish media. Just as Goretti's story remains unresolved, the film raises the question of an enduring national-feminist struggle in a scene where Fidelma switches off the TV as the credits to a film roll up its screen. The credits are accompanied by Peter Cadle and Christy Moore's "Unfinished Revolution," which is the end credit song for *Mother Ireland*. In Cadle's lyrics, women from Nicaragua, Afghanistan, and Northern Ireland are united in their contribution to global struggles against oppression. They bravely fight injustice, but they also benefit from revolution, which brings literacy and better healthcare for the poor. In the case of Northern Ireland, as far as the song is concerned, the unfinished revolution is continued resistance to British occupation. Cadle and Moore celebrate women's stoicism in the face of a British state that made women vulnerable to the army by removing men from the home, repeatedly violating the borders between public and private spaces, and calling into question women's sexuality:

Soldiers kicked down the door, called her a whore
While he lingered in Castlereagh
Internment tore them apart, brought her to the heart
Of resistance in Belfast today
Her struggle is long, it's hard to be strong
She's determined deep down inside
To be a part of the unfinished revolution
She's the key to the unfinished revolution

Here, like Pearse's mother, the anonymous nationalist woman bears personal pain—in this case home invasion, sexual harassment, and separation from her husband (who, like Ciaran, is rendered ineffective by "lingering" in Castlereagh)—for the higher cause of Irish liberation. But unlike Pearse's mother, Cadle's woman is an active part of resistance; she has much more to offer the nation than stoic grief and male children.

The unfinished revolution in the song refers to the occupation of Northern Ireland, but in the context of Harkin's film within a film, it raises questions about unfinished business in Ireland and Britain. "Unfinished Revolution" comes at the end of *Mother Ireland*, the Derry Film and Video Collective's first film, which interrogated the image of Mother Ireland and her relationship to republican women. As Fidelma goes to turn the TV off, the words "Derry Film and Video Collective" appear on its screen, making clear that the film that has just ended is in fact *Mother Ireland*. This moment of reflexivity is also an anachronism—Fidelma is turning off the TV in 1984, while *Mother Ireland* was not made until 1988. As such, this reference functions almost extra-diegetically, as a moment of protest that triggers another obscured historical memory: the censorship of republicanism by both Britain and the Irish Republic. Britain's censorship legislation was passed the year *Mother Ireland* was finished, which was also the year Mairéad Farrell was shot to death by the SAS at Gibraltar. *Mother Ireland* became the first film produced in the North aided by the Workshop Declaration legislation, and it was banned by the government that helped sponsor its production. But the legislation that prevented *Mother Ireland* from airing on British television was actually modeled on restrictions initiated in the Irish Republic (Gogan 1988–89b, 11). In both island nations, Radio Telefís Éireann (RTÉ), the British Broadcasting Company (BBC), and Channel 4 as well as other broadcasters in Ireland and the United Kingdom before 1996 were forbidden to air material that contained "direct statements" from members of specific proscribed groups, including Sinn Fein, the only political party silenced under the ban (Gogan 1988–89a and 1988–89b, 10–11). One way around this legislation was to dub the voices of people banned by the legislation, so that their statements would no longer be "direct." Because Derry Film and Video refused to do this, *Mother Ireland* was not aired in either Britain or Ireland.

This jarring moment of deliberate protest in the middle of a fictional narrative[29] is a fragment that cannot easily be reabsorbed into the story. As such, it opens up avenues for comparison between the treatment of nationalism in Northern Ireland and other false states of emergency in Ireland and Britain, especially those concerning questions of gender, race, and ethnicity. A manifold unfinished revolution thus awaits Goretti and other Irish women in the North. Not only is there the work of "finishing" the 1918 war of independence by undoing partition but there are also the tasks of fully liberating women and opening the channels of communication so that the public has access to information uncensored.[30] Although censorship of both sexual and national knowledge has largely been lifted, the questions of gender and state partitions remain.

29. In an e-mail to me, Harkin confirmed that this reference to *Mother Ireland* was a protest against the film's censorship.

30. Although she does not discuss the presence of *Mother Ireland* in *Hush-a-Bye Baby*, the regulation of information is a central focus of Conrad's entire critique of the family in Irish nationalism, including her reading of *Hush-a-Bye Baby*. See Conrad 2004 for an extensive discussion of the relationship in Ireland between information, informing, censorship, and what she calls "the family cell."

2

"Blessed Are Those Who Hunger for Justice"

Martyrdom, Masculinity, and the H-Blocks

> "My death will only be in vain if you as republicans fail to under-
> stand what you're about . . . and fail to teach it to others. . . . I am
> dying for those people who I'm proud to know as the risen people."
> —Bobby Sands on his imminent death on hunger strike

A 1981 MURAL on Belfast's Rockmount Street (fig. 3) offers a salient example of the constellation of religious, mythological, and historical symbols deployed in order to rally support and sympathy for Irish republican
prisoners on hunger strike in the H-Blocks of Her Majesty's Prison (HMP)
the Maze. A bearded man with long brown hair lies dying in a prison hospital bed. His large brown eyes stare out at pedestrians from behind the
rosary beads clutched in his hand. His dying body, propped by pillows and
covered in blankets, presses against the limits of the mural's foreground,
forcing his presence on passersby. Behind him, a white "H" encased in
cement and barbed wire recedes far into the background, its lines almost
meeting. Mediating between the fortified H and the hunger striker stands
the Virgin Mary, whose body has been painted to mirror the letter's lines,
her outstretched arms emitting beams of divine light. The benediction inscribed above the image reads, "Blessed are those who hunger for Justice."

The prisoner, with his prominent almond eyes, flowing brown hair,
and full beard recalls Byzantine mosaics of Christ and the apostles, but
he also resembles the pre-colonial Celtic Irish for whom long hair was a
mark of virility, and who mocked the newly arrived English settlers for

3. *Blessed Are Those Who Hunger for Justice*, 1981 mural on Rockmount Street, Belfast, from Bill Rolston, *Drawing Support: Murals in the North of Ireland* (Belfast: Beyond the Pale, 1992). Courtesy of Bill Rolston.

their unmanly cropped hair. By the sixteenth century, as English and Irish cultures began to mix, long hair and the masculinity it signified also became a mark of resistance to an increasingly colonialist culture. The Irish who cut their hair and adopted English styles became the emasculated objects of ridicule in poems such as Laoiseach Mac an Bhaird's "O Man Who Follows English Ways" ("A fhir ghlacas a ghalldacht") (McKibben 2010, 24–36). The hunger striker in the mural thus becomes a virile Christ figure whose suffering is as much a mark of his strength and powerful resistance to the state as it is an act of martyrdom for his community. The fortified "H" looming in the background is a clear reference to the H-Blocks of Long Kesh (so named because of their shape). But "h" is also the first letter of "hunger," alluding to the hunger striker, to a communal hunger for the justice lacking in the British state, and to the recurrence of hunger in colonized Ireland. In an Irish nationalist context such as that of the mural, hunger—as an act and as a condition—is laden with associations to British colonial domination. "The Irish," Maud Ellmann writes, "have a long tradition of starving and the English a scandalous tradition of ignoring it" (Ellmann 1993, 11). This "tradition" is passive hunger from famine and food shortages exacerbated by colonialism, and it is also the political act of the hunger strike, which has been a central weapon in the arsenal of republican prison protests since the 1910s.

The inscription "blessed are those who hunger for justice," which appeared in support of the hunger strikers on walls in Derry and Belfast, does more than mimic the tone of the Beatitudes, it also bestows a benediction on the entire nationalist community that follows the logic of the Sermon on the Mount: those who suffer are blessed through the fact of their anguish. In Northern Ireland, those who hunger for justice are those starved for it—the objects of hunger, who as a result of emergency legislation have no access to justice. But the hunger striker is actively hungering for the cause of justice. He is thus blessed in his capacity as a martyr assuming the suffering of his people on a public and symbolic level. The mural invokes the spiritual authority of Christian millenarianism as expressed in the Beatitudes, which imagine an apocalyptic reversal of power relations (the meek shall inherit the earth, the last shall be first). In doing so, it resonates with what Allen Feldman has identified as the eschatological intent of the 1981 hunger strike: to rid the North of the British Army and ultimately issue in the messianic triumph of Irish nationalism (1991, 218).[1] The mural thus introduces a new allegorical figure to Irish nationalism: that of the Blanketman (the H-Block prisoner), who, like Mother Ireland, expresses the subjugated status of a population by blending Irish history, Celtic tradition, and Catholicism. But because the emblematic figure of the Blanketman is also a transformation and representation of actual men on protest, it contains a level of insurrectionary energy typically absent

---

1. On the surface of things, the prisoners were hunger striking for five demands: (1) the right to wear their own clothes, (2) the right to abstain from prison labor, (3) the right to associate freely with other prisoners and to segregate themselves according to paramilitary affiliation, (4) reinstatement of remission lost as punishment for their protests, and (5) reinstatement of standard visiting schedules, parcel allotments, and access to prison facilities. But Feldman convincingly argues that the protest's motives went much deeper than these demands.

from Mother Ireland. Fusing two traditions—Christian martyrdom and Irish resistance—into this contemporary republican figure, the mural establishes the Blanketman as the rightful heir to heroic Irish history, and it recasts suffering as a form of action. Gazing intently at the viewer, with the spiritual authority of the Virgin visually and symbolically behind him, the Blanketman reminds his community that his death is for their political resurrection.

The religious iconography that proliferated in representations of republican H-Block prisoners imagined the Blanketman as a national martyr, thus cementing the problematic link between Irish nationalism and Catholicism. But, in reviving Pádraig Pearse's figure of the ascetic nationalist martyr, such images also contradicted Britain's version of the conflict in which a bloodthirsty, hyper-masculine IRA—Margaret Thatcher's nebulous "men of violence"—holds its community hostage to its own self-destructive rage. The masculinity at the core of representations of the H-Block protests eschews a phallic, militarized body and instead foregrounds the capacity of the male nationalist's body to be wounded and degraded while his faith in the inevitability of a liberated, united Ireland remains steadfast. The Blanketmen's experience became, as Ellmann observes, a living example of Terrance MacSwiney's famous assertion, "It is not those who can inflict the most, but those who can suffer the most who will conquer" (Ellmann 1993, 60).[2] Embodying this claim, the Blanketman witnesses the suffering of his community and actively shoulders that burden in order to reveal it to the world. In doing so, he becomes the antithesis of the familiar green-clad volunteer who raises his rifle triumphantly on other republican murals. Whereas the bulkiness of the gunman's body signifies his imperviousness to wounds, the Blanketman's body is exposed, emaciated, and highly vulnerable.

This chapter addresses the relationship of heroic memory to representations of masculinity under incarceration in three films about the H-Block protests—*Some Mother's Son* (Terry George, 1996), *H3* (Les

---

2. Terrence MacSwiney, Lord Mayor of Cork, died on hunger strike in Brixton Prison in 1920.

Blair, 2001), and *Hunger* (Steve McQueen, 2008). Despite their diverse audio-visual styles and political viewpoints, each film places the 1981 hunger strike at its narrative climax, ends with the hunger strike unresolved for its characters, and offers concluding titles that explain the changes implemented in the North as a result of the deaths of ten men. The placement of the hunger strike at the film's dramatic peak positions the actual historical event on the cusp between an oppressive past and a brighter, better future. Therefore, I argue, in its narrative structure, each of these films is consistent with a heroic approach to republican history, wherein death is rewarded with tangible political gains and thus becomes a form of victory. But the films are not simply heroic celebrations of the Blanketmen's ordeal. Each film also attempts to qualify the heroic discourse of nationalism. How it accomplishes this complexity depends in part on how it engages with the preponderance of what Feldman refers to as "Christological models" for narrating the history of the hunger strike—the tendency to interpret the protest as the IRA's penance for prior acts of violence (Feldman 1991, 219).

Critiquing journalists who wrote about the hunger strike as a fatal act of contrition and linked it to Gandhi's nonviolent fasts, Feldman argues that such interpretations are problematic because they sever the hunger strike from the military campaign that continued outside the prison walls, thus missing the fact that Bobby Sands intended his death and the deaths of those who followed to provoke a violent sense of injustice and anger toward the British government, which would then provide the PIRA and INLA with fertile recruiting ground. But, as he notes, while the Blanketmen "insist[ed] on a secular interpretation of the Hunger Strike, [they were] well aware of the political benefits of the protest's sacralization" (Feldman 1991, 219). In fact, Sands, who organized the protest and guided its interpretation by the prisoners and by the outside community, deliberately drew on the language of death and resurrection to frame the Blanketmen's approaching ordeal. This rhetoric becomes blatant in his instructions to the Blanketmen to go out and preach the gospel of republicanism after his death. As one former prisoner recounted: "Bobby said out the door, 'I'm going to die, make no two ways about it. I know I am dying and I want to make it clear what I am dying for. It's not about a suit of clothes or a food parcel. I'm dying to make sure that the struggle continues, that the struggle lives. . . . My death will only be in vain if you as Republicans fail to understand what you're about and where you're going and fail to teach it to others. It had fuck all to do with the uniform. For anybody to believe I died for five demands is madness! I am dying for those people who I'm proud to know as the risen people!" (Feldman 1991, 243–44).

Although Feldman limits his discussion of the Christological to written texts, his arguments work for visual ones. The language of the sacred finds its way into all discourse on the H-Block protests, and it is often linked to a heroic framework wherein the prisoners successfully resist the prison system and ultimately triumph. The films I cover both facilitate and thwart this heroic understanding, and the extent to which they do so is connected to how the male body is portrayed. This chapter thus examines the question of political cinema in relation to a central problem facing cinematic representations of the H-Block protests: the opposition between, on the one hand, an artistic medium that tends toward the dematerialization of what it represents and, on the other, the brute physicality of life in the blocks. While I agree with Feldman that the hunger strike was an act of insurrection rather than one of expiation, religious iconography is not necessarily at odds with political expression in cinema. Political film has at times turned to Christological imagery to make its point, particularly in Italian neorealist and art cinema, where Gramscian ideas often coexist with Catholic iconography. Even *Hour of the Furnaces*, the film by Fernando Solanas and Octavio Getino that inspired the very concept of "Third Cinema," fuses the socialist and the sacred. The film's final shot features a close-up of a post-mortem photograph of Che Guevara. Accompanied by rhythmic drumming, the image lingers on screen for three minutes. The audio-visual combination of mesmerizing bongo beats with a long take of the dead rebel's face turns this shot into a religious icon and metaphorically resurrects Che to implore the spectator to take action. Even if, as Robert Stam and Ella Shohat argue, such an address romanticizes death as heroism (Shohat and Stam 1994, 267), the fusion of religious iconography with a revolutionary call to arms and the rewriting of death as victory speak to a radical exclusion wherein martyrdom is imagined as a way to blast open a space for political inclusion.

In this sense, the Blanketmen used Catholicism tactically, appropriating religious discourse to convey a politically and historically specific protest against British occupation.[3]

Convicted of terrorist offenses in a judicial system that had been retooled to all but guarantee guilty verdicts, republican prisoners were physically relocated into a space of exclusion (prison), where they faced political invisibility. However, the Blanketmen resisted this *homo sacer* status by embodying it. Pulling from the rich archive of images of suffering in Catholicism and Irish nationalism, they drew comparisons between their struggle and the historical struggle for Irish liberation. Republican prisoners were genuinely bodies in pain, subjected to the arbitrary power of the prison authorities, but they also performed that agony and disempowerment, while relatives and supporters on the outside helped to locate this pain within the pantheon of Irish and Christian martyrs. Spanning five years, the struggle of republican prisoners to regain political status took place on an ever-shifting terrain, generating an intimate, embodied history of Ireland in which the tiniest maneuvers were recast as victories. This history was self-inscribed on the bodies of the Blanketmen but also imposed on their bodies by the prison regime. It was rewritten on the bodies of the Blanketmen's relatives—who marched and demonstrated dressed in blankets and carrying photographs of the incarcerated men— and again on the walls of Derry and Belfast in order to be transmitted to the larger republican community. In the context of the H-Blocks, the prisoner's body is a screen for the projection of a republican understanding of Irish history, but it is also a site of violence and a weapon against the state. The Blanketmen's unique situation as prisoners whose bodies formed their entire world and means of expression provoked a fusion of

---

3. Michel de Certeau defines a tactic as a means of "making do" within prescribed circumstances. Distinguishing tactics from strategies, he explains that strategies produce specific spaces in conjunction with particular abstract models of power or capital, but tactics are maneuvers within such constructions. A tactic lacks a stable power base; it "must play on and with a terrain imposed on it and organized by the law of a foreign power." An "art of the weak," a tactic "must vigilantly make use of the cracks that particular conjunctions open in the surveillance of the proprietary powers. It poaches in them" (Certeau 1984, 37).

republican activism and symbolic communication; "to symbolize in the H-Blocks," argues Feldman, "was to act politically, and with finality" (1991, 165).

Within the H-Blocks, the prison administration reduced the Blanketmen's existence to a form of bare life, in an attempt to recode them not just as offenders but also as objects, "as mere biological life and not as political subjects" (Kearns 2007, 8). Agamben ascribes the condition of bare life to those living outside of the political and juridical order, where the continuance of life itself is dependent on the sovereign (Kearns 2007, 7). While the Blanketmen were not under threat of actual death, the prison system did overtly attempt to terminate their political and intellectual lives. In an essay discussing the hunger strike and the Irish Famine of 1847, Gerry Kearns expands Agamben's concept to allow for degrees of bare life wherein the state might not be overtly genocidal but it is also clearly not interested in protecting the life of all citizens equally and, in fact, it actively destroys political life for excluded populations. In states that claim to be run by rational, representational governments, bare life is justified through discourses of security, and in the H-Blocks, security measures were so excessive that they became superfluous to any real threat posed by the prisoners. The body-cavity searches when prisoners were moved from one cell to another, the one-towel rule, the restricted access to toilets and hygiene, and the exclusion of non-religious reading materials all had a function other than legitimate security. Like the greater environment of Northern Ireland, the H-Blocks existed in a constant state of emergency. The Blanketmen's task was to reveal the connection between these two routine states of emergency, thus bringing about a real crisis in state power. They resisted their reduction to mere biological life, paradoxically, by using their bodies, bodily waste, and body cavities as sites for political expression.

Emergency Legislation

The Blanketmen conceptualized their incarceration as a reenactment of the mechanisms of British colonization (Feldman 1991, 227), but in refusing to bathe, shave, go to the toilets, and eventually refusing to eat, they also performed the condition of being colonized and brutalized, which is the condition of Irish history as seen through a republican lens. The link between the degradation in the prison and the occupation on the outside achieved its highest degree of visibility on May 5, 1981, with the death of Irish republican prisoner and member of parliament Bobby Sands after sixty-six days of starvation. Sands's death focused international attention on the H-Block hunger strike, which he had begun on March 1. Sands was joined at regular intervals by other republican prisoners. The death of ten men (whose ages ranged from twenty-three to thirty) between May and October 1981 captured sympathetic international media attention for the PIRA and INLA prisoners[4] and, by extension, the wider Irish republican community. Like Bloody Sunday, the hunger strike stands out as a pivotal moment in the convoluted history of the Northern conflict,[5] one that offered a public glimpse of the exceptional status conferred on northern nationalists. The hunger strike helped to swing media coverage around (albeit briefly) to a sympathetic Irish community victimized by an intractable and heartless Margaret Thatcher.[6] The final and most extreme

4. The protesting H-Block prisoners came from the ranks of the Provisional Irish Republican Army (PIRA or Provos) and the Irish National Liberation Army (INLA). The Provos split from the "Official" IRA or Sinn Fein in 1970 over the issue of what was euphemistically termed "physical force." The PIRA and Provisional Sinn Fein quickly became the dominant factions of the various versions of IRA or Sinn Fein. The INLA, affiliated with the Irish Republican Socialist Party (IRSP), is much smaller than the Provos. Despite ideological differences between the PIRA and INLA, the two groups held solidarity in the prison.

5. This familiarity on a global scale is due partly to the volume of publicity focused on Sands's death, which sparked official and unofficial expressions of sympathy for the hunger strikers and outrage against Britain. The New York State legislature passed a resolution censuring the British government; the parliaments of India and Portugal observed a minute of silence; France renamed a street for Sands; and the Iranian government offered perhaps the most cleverly sardonic response when it renamed the street of the British Embassy's Teheran address "Bobby Sands Street" (Adams 1996, quoted in McKeown 2001, 78–79).

6. It is worth keeping in mind that media representations of Thatcher as coldhearted and irrationally stubborn are saturated with gender stereotypes. Thatcher was no doubt

of a series of body-based protests that prisoners had begun in response to the British government's revocation of their "special category" (political) status, the hunger strike of 1981 was also the most spectacular, relying on public funerals and the proliferation of images outside the prison to find a way out of the invisibility and isolation imposed by cellular incarceration.[7] Deploying the religious and nationalist-historical significance of martyrdom and hunger, Sands's protest mobilized a powerful narrative of Irish suffering with which the republican community could confront the master narrative of the Irish terrorist propagated by Britain and circulated in journalism and popular film.

The hunger strike, its preceding protests, and visual representations of prisoners at the time thwarted the British efforts to hide the existence of war in Northern Ireland, which the government had initiated in 1972 (the same year as the global coverage of Bloody Sunday) with a three-pronged strategy of "Ulsterization," "normalization," and "criminalization" that effectively entrenched the state of emergency in the North. Under Ulsterization, "primacy of policing" was given to the Royal Ulster Constabulary (RUC), granting them the authority to decide how best to deploy the British Army. This transfer of power meant that Britain's army was now under the orders of a sectarian police force similar to the white South African police under apartheid. RUC officers were also solicited to become part-time soldiers for the Ulster Defence Regiment, a locally recruited branch of the British Army, whose members often had close ties to loyalist paramilitary groups (Feldman 1991, 278).[8] With "normalization," the

seen as a female anomaly—a callous *woman* as opposed to a callous leader—as the nicknames "Tin Knickers" and "The Iron Lady" attest. However, to call out the sexism at work in how she was perceived is not to defend her policies, actions, or beliefs.

7. Feldman writes that because corpses "had become customary spectacle of political power on the 'outside' . . . the media through which the PIRA (inside) was to establish its legitimacy and hegemony on the 'outside' would be the externalization and production of corpses" (1991, 235).

8. The full quotation from Feldman's book about this evidence is given in the introduction.

government re-opened town centers and removed the security barriers from many smaller towns and villages (McKeown 2001, 239n8).

Criminalization evolved as an answer to the problems created by internment and the subsequent restructuring of the court system. Introduced in 1971, internment had enabled the government to imprison people suspected of anti-state activities against whom it could not procure legal convictions, but it also clogged the legal and penal systems with prisoners awaiting trial, some for up to a year (Feldman 1991, 86). In 1972, the Diplock Commission was formed to study the issue, and it recommended that the courts be changed to accommodate the "special" circumstances internment had created. The commission advised a streamlining of the conviction process by dispensing with juries and having trials for men and women accused of terrorism presided over by a single judge endowed with the authority to pronounce guilt and sentence the prisoners at his or her discretion. These "Diplock courts" were put into effect in 1973, when the government passed the Emergency Provisions (Northern Ireland) Act. Through the magic of rushed convictions, they reduced the number of remand prisoners but they also increased the number of prisoners with special category status.[9] The vast majority of male political prisoners were detained at Long Kesh, a World War II air force base that had been converted to a prison camp. Political prisoners were separated from the Ordinary Decent Criminals (ODCs)[10] and were further segregated according to political affiliation. They slept in dormitory-style Nissen huts ("the Cages") and they lived like prisoners of war; prison guards acknowledged the paramilitary command structure by addressing the prisoners through the Officer Commanding (OC) for each unit (Feldman 1991; McKeown 2001; Campbell, McKeown, O'Hagan 1998).

In 1975 Long Kesh housed just over a thousand special category prisoners and more than five hundred detainees, statistics that undermined the legitimacy of the prison system and revealed the extent to which the

9. Prisoners had won special category status in 1972 by going on a hunger and thirst strike (Feldman 1991, 219).

10. Mervyn Rees, Britain's Secretary for Northern Ireland, coined the term in 1976.

state had excluded republicans from political life. That same year, the Gardiner Commission was formed to study problems created by special category status (McKeown 2001, 15). Rather than question the transformation of the court system from an implement of justice to a weapon in the arsenal of counter-insurgency, the commission recommended the revocation of special category status and the construction of a cellular prison complex (Feldman 1991, 151). Britain's Labour government put these recommendations into effect, announcing that anyone sentenced for terrorist offenses after March 1, 1976, would be denied political status and incarcerated in the new H-Blocks, built alongside the compound at Long Kesh. Prisoners already incarcerated in the Cages would remain there with political status unless they were caught trying to escape or were released and convicted for new offenses. In order to erase previous associations of the site with political status, the prison was renamed HMP the Maze, and the two separate areas became known as Maze Compound and Maze Cellular (McKeown 2001, 16). In the entire Maze prison complex, the history of England's contradictory stand on Irish insurgency was manifest in architectural form: Irish people accused of acts against the state found themselves in a no-man's land between the discourses of war (extraordinary violence with a nationalist-political thrust) and crime (ordinary violence that requires due process in prosecution). This metaphorical space created by emergency legislation is the space ascribed to the *homo sacer*, the point where "the law suspend[s] itself" (Gregory 2004, 62). After their all but guaranteed convictions, republican prisoners found themselves in an actual, physical zone of abandonment: the H-Blocks.

Tactics of Resistance

Hunger acknowledges the routinization of the state of emergency in Northern Ireland by resisting temporal linearity and withholding narrative context. The film begins with a rhythmic clatter over a black screen. Titles soon convey the place and year—Northern Ireland, 1981—and provide some historical background: "2,187 people have been killed in 'the Troubles' since 1969. The British government has withdrawn the political status of all paramilitary prisoners. Irish Republicans in the Maze prison are on a 'blanket' and 'no wash' protest." After this orientation, a close-up of a hand slamming a metal dustbin lid against the asphalt reveals the source of the noise and the following shot depicts a group of people crouched on the ground and banging bin lids together. However, of this group, only one person is in focus—a woman in the foreground who occupies nearly half the frame. The film returns to a close-up of the mechanical move-ments of the lid, before abruptly cutting out all sound to reveal the title, after which come a series of shots depicting a man's morning routine. The relevance of these images to the preceding ones becomes clear when we discover the man, Raymond, works as a prison guard in the Maze.

An overpowering, visceral sound, the bin-lid banging is initially dis-orienting. While the film's insistence on giving the specific year as 1981 suggests that this action is in response to the death of Bobby Sands, the juxtaposition of these shots with Raymond's habitual tasks and the fact that the film's story actually begins in 1980 help to dislodge this sequence from a specific instance in time. The woman who stares intently off screen as she rattles her lid against the ground never appears in the film again. As the only person in focus, she becomes a representative of the blurred forms behind her. Her gender, her iconic function in the shot, and the way McQueen simply drops any narrative thread initiated by this scene suggest a more emblematic purpose to this sequence; it becomes an audio-visual shorthand for Northern Ireland under British occupation. Through this opening sequence, *Hunger* alludes to the wider republican community in whose name the Blanketman suffered. The film thus establishes the state of emergency not as a rupture, but as part of the fabric of everyday life.

In Northern Ireland, the prison's existence as a "closed space" (Fou-cault 1995, 236) reflected the closed-circuit logic of the state, which turned the judicial system into an echo chamber of its own pronouncements. Everything about the process that brought Irish republican prisoners to British jails was controlled by a state that had as its goal the end of Irish nationalism. Regardless of what prisoners had done on the outside, their guilt was predetermined and then affirmed in the Diplock courts. The inevitability of a conviction meant that the government could shift the center of the conflict from the streets to the jails, where it would presum-ably become invisible. Cellular incarceration was designed to break not only the prisoner, but also the struggle to which he belonged, the chain of nationalist heroes to which he attached himself. This began with the new regime at Maze Cellular, where unlike at Long Kesh or Maze Compound, the guards and the prison administration refused to recognize "any social unit greater than the individual," a refusal that was repeated architecturally with cells designed to house only one prisoner each (Feldman 1991, 161). For militant republicans, the H-Blocks threatened to break the back of not just the IRA—as touted in the press—but the entire republican community as well (Feldman 1991, 161). To illustrate the extent of this danger, Bobby Sands developed the concept of the "Breaker's Yard," which understood the Maze as a site designed to kill political life not only while the republican prisoner was incarcerated, but also after his release.[11] As one former prisoner explained: "The idea of the Breaker's Yard is that they'll get IRA volunteers into jail. They'll isolate them from the struggle by putting them through the fucking mill. Even if the brutality is not there, they'll get you in and individualize you and isolate you within the prisons. They'll divorce you from your structures and divorce you from your roots. They'll turn out apathetic people who'll be doing nothing all day but watching the gate for their day of release, and when they do get that day of release, all that's going to be in their heads, 'I'm not going back in there'" (Feldman 1991, 161). Sands's insight into the dynamics of the Breaker's Yard and the resistance tactics prisoners developed in response, Feldman argues, ensured that the prison became the regenerating center of the republican movement, not its final resting place (1991, 162–65). This shift cemented the connection between resistance in the prison and violence in the street, placing the Blanketmen "into an emblematic and sacrificial structure of action" (Feldman 1991, 162–63).[12] The link Sands made between prisoners on the inside and militant republicans on the outside was designed to counter the machinery of the Breaker's Yard, and

11. I use "his" alone here because neither Sands nor Feldman addresses the breaking of women prisoners in Armagh (Feldman 1991, 160–61).

12. An unfortunate side effect of this radical rethinking of the struggle was that women combatants and prisoners seemed to become even less visible. How were women to remain connected to the struggle if its nerve center had shifted to a men's prison?

it offers evidence refuting the arguments of authors and filmmakers who see the H-Block protests as "passive" or nonviolent resistance.[13]

Although *Hunger* opens with a shot of the wider republican community, once inside the H-Blocks, the film removes that community from view, except as visitors to the Maze. Likewise, *H3* remains inside the prison from beginning to end, leaving only briefly through a character's dream. Both films keep their audiences firmly within the space of the exception. In doing so, *Hunger* and *H3* shift ideas of narrative scope and visual scale from the grand to the minute. Tiny moments function as major plot points, as when in *H3* prisoners pass contraband from cell to cell by "shooting the line"—flicking a button tied to a thread from under one cell door to another and using the thread to distribute cigarettes hand-rolled with pages from the Bible. In *Hunger*, a prisoner scoops a fly onto his finger, and the film takes time to depict this interaction between inmate and insect. Through their frequent use of close-up and extreme close-up shots, both *Hunger* and *H3* complicate Foucault's characterization of the prison as an "exhaustive apparatus with complete authority over the prisoner." For Foucault, in its function as a closed space, the prison has "neither exterior nor gap; it cannot be interrupted" (Foucault 1995, 236). But the Blanketmen did find gaps in the system and ways to interrupt its logic.

Visibility as a military unit was central to the prisoners' struggle against the breaking process; therefore, the choice of a blanket over a uniform was essential in initiating individual republicans into the collective identity of Blanketmen. Once a prisoner put on the uniform, his history and identity dissolved into the history put forth by Britain and unionism, which within the framework of Irish republicanism is one that criminalizes the wish for Irish sovereignty and charts the triumph of the state (Feldman 1991, 156). Feldman explains, "The Blanketmen saw their passage through the disciplinary machinery of the prison system as a journey to the inner truth of the British state. The prison system for them encapsulated a wider

---

13. The terms "passive" and "nonviolent" resistance are inherently problematic; there is nothing passive or nonviolent about refusing food or deliberately putting your body in the destructive path of the police or army.

colonial power which had imprinted discourses of domination upon their bodies" (Feldman 1991, 227). By choosing nakedness over the uniform, the Blanketmen initiated a political struggle against expanding circles of power that overlapped across multiple planes of time and space. From the Blanketman's body emanated resistance against the guards in each wing, the prison system, the unionist state, Britain's presence in the North of Ireland, and the history of Britain's colonial domination of all of Ireland.

Some Mother's Son, *H3*, and *Hunger* all establish the refusal to wear the uniform as the individual prisoner's first act of resistance to penal inscription, but the extent to which this act is successful varies. Each film details the induction process through newly incarcerated characters, but in *H3* and *Hunger* the audience is exposed to the prison before these characters arrive, while in *Some Mother's Son*, we see the H-Blocks for the first time through the eyes of new prisoners. While this shift might seem minor, establishing the violence of the H-Blocks before new prisoners arrive limits the extent to which their resistance to the prison regime can be seen as reassuringly triumphant. In *Some Mother's Son*, Frankie Higgins and Gerard Quigley are arrested, tried in a Diplock court, and convicted. After sentencing, they are taken to the H-Blocks and processed into the prison system along with an ODC. The film cuts from an exterior establishing shot of H5 to a fluorescent-lit room painted institution gray, as Frankie, Gerard, and the ODC walk in, wearing towels and holding their uniforms. They step into three separate stalls, and a pockmarked guard paces in front of them. The camera tracks in medium close-up across all three as the guard checks their progress. He first approaches the ODC, who pulls on a prison shirt, and greets him with a friendly, "Murphy, you're back again." He strolls over to Frankie, who holds the folded pile of prison clothes out in front of his chest as if they were contaminated, and asks, "What's your problem?" Frankie, shot in medium close-up and from a slightly lower angle than the guard, stands at military attention, stares straight ahead and declares, "I'm a prisoner of war. I refuse to wear a criminal's uniform," and drops the uniform on the floor. The guard steps over to Gerard and, thrusting his baton in Gerard's face, asks, "What about you? Do you refuse?" To which Gerard sneers, "I refuse," and lets the uniform fall.

After Gerard and Frankie reject the uniforms, the following shot begins with the abrasive buzz of an alarm as a metal grille rolls open. Clad in towels and led by the guard, the two men strut through the door, as what sounds like a synthesized *bodhrán* beats out a generically Celtic rhythm on the soundtrack. When they turn onto the wing, they are bombarded with the sights and sounds of tall, shaggy, bearded Blanketmen who crowd the corridor to cheer hello before being herded back into their cells. Frankie and Gerard walk through another grille, and a Blanketman pops out of his cell, empties his chamber pot, smiles, and waves to Frankie. This entire sequence depicting their first glimpse of the H-Blocks is edited in a point-of-view and reaction shot pattern; Frankie and Gerard are shot from a slightly lower angle, which endows them with an air of power and control that the film bolsters in its narrative. Frankie and Gerard are among friends in the H-Blocks; they have joined a community of volunteers all cheerfully doing their bit for Ireland. From the moment they enter the prison, the Blanketmen have secured a victory over the Breaker's Yard. *Some Mother's Son* further protects its characters by removing the aspect of life in the H-Blocks that made prisoners feel especially vulnerable—the constant exposure of their genitalia to the gaze and violence of the guards. Possibly to avoid an NC-17 rating, the film tastefully shoots Frankie and Gerard from the waist up or ensures that, contrary to historical fact, they are discretely covered in towels.

In *Some Mother's Son*, Hollywood's terror of full-frontal male nudity becomes a way for the film to hold on to a heroic masculinity for its characters, while in *H3*, male nudity functions as a way to portray male vulnerability. The film opens with a series of shots depicting the prison's eerie morning stillness; a horde of screws[14] disturb the prisoners with a wing

---

14. According to McKeown, the term "screw" derives from nineteenth-century prison labor: "When tread-wheels and hand cranks were introduced as punitive labour . . . they could be adjusted to make them heavier to turn/push in order to make the penal labour more arduous. Hence . . . 'tightening the screw.'" The guards who came in to tighten the apparatus became known as screws (McKeown 2001, 240n1). I alternate between the terms "guard" and "screw" in this and chapter 3, using "guard" for the abstract relationship between prisoner and warder and "screw" for the men and women

shift and anal mirror search—hygiene and security measures that in actuality were opportunities for violence against the prisoners. The torture of the Blanketmen in this sequence is intercut with the arrival of eighteen-year-old Declan McCann to the H-Blocks, which elicits a sense of dread for Declan's future and a painful longing, in sympathy with the prisoners, for the community and relative corporeal autonomy they had on the outside. As screws push four Blanketmen into the prison corridor, the film cuts to a shot inside the van transporting Declan, where a gray-haired officer comments on Declan's young age, shaking his head at the "shameful" waste of a life. He contrasts Declan's activities with those of a "normal" young man when he offers an example from his own upstanding life, "When I was your age, I was chasin' girls at the dances and not placin' bombs in shops and shootin' soldiers," imagining youth as a universal time of innocence and refusing to recognize the power imbalances that allowed the guard the luxury of choosing heterosexual romance over insurgency. When Declan is brought to the prison, the guard hands his papers over to another screw, turns to Declan, and says, "Good luck, son." However, his fatherly concern is undermined by the preceding sequence in which his colleagues had beaten naked prisoners and kicked them over the foam-padded search mirror. As the film cuts between Declan's transport and the extended body cavity searches of each of the four prisoners, it inserts Declan into a chain of brutalized bodies onto which the state inscribes its presence, despite their lack of uniforms.

Declan is handed over to more screws, who greet him mockingly as "a baby Provo." A tall, middle-aged officer with broad shoulders and a thick, freshly scrubbed neck stands over Declan in a shot that emphasizes the latter's youth. Declan looks straight ahead and declares, "I won't be wearing the prison uniform or doing prison work. I'm not a criminal. I'm a political prisoner." His statement is as impassioned as Frankie's in *Some*

---

who had daily violent interaction with the protesting prisoners. "Screw" is consistent with the language the prisoners use in their narratives, and I think it is a more accurate description of the relationship between protesting prisoners and the guards. "Screw" also carries a violence associated with both penetration and resistance (as in "to screw" and "screw you"), whereas "guard" is too benevolent a term for the H-Blocks and Armagh.

Mother's Son, conveying the same sense of commitment to the republican movement and determination to resist the prison system. But Frankie's statement was backed by his thirty-something age and by the size and strength of his movie-toned body. In *Some Mother's Son*, Frankie's refusal to wear the uniform demonstrated his mastery over the guard, which the film reinforced with a slightly lower angle on Frankie and strengthened in the following sequence through the crowd of jovial Blanketmen. By contrast, the force of Declan's statement as an assertion of power is under-cut by his shorter stature in relation to the officer, by the baby fat on his smooth, pale cheeks, and by the anxiety in his wide eyes. After this state-ment, he is led into a room and surrounded by a group of screws who order him to strip and smack him on the back of the head. When he removes his underwear, one screw eyes his pale, adolescent body and laughs deri-sively. Shot from behind and surrounded by a group of overdressed men in shiny black boots, Declan seems even younger than his age of eigh-teen. After being admitted into the prison system, a stark-naked Declan is escorted down the prison wing by two burly screws who yell, "Here comes a streaker!" and throw him into a cell with the wing OC, Seamus Scul-lion. Scullion greets him, hands him a blanket, and grimly jokes, "Don't worry, the first ten years are the hardest."

The blanket shielded the prisoners from the gaze of the prison regime physically by covering their bodies and symbolically by making their pre-sumed criminality illegible. The protests that followed it grew out of a need to counter the deepening surveillance and increasingly violent and invasive measures taken to force the prisoners to conform. These protests became important aspects of the struggle between visibility and invisibil-ity central to any prison dynamic. Because "instructions to break the pris-oners came from the highest levels of government" (according to a Prison Welfare Officer at the time), the Blanketmen were unprotected by any authority higher than the guards on individual wings and found them-selves in a system that frequently changed its rules of operation (Feld-man 1991, 191). For example, the Blanketmen were initially issued two towels, one of which they wore at the showers while bathing. In 1977, the prison regime announced a one-towel rule at the showers, demanding that republican prisoners be naked before their loyalist warders. Although they successfully resisted this regulation at first, it ultimately became institutionalized, and the Blanketmen stopped going to the showers altogether, beginning the no-wash phase of the protest. However, even before the no-wash protest began, the Blanketmen had been granted only limited access to washing, shaving, and dental hygiene. In between their weekly trips to the showers, the Blanketmen were issued a single basin of water with which to wash and shave. Rather than use the same dirty water for these daily tasks or risk shaving in mirrorless cells, the republican prisoners grew beards (Feldman 1991, 173; Campbell, McKeown, O'Hagan 1998, 20–21).

According to a British government pamphlet issued in the 1970s, the H-Blocks offered all the comforts and amenities of modern life. But the individual cells lacked toilets. As "category A" (terrorist) prisoners, the Blanketmen were locked up twenty-four hours a day, and any trips to the toilet required the indulgence of a guard. As an interim solution, they were issued chamber pots that would be emptied each morning by orderlies—conforming prisoners who performed menial labor that the guards refused to do and received special privileges in reward. The chamber pots full of urine posed a threat for the Blanketmen, since screws would often kick them over, spilling their contents onto the cell floor. In 1978, the prison authorities made two significant changes to toilet regulations: the Blanketmen would not be allowed to the toilets at all without a uniform, and they would now empty their own pots. For republican prisoners, to don so much as a prison sock put them on a slippery slope to criminalization. Emptying their own chamber pots technically constituted performing prison labor and was, therefore, a step toward conforming to the prison regime. Instead, the Blanketmen poured their urine through gaps around the cell door into the corridor, and they broke their cell windows to empty excrement into the yard. The screws responded by squeegeeing the pool of urine back under the cell doors and by spraying the yard walls with high-pressure hoses that they usually aimed at the open cell windows, soaking and bruising the men inside. Eventually, the prisoners found a better means of waste disposal and began smearing their feces on the cell ceilings and walls, a method that enabled it to dry quickly, thus taking the edge off the intensity of the odor. Urine disposal was more problematic, and often cell floors would be covered in inches of a urine-water-disinfectant solution (Feldman 1991, 173; Campbell, McKe-own, O'Hagan 1998, 20–21).

The "dirt" phase of the H-Block protests has received a great deal of commentary, and in some ways, this protest is even more spectacular than the hunger strike. Historians of the hunger strike, many of whom were journalists at the time (such as Beresford, O'Malley, and Coogan), frequently refer to this phase as the "*dirty* protest," a phrase that seems to have originated in the British and Irish press. Prisoners themselves occasionally use the phrase in interviews, but the writing coming out of the prisons and out of the republican community at the time uses "*dirt* protest" or simply "no-wash protest" to refer to both phases. The difference is significant because while "dirt protest" alludes to the materials used in the protest, "dirty protest" characterizes the protest itself as vile and dangerously taboo, as if there were something dirty—something sinful—about defying the will of the state. Such a conceptual framework reinforces the image promulgated by the British and Northern Irish state of itself as rational and above violence and of the republican community as irrational and undisciplined—an image that owes its genealogy to colonialist tropes that portrayed the colonized as filthy, infantile, and animalistic.

By 1978 "Europe's most modern prison" housed over three hundred protesting republican prisoners who were usually doubled up in cells designed to hold only one man. Unwashed and unable to brush their teeth for over a year, the Blanketmen lived in cells devoid of furniture, except for a bare foam mattress, and empty of reading material, except for a Bible (from which they tore pages for rolling contraband tobacco). The foam mattresses acted like sponges, sopping up the squeegeed urine, and each prisoner's cell walls and ceilings were lined with his own and his cellmate's excrement. The glass in the cell windows had never been replaced, and snow and rain blew into the cells until the government solved that problem by barricading the windows with sheets of corrugated metal, blocking out *all* natural light and fresh air. The Blanketmen's daily life consisted of brutal torture including beatings, forced bathing, and violent body cavity searches. But it also involved multiple forms of petty torture that used the vulnerability of the prisoner's body against him. For example, the prison authorities would turn the heat off in winter only to blast it in summer. Prisoners were given only three pints of water daily, and meals were minimal, undercooked, cold, tampered with, and often arrived with the protein portion missing. By law, prisoners had a monthly salt ration, and screws, in a technical adherence to the letter of the law, would often deliver the whole ration on one meal, thus making the food inedible.[15] Defined as privileges in the British penal system, cigarettes, pens, paper, pencils, non-religious magazines, and books other than the Bible were all banned. Prisoners could receive only one parcel a month, and only three packets of tissues from the monthly parcel usually made it past the censors. The Blanketmen were allowed out of their cells once a week for a forty-five-minute mass and once a month for a half-hour visit. Both "outings" required a prison uniform and were preceded and followed by extensive strip and body searches. The smallness typical of prison life was reduced in the H-Blocks to the miniscule (Maloney 1978, 24–25; Feldman 1991, 173; Campbell, McKeown, O'Hagan 1998, 20–21; McKeown 2001, 51–63).

The Art of Politics

Hunger, artist Steve McQueen's first feature film, expresses incarceration through the tiny details of a barren prison life. The film retains what Okwui Enwezor has identified as the haptic quality characteristic of McQueen's film and video installations (1999, 38). McQueen's adeptness at evoking the sense of touch through sight and sound has tremendous potential for a film about the H-Blocks, where the Blanketmen were reduced to the brute physicality of bare life. Unlike the other H-Block films, *Hunger* mines urine, excrement, food, blood, and wounds for their audio-visual potential, foregrounding the assault on multiple senses that confronted both prisoners and prison personnel inside the Blocks and offering a cinematic

---

15. The list of incidents of petty and violent harassment is endless, and I have included only a relatively small number here. For a more comprehensive image of the prisoners' ordeals, see Maloney 1978; Women Against Imperialism 1980; D'Arcy 1981; McCafferty 1981; Sands 1997; Campbell, McKeown, O'Hagan 1998; Murray 1998; and McKeown 2001.

study of bare life. In an interview for the Criterion DVD, McQueen discusses the problem of holding onto the body in a medium made of light and shadow: "For me, the physical aspects of, for example the urine, the feces, the beatings . . . has to come across to the audience in a real sort of direct manner. How can you make that movie smell of shit? How can you allow people to feel the cold? Those are those sort of sensual elements which have to come through this film."

In McQueen's film, the Blanketmen become their bodily pain and waste. Consistent with the many paradoxes of the H-Blocks, *Hunger* illuminates the Blanketmen's materials of political signification without much verbal language. In a departure from earlier portrayals of the H-Blocks— as well as from former prisoners' own recollections of their experiences— the Blanketmen of *Hunger* are strikingly quiet. In fact, as Caoimhín Mac Giolla Léith notes, one character, Davey, responds with "blank incomprehension" to his cellmate's "attempt[s] to communicate in Gaelic, the *lingua franca* of Irish Republicanism" (Mac Giolla Léith 2008). This verbal reticence on the part of the film foregrounds the inadequacy of language in a zone of abandonment, where the prison administration has the power to rename torture "security measures" and political prisoner "ordinary decent criminal." Stylistically, the film's almost non-existent script is consistent with the lack of speech in McQueen's installations, and it frees the spectator to focus on the film's images and sounds, a rare opportunity in narrative cinema. Through a selection of minimalist shots and a willingness to torture the bodies of its actors, *Hunger* allows the evidence of the prisoner's body to speak volumes.

McQueen conveys a visceral sense of physicality through close-ups of bodily waste and of wounds that serve as evidence of brutality, and through scenes of physical violence. The film eloquently captures the austerity of life in the H-Blocks, revealing the Blanketmen's ingenuity in transforming bare life into political language. For example, after a sequence in which the newly convicted Davey is registered in the office of the prison governor, the film cuts to a shot of him being led naked to his cell. The camera follows him from over the top of his head, focusing on a fresh wound. Amid a mass of matted black hair, blood oozes across his scalp and trickles down the side of his face, clearly the result of a baton blow. Later, *Hunger* uses urine as a metonym for the Blanketmen when Davey and his cell-mate, Gerry, empty their chamber pots. Using leftover mashed potatoes, Gerry builds a dam along the gap between the cell door and the floor, taking care to construct a chute through which to pour the urine. As he pours the contents of the pot through the mashed-potato sluice, the film cuts to a floor-level long shot of the prison corridor. Quietly, streams of urine seep out from under various cell doors, converging into a collective pool that slowly covers the polished floor of the hallway, suggesting a ghostly collective of Blanketmen. Here, McQueen substitutes urine for the voice as the disembodied trace of a political community whose members rarely saw one another but nevertheless felt the presence of their comrades. When this shot of the urine-filled hallway reappears later in the film, an orderly begins to clean the floor, far from the camera. His footsteps and the rhythmic scraping of his squeegee form the only soundtrack. He works his way toward the camera, pushing the urine back under cell doors, until his squeegee arrives at the camera's lens. The silence and duration of this take focuses attention on the actions of the orderly, who is in effect driving the collective of Blanketmen back into their cells. Like in *Some Mother's Son*, the presence of the Blanketmen in the prison corridor disrupts the order of things, but here they are represented unheroically, as piss.

But while the Blanketmen may be portrayed through their own waste, throughout *Hunger* there is an odd beauty to the bodily substances that fill the frame. In the hands of McQueen the artist, shit becomes oil paint—the feces covering the walls of the prison cells varies in shade, thickness, and texture. In one scene, it functions almost as form of communication between a prisoner and an orderly in a way similar to abstract expressionism's conception of the gesture in painting—as a biographical (and biological) trace of the person who had made it. After a harrowing scene where Sands is forcibly shaved and bathed, a guard dressed in a green hazmat suit goes into a cell to hose down the walls. He stops, removes his protective visor, and stares. The film cuts to the object of his gaze, a wall where a prisoner has used his excrement to create a giant, swirling spiral. The orderly follows the curves of the spiral with his hose, repeating in reverse the gestures of its creator. In this respect, *Hunger* is consistent with McQueen's wider body of video work, where the representation of people and histories marginalized by colonial and postcolonial power structures acquires a transcendent beauty befitting a modern Manhattan gallery space. As Mac Giolla Léith notes, McQueen's work is "inflected by the politics of post-colonialism" but also contains "an underlying aspiration somehow to transcend politics" (2008). In *Western Deep* (2002), for example, McQueen shoots workers of one of the deepest gold mines in the world, South Africa's TauTona (or Western Deep) mine. Like *Hunger*, the video subordinates narration to the sensory aspects of cinema. Shots of the mineshaft from within its crowded elevator, water running over tracks, a metal grate, cracks of light, and pieces of stone are accompanied by a soundtrack that alternates between industrial and natural sounds and complete silence.

If McQueen's work seeks to transcend politics for the realm of art, the distracting beauty of his images and the haunting crispness of his approach to sound also foreground the artifice of representation itself. In this respect, *Hunger* undermines McQueen's own claims to place the audience in the H-Blocks. The film seems acutely aware of the impossibility of reconstructing history "the way it really was" on screen and the falseness of passing off representations of reality as actual experience. Like Pat Murphy's *Maeve* and *Anne Devlin*, *Hunger* offers mute tableaux, shots with little to no movement that last a few beats too long on screen, so that their artificiality becomes apparent.[16] For example, after one of Gerry's aborted attempts to converse with Davey, the film cuts to a quiet shot of the cell. In the center, light streams in from the cell window, struggling to illuminate the deep-brown walls and casting a golden, almost saintly light on the two blanketed men, who sit without moving or speaking on their bare foam mattresses. The political potential of McQueen's overt artifice is strengthened in his body of work by his radically anti-linear approach to time, which carries over into *Hunger*. Toward the end of *Western Deep*

16. Luke Gibbons writes of the scene in *Anne Devlin* where Anne cradles her brother, "The 'natural' role of mother is offset by the deliberately posed and 'artificial' character of the shot; so far from depicting woman as nature, it points to woman as *representation*, the coded, tableau-like composition constituting what is virtually a direct, iconographic quotation from the history of art" (1996, 113).

are a series of shots of men stepping up and down on a bench to the noise of a buzzer. The men are in two straight rows, each row facing away from the other, and naked except for a cloth around their waists. Their pace increases and decreases according to the alarm, which is accompanied by a flashing red light. No explanation is given for their actions, and the only context we have is that of the mine. As Jean Fisher writes about this work and its companion piece, *Carib's Leap*, time in McQueen's films becomes "a non-chronological, pure cinematic time in which we lose ourselves not to narrative, as in orthodox cinema, but to the intensity of the image itself, or its serial sequences" (Fisher 2002, 120), and, I would add, to McQueen's mastery of sound. She argues that this lack of narrative structure and clear sense of time opens McQueen's work to accommodate and even provoke a viewer's associations with other contexts (123). Thus, the lines of men moving up and down on command in the mine's examination room are not only evidence of contemporary brutality, but they also call up images of past historical trauma, allowing the spectator to link past and present in ways consistent with the concerns of political film.

As noted earlier, McQueen's approach to temporality, whereby similar if not identical shots are repeated with increasing amounts of context, enables *Hunger* to portray how the exceptional became routine in the H-Blocks. He achieves this through his treatment of the prison staff rather than the prisoners. *Hunger* explores the power dynamic between the guards and the Blanketmen, and in this project, McQueen's fascination with detail becomes vital to understanding how a state of emergency gets woven into the fabric of everyday life for those in power as well as for the objects of power. Initially, the film establishes a series of parallels that seem to imply that the guards and the prisoners are equally captive in this system. While the first shot on screen depicts women banging bin lids, presumably after Sands's death, the narrative opens with the morning routine of H-Block guard Raymond, who soaks his swollen knuckles in a sink. Raymond sits at the breakfast table and his wife sets out a plate of eggs, sausage, and toast in a shot that foreshadows the steaming hot, alluring breakfasts laid out before Sands to tempt him off his protest and amplify his suffering. While Raymond consumes the food alone, McQueen's camera focuses on the crumbs that fall into the napkin on his lap, suggesting the disparity between the guard's feast and the starvation of the title. After breakfast, Raymond steps outside to his car, drops to the ground to check for bombs under the engine, opens the car door, and puts the key in the ignition. His wife watches anxiously inside the house, shot behind a pane of glass while he turns the key. Avoiding assassination is part of their morning routine, and both Raymond and his wife are visually confined in this sequence. Having survived starting up his car, Raymond departs for work.

Once inside the Maze, he puts on his uniform and steps onto the wing; like the UDR men in *Four Days in July*, Raymond must hide all traces of his occupation from the public since he too is a "legitimate target" for republican violence. His workday is conveyed in a series of shots whereby temporality becomes difficult to discern, implying a routine aspect to these images. Shot through a metal security screen, he leans against a wall in the prison yard and smokes a cigarette. Framed in a mirror, he soaks his hands, swollen and covered in abrasions, while a large pair of metal scissors rests on the edge of the sink. This particular image repeats in the film as if to elicit sympathy for the physical pain caused by the guard's work. However, as the film progresses, it fills in narrative gaps that explain how Raymond's hands came to be battered—by punching Irish prisoners in the face. Likewise, the scene of Raymond smoking is also repeated with more context: Bobby Sands is brought to the bathroom, where two screws hold him down while Raymond takes the enormous metal scissors from the earlier shot to Sands's scalp and face, cutting flesh as well as hair. Sands is tossed into a tub, and Raymond scrubs his body with the kind of heavy wooden broom/brush intended for scouring floors. As Raymond aims the broom at the center of Sands's body, the sounds of splashing water and Sands's agonized groans turn this scene into a harrowing adaptation of Sands's "One Day in My Life": "Every part of me stung unmercifully as the heavily disinfected water attacked my naked, raw flesh. I made an immediate and brave attempt to rise out of the freezing, stinging water, but the screws held me down while one of them began to scrub my already tattered back with a heavy scrubbing brush. . . . They continued to scrub every part of my tortured body, pouring buckets of ice-cold water and soapy liquid over me. I vaguely remember being lifted out of the cold water—the sadistic screw had grabbed my testicles and scrubbed my private parts. That was the last thing I remembered. I collapsed" (1997, 49). The screws drag an unconscious Sands away, and Raymond is left alone in the bathroom. In a low angle shot that includes a section of the bloody bathwater still churning from the violent struggle, Raymond soaks his hands. The disparity between the terrifying violence he has just inflicted on a naked prisoner and the superficiality of his own injuries prevents this moment from being merely one of appreciation for the fact that guards had a hard time in the Blocks too. The visible evidence of Sands's pain in the foreground undermines identification with and sympathy for Raymond's sore knuckles.

Hunger portrays the fact that guards and prisoners were locked in an escalating struggle in wretched conditions, but it also acknowledges the radical asymmetry of that contest. In this respect, the film—which diverges from *H3* and *Some Mother's Son* in its willingness to portray the misery of prison employment—is able to explore how the H-Block protests achieved a degree of success in throwing the role of incarceration into crisis, and it lays bare the brutality at the core of the state of emergency. In addition to Raymond's repeated grimaces while tending to his knuckles, the film includes a sequence in which screws in full riot gear stand in two neat rows in order to beat naked Blanketmen. After the Blanketmen destroy their furniture in protest over the swindle following the 1980 hunger strike, a riot squad is brought into the prison to oversee a mirror search. As Raymond inspects and sucks his injured thumb, members of the riot squad line the prison corridor leading to the foam-padded mirror and begin to beat their batons against their plastic shields. The film cuts to a shot of the hallway in time to catch Gerry being flung out of his cell and against a concrete wall; his face smashes against the wall with a thud loud enough to be heard over the incessant clattering of the batons, and he falls while two guards drag Davey toward the gauntlet of screws. Davey is thrown to the floor, and as the actor (Brian Milligan) crawls through the double line of truncheon blows, large red welts start to appear on his naked body. Against the audio background of batons on shields, Davey is dragged over the mirror, and McQueen highlights the pain of a rectal search with sound effects and groans from

Davey. He is jerked back up so that a guard can probe his mouth, using the same gloved finger that was used on his anus.[17] Davey is dragged away, and Gerry is brought out over the mirror. When he head-butts a screw, a helmeted guard breaks out of line in order to thrash him with a baton, grunting as he repeatedly beats Gerry (who is out of the frame), his exertion revealing the physical strength required to be a guard in the H-Blocks.

Toward the end of the beating, the sound becomes distorted and then vanishes entirely when the film cuts to a shot of a cell door being opened. Sands is tossed through it and onto the floor. The film cuts back to the scene of the mirror search, where a younger member of the riot crew also leaves the clattering violence, to get some fresh air in the prison yard. The wall of the prison cuts the frame in half, maintaining an image of the riot crew battering Bobby Sands in slow motion on one side of the wall, while on the other side, the solitary gentle guard cries, shattered by the scene he has just participated in. The guard's tears may evoke sympathy and work as an attempt to humanize the "screw," but the physical and psychological torture happening on the other side of the wall serves as a reminder of his role in the violence. Furthermore, the shot of Sands being beaten is out of chronological order, and McQueen's resistance to a cause-effect narrative structure throughout the film helps to turn the screws' actions into moments of sheer brutality. "Security" measures are revealed to be instances of violence for its own sake[18] as the film portrays the arbitrary application of power that characterizes the space of the exception for Agamben.

Pressure to end the protests combined with the Blanketmen's unexpected success at resisting total assimilation into the prison system led to increased violence by the guards. The Blanketmen had a standing order from their OCs to refuse to comply with any instructions to be searched.

17. This added measure of degradation was common during the mirror search.

18. Feldman characterizes the mirror search as "a ceremony of defilement" and "the reorganizing ritual upon which new strategies of compulsory visibility and hierarchical observation revolved" (1991, 174–75).

To get prisoners to obey orders for body cavity searches, guards had to beat them into position—it often took several guards to hold down and search just one prisoner. As the protest wore on, the role of "guard" became more accurately described as that of "screw," and their primary function was eventually reduced to the perfunctory repetition of violence for its own sake, a robotic role picked up in the mechanical metaphor "screw." With mounting demoralization among prison staff, their work conditions affected the government financially. The position became harder to fill, and as an incentive to stay on, the government raised their salaries and offered hiring bonuses. During the no-wash and dirt protests, H-Block prison officers made as much money as general practitioners (Feldman 1991, 193).

Inside the Maze, the blanket, no-wash, and dirt protests thwarted the goal of isolation, transformed the prison staff's work environment, and raised the cost of running the H-Blocks. The fact that prisoners were often doubled up in a cell enabled their resistance to total isolation. By refusing to shower or slop out, the prisoners created a protective force field of odor that made their presence palpable even when they were invisible behind locked doors.[19] On the no-wash and dirt protests, republican prisoners transformed the conditions in which the guards had to spend their twelve-hour shifts. Prison staff patrolled wings that reeked of body odor, excrement, urine, and rotting food. The smell from the prison clung to their uniforms and their bodies, assaulting their senses, affecting their feelings about the cleanliness of their own bodies and interfering in their relationships with spouses and children (Feldman 1991, 192–93). "The guard who spent four hours every working day attempting to rid himself of the stench of the H-Blocks, and who had to bring that stench home to his family, had become an inadvertent emissary of the Blanketmen" (Feldman 1991, 195). He became an infectious agent carrying the contagion of the prison, the taint of republicanism, beyond the walls of the institution that strove to contain it and into loyalist and Protestant neighborhoods. Thus, as

---

19. Feldman writes that through the dirt and no-wash protests, the prisoners "reclothed their naked bodies with a new and repellant surface of resistance" (1991, 175).

Feldman observes, prison guards became increasingly isolated from their families and their surrounding communities, an isolation that mirrored the aim behind criminalization for the PIRA/INLA man. Ironically, as they became more violent against the prisoners in their attempts to re-assert power, the screws were "inserted deeper into the closed systems of the prison situation, the only social institution in which they participated in an unambiguous, fixed social relation" (Feldman 1991, 196).

But if the Blanketmen's resistance to prison regulations disrupted the processes of institutionalization and frustrated the view of surveillance, their tactical victories should not be mistaken for triumph over penal inscription. Their refusal to wear the uniform was a refusal to allow the prison regime to inscribe its version of history onto their bodies. Their refusal to wash and shave afforded them another layer of protection from penal inscription. Ultimately, the excrement on their cell walls from their refusal to go to the toilets hindered the cell's function as "a theater of observation" (Feldman 1991, 157). The prison was denied access to inscribing itself upon the surfaces of the Blanketmen's bodies to the extent that the Blanketmen resisted being turned into state texts by the uniform. But it found other ways to write its presence and display its power on their bodies. Beatings did, in fact, give the prison system access to the surfaces of the Blanketmen's bodies. The Blanketmen were scalded, pummeled, gashed, scraped, and scrubbed by the screws; their noses and limbs were broken; their heads and faces were forcibly shaved, and they were forcibly bathed in either blistering or freezing water. The scars, bruises, black eyes, and disfigurement of the Blanketmen's bodies constituted a palpable form of penal inscription not unlike Kafka's machine in "The Penal Colony." The republican prisoners' bodies were bodies in pain, and like Eugene's body in *Four Days in July*, they were violently inscribed with a history of brutality, disfigurement, and death at the hands of the occupying state.[20]

The Blanketmen's "victory" over the penal system lay in their ability to suffer pain and degradation, to force the prison system to engrave its

---

20. Feldman writes of the "colon-ization" of the prisoner's body as the state invaded it through measures including anal cavity searches (1991, 174).

presence into their flesh rather than letting it rest on the surface. Refusing the superficial inscription of the uniform, the Blanketmen provoked the prison to reveal its deeper violence; they goaded the state into dropping its mask of civilization and exposing the utter hostility with which it viewed Irish nationalists. This animosity, in a republican framework, was merely the most recent manifestation of the genocidal contempt with which the British had historically viewed the Irish. Thus, by suffering the daily tortures of the H-Blocks, the Blanketmen used their ordeal to discredit the state as a guardian of reason, thus destabilizing the pseudo-rationality of the state of emergency. By performing their subjugation (through messages, poetry, songs, essays, and images smuggled out of the prison), the Blanketmen encouraged associations between their history, the history of Ireland, and the passion of Christ. By the time the protest was elevated to the level of a hunger strike, the Blanketmen's bodies had become allegorical ones.

Holy Marxists: The Starving Blanketman on Screen

If a preoccupation with the phenomenology of shit surrounds written and cinematic portrayals of the dirt protest, then an equally uncritical focus on the purity of self-sacrifice and spiritual transcendence haunts representations and analyses of the hunger strike. Feldman mentions Collins and O'Malley as chief offenders, and to his list I would add Maud Ellmann, who, in comparing Bobby Sands to both the title character of Samuel Richardson's *Clarissa* and religious fasters, at times presents hunger striking as a form of corporeal transcendence bordering on the ecstatic. Starvation understood as transcendence, hunger imagined as pre-colonial Gaelic practice, and the value placed by Christianity on holy fasting and sacred degradation all help to dislocate the H-Block protests from their contemporary political context, positioning them as a poetic struggle, a noble sacrifice occurring in epic time along with the death of Cúchulainn and the martyrdom of saints. While these representations became important for marshaling support for the hunger strike, they contradict the radical politics and insurgent violence that was at the heart of the protest. The hunger strike, Feldman argues, was "ethically and semantically" linked to the street violence that preceded it and was expected to coincide with and follow it (1991, 220). Feldman's de-poeticized understanding of the hunger strike brings into focus the protest's vital link to the state of exception that was the condition of northern republicans. The hunger strike tied the Blanketmen's immediate material needs (the five demands) to the needs and goals of the republican movement—goals that ranged from the cessation of state violence and discrimination (such as gerrymandering and emergency legislation) to a United Ireland.

The multitude of meanings that converge on the emaciated flesh of the hunger striker do not come only from interpretations of the protest; they were also present at the outset of its production. If the hunger striker's death was an act of violence against the state, it was also a manifestation of the republican community's exceptional status in relation to the state. In fact, in order to be an effective weapon against the state, the hunger striker's emaciated corpse required this other meaning. The stream of dead bodies released from the prison and bound for the grave was intended to "reawaken an overwhelming sense of historical violation in the Catholic communities, which would push this population over the edge into an apocalyptic display of street violence, intensified terrorist activity, and open armed revolt to be led by the cadres of the PIRA and INLA" (Feldman 1991, 254). With this objective in mind, the link between Ireland's past and the Blanketmen's present became integral to readings of the hunger strike. In letters and stories smuggled out of the prison and reprinted in *An Phoblacht/Republican News*, pamphlets, flyers, and other unofficial media outlets, the Blanketmen connected their immediate experience of life in individual cells of the H-Blocks to the broader history of British colonialism in Ireland. The H-Blocks became part of a series of equations that connected the Blanketmen to the national struggle in ways that defied temporality. The Maze was a microcosm of the British state; it repeated with intensified violence the forms of restrictive governmentality practiced by that state against Northern nationalists. Furthermore, seen in a republican framework, the British Army of 1980 was a continuation of the dynamics of colonial power set into motion some eight hundred years earlier (as expressed in "The H-Blocks Song.") In short, the Blanketmen became history embodied, surfaces on which the violence of Irish history materialized. These dynamics began with the blanket protest but became most intense during the hunger strike, which, Feldman argues, "would stage the abuse and violence of the Other in the eviscerated flesh of the dying protester" (1991, 236). Paradoxically, as the body of the hunger striker slowly, agonizingly, and publicly consumed itself, the abstraction of colonial power was transformed into flesh. "In the form of the dying hunger striker, the Blanketmen now possessed an encapsulating public bearer of their institutional defilement" (Feldman 1991, 247).

Some Mother's Son, which already sanitizes the H-Blocks to some degree by minimizing the no-wash and dirt protests, uses Christian iconography in order to cleanse the Blanketmen of their physical and moral stains in a sequence depicting Mass in the prison. The sequence opens with a shot of prison workers wearing green hazmat suits as they scrub down the cell walls with steam and antiseptic chemicals. A priest and cardinal, covering their noses and mouths with white handkerchiefs, set up a makeshift altar in the prison corridor. Historically, Mass was held in an actual room on a separate wing of the prison, and republican prisoners would put on at least the uniform trousers and submit to strip and body-cavity searches in order to attend. But in this sequence, George departs from historical accuracy, and as guards unlock the cell doors, the prisoners emerge onto the corridor barefoot and blanketed. Visually, they resemble Edmund Spenser's paranoid description of the pre-famine Gaelic nobility. In his *View on the Present State of Ireland,* written in 1596 for Elizabeth I, Spenser objected to what he saw as the obvious wildness of the Gaels, manifest in "their glibs of overhanging hair (which concealed their plotting faces)" and their mantles (instead of cloaks), which "often concealed offensive weapons" (Kiberd 1995, 10).[21] But the prisoners also resemble representations of early Christians who—like the Catholic Irish before the repeal of the Penal Laws (in 1830)—were persecuted for their beliefs and held clandestine masses. Iconographically, the sequence collapses the imagined nobility of the pre-colonial Irish with the persecution of the colonized Irish in the eighteenth and nineteenth centuries and

---

21. My thanks to Orla Ryan for pointing out the mantle connection to me.

the persecution of Christians before Constantine. Because to suffer in the name of God is the purest form of physical abjection and corporeal sacrifice, the film uncritically places the Blanketmen on the same level as religious martyrs.

This transformation of the Blanketmen from a political to a religious community is strengthened when the film cuts to a close-up of the Eucharist accompanied on the soundtrack by the ringing bell that signals the arrival of the Holy Spirit and the moment of transubstantiation. The cardinal breaks the Host, recites "This is the lamb of God, happy are those who are called to His supper," and the Blanketmen respond, "Lord, I am not worthy to receive You, but only say the Word and my soul shall be healed." As steam billows like incense from the cells behind the cardinal, he and the priest walk among the kneeling Blanketmen in order to place the Host on the prisoners' tongues. This sequence sacralizes not only the Blanketmen, but also the clergy, who humbly and solemnly administer the Eucharist in the most traditional and intimate way possible. The Blanketmen, streaked with dirt, are visual reminders of centuries of colonization and persecution on the basis of both national (Irish) and religious (early Christian and then Irish-Catholic) identities. They are further abased by the filth and excrement of their environment—to which the cardinal constantly alludes by delicately covering his nose and mouth—and by the fact of their imprisonment. They kneel before the Eucharist, and the benevolent clergy walk among them. All are men united in their humility and reverence before the body of Christ, rather than in the cause of Irish republicanism.

While Catholicism was an important aspect of the Blanketmen's lives, like everything else in the H-Blocks, it also had a political function. The Christian Bible, the only reading material allowed, could also be used as paper for rolling cigarettes or writing political and personal messages to be smuggled out of the prison. As the only form of assembly the Blanketmen were allowed, the forty-five-minute weekly Mass became a vital form of socialization and a means to exchange information and contraband. The mass in *Some Mother's Son* remains consistent with the film's overall project, which is to depict the hunger strike as an individualized melodrama. In its compassionate aim to represent the personal anguish of hunger strikers' relatives, the film ultimately sacrifices the politics of the protest to the spectacle of grieving mothers, in the process sacralizing the sons who will ultimately die at the hands of republican ideology or be saved by their mothers, who were given power of attorney should the men lapse into a hunger-induced coma. Since the Crucifixion was pre-ordained, the film's visual and narrative comparisons of the Blanketmen to Christ adds a highly problematic layer of inevitability to their deaths that is consistent with fatalistic representations of republicanism in films such as *Cal, The Crying Game, Odd Man Out*, and *Michael Collins* (to name but four). Unlike Christ, the hunger strikers were not born to die; they died in combat against agents of the state for an expressed political cause.

Some Mother's Son is aware of how Christological comparisons cemented the connection between the hunger striker and his community, but it offers a naïve version of this Christology, as seen in the sequence depicting Bobby Sands's death. As Sands lies emaciated and blind in the prison hospital, the film cuts between close-ups of his cavernous bearded face and long shots of an evening prayer vigil and march. A priest stands over Sands and begins to pray, "Hail Mary full of grace," and the film cuts to the crowd holding white candles and reciting the refrain, "Holy Mary, Mother of God, pray for us sinners, now and at the hour of our death. Amen." The film continues to cut between shots of Sands, close-ups of his heart monitor, and shots of the marchers as they pass posters and murals of Sands's smiling face on their way to the local police station. Although miles apart, the two spaces are united on the soundtrack by the Hail Mary and a staccato, wooden-flute motif. The film cements this unity visually when Sands dies. His heart monitor displays a flat line, and the film cuts to a series of shots: of the crowd marching, a close-up of the priest closing Sands's eyes, and a high-angle shot of the crowd assembled in front of the police station, almost as if from Sands's point of view as his soul ascends. In this last shot, Sands is absent in body, but he appears iconographically, blessing the crowd through a large poster in the upper right corner of the frame that hovers over them, just as in the following shot the priest blesses his corpse by anointing it with holy oil.

Some Mother's Son depicts the hunger strike in sweeping gestures. The able-bodied Blanketmen refuse to let the H-Blocks break their sprit.

The film protects its male bodies from the penetrating gaze of the screws and the scrutiny of the spectator, lowering the material stakes in the protest and rewriting it as a high-minded, moralistic stand against the prison uniform. Significantly there are no mirror searches, no gruesome beatings or forced baths, and no temptation to leave the squalid protesting blocks. In minimizing the violence of the H-Blocks, the film adheres to a rendering of the high-spirited "lads" on the blanket. But while George may construct heroes in the prison, he curtails the heroics of nationalism by shifting the focus from the Blanketmen to their mothers. Immediately following Sands's death, Kathleen Quigley, who will eventually take her son off the hunger strike, emerges as the lone voice of reason. When whistles and bin lids announce Sands's death at the prayer vigil, the riot the Blanketmen had relied on breaks out. As the RUC storm the protesters, who retaliate by lobbing stones at tanks, Kathleen is separated from her youngest son, Liam. When she finds him, he is about to hurl a rock at a tank. Realizing how perilously close her involvement in Northern politics has brought her to the possibility of losing another son, she grabs Liam's arm and forces him to drop the stone. She wraps her arm around him and leads him away from the riot. After this moment, Kathleen becomes increasingly disillusioned with political activism, a disillusionment that will enable her to take Gerard off the hunger strike. Following her perspective, the film's mood shifts to despair over what it presents as the futility in political engagement. Kathleen makes her decision to take Gerard off the hunger strike out of a perception that all political roads in the North lead inevitably to violence. The film thus constructs the riot as antithetical to the meaning of Sands's saintly sacrifice. The shift in mood to despair at a mounting death toll qualifies heroic representations of the protest by emphasizing loss over success. But the film's epilogue explains that the hunger strike of 1981 ended "after several mothers intervened to save their sons' lives," and that the British government granted all of the prisoners' demands shortly afterward. Rather than question the nature of heroic representation, *Some Mother's Son* simply substitutes mothers for Blanketmen. Limiting the aim of the hunger strike to the five demands establishes Kathleen as the film's true hero, and in valorizing its only apolitical character, *Some Mother's Son* is consistent with "troubles" films that advance a critique of Irish republicanism through a critique of atavistic violence by equating the two.

Despite its radically different audio-visual style and narrative structure, *Hunger* also turns Sands into a religious martyr, one whose ideological fervor makes him impervious to pain. In the mirror search sequence, after the split-screen shot of the crying guard, the film cuts back to Sands on the floor of his cell. Shot from above, Sands rolls over onto his back. As he does, his battered face comes into view: Sands is faintly smiling, and the trail of blood that runs upward from the corner of his mouth only seems to make his smile wider. The rattling sound of batons on shields continues over the shot, as if Sands were savoring the memory of the beating. In contrast with the fragile nerves and injured hands of the prison guards, this shot implies that Sands relished his pain and that, like any good martyr, he drew strength from being injured.

Before Sands goes on hunger strike, he meets with a priest, Dom, who is sympathetic to the republican cause but concerned for the deaths that will ensue with a second hunger strike. Like Pat Murphy's depiction of Major Sirr's interrogation of Anne in *Anne Devlin*—where she is questioned not only for information but also for the depth of her commitment to an independent Irish nation—*Hunger* portrays this scene in a long shot that is also a very long take. Sands and Dom meet in an empty association room; the priest is in black and Sands wears only tight-fitting prison trousers, emphasizing the leanness of his revolutionary's body. A hazy light comes in from a window behind them, making the two men almost silhouettes. The camera remains stationary for the entire take, which focuses attention on the conversation taking place directly in the center of the frame. While the scene seems to function as a parallel to Christ's temptation in the desert, Dom makes a compelling argument against hunger striking, so that this moment also becomes a way for the film to include a critique of the practice of hunger striking from within a republican perspective. Dom points out that given Sands's awareness that Thatcher will not capitulate easily, a hunger strike could only be "destructive" and men would be "pre-designed to die." He asks Sands if he is looking to obtain martyr status, and he points out that the work Sands did as a community activist before his involvement with the PIRA was his real contribution to the struggle. "Freedom fighter?" Dom ask. "They're the men and women working out there in the community." Through Dom's perspective, *Hunger* questions the heroic legacy of the hunger strike, which is an important step away from constructing an amnesiac nationalist history of the troubles. But Sands counters Dom's concerns by invoking Christ (and implicitly Che Guevara), "Jesus Christ had a backbone. But, see, them disciples? Every disciple since—you're just jumping in and out of the rhetoric and dead-end semantics. You need the revolutionary, you need the cultural-political soldier to give life a pulse, to give life a direction."

The Bobby Sands of *Hunger* is like the Christ of Pasolini's *The Gospel according to Matthew*. Both films study a man whose image has become iconic, in the original religious sense of the word as well as its broader cultural applications. In Pasolini's film, Christ has no psychological interiority; characters love him but do not get close to him. All of his lines are direct quotes of statements attributed to Jesus in Matthew's Gospel, and the actor delivering them consistently looks far into the distance. Pasolini's Christ loves humanity as a sum total, not as a series of individualized relationships. Likewise, when Sands explains the necessity for a fatal hunger strike to Dom, he has already left behind any immediate, earthly concerns. Even before he begins to fast, Sands's focus is on what will happen after his death. *Hunger* endows Sands with the long vision of the revolutionary, which the film portrays as having been prophesized by his childhood passion for cross-country running. His way of understanding time extends into the future far beyond the grasp of the other characters and thus serves to distance Sands from humanity, which is in turn emphasized by the stoicism of his parents. In Northern Ireland, the photograph of Sands's smiling face, taken shortly before he was incarcerated, has come to function like Alberto Korda's famous image of Che Guevara—endlessly re-created not only in murals but also on T-shirts, buttons, posters, calendars, and any other item (including refrigerator magnets) available for consumption through various republican websites. McQueen's film shrewdly recognizes the impossibility of any cinematic portrayal of Sands other than the symbolic, and the film pushes an image of Sands as committed to his community but also remote from it. These aspects are an acknowledgement of limits of narrative film, and they become the means by which the film transforms Sands into a republican Christ. The drawback to this, though, is that in the process, *Hunger* limits its analysis of the hunger strike exclusively to Bobby Sands and his emaciated body while also reproducing the troubles film trope of the masochistic Catholic, nationalist Irishman. Throughout the film, Sands is isolated from other republicans visually and within the narrative, and he ceases to speak once his hunger strike begins.

Ultimately, *Hunger* seems to be seduced by the spectacular dynamics of martyrdom, and the film portrays the decomposition of Sands's body in painful, exquisite detail. After his meeting with Dom, Sands never speaks again. His election as a member of parliament is neither portrayed nor acknowledged in the story, a significant omission since the campaign to get Sands elected became one of the first wide-scale moments of political action since the Widgery verdict on Bloody Sunday maimed the civil rights movement. A prison doctor explains to Sands's parents what happens to a starving body, and the film offers a series of shots of Sands slowly dying in a sterile white prison hospital room. Angry pink bedsores erupt on Sands's sinewy body in spots where the weight of his bones pushes his fragile skin against the bed sheets. When the wounds on his back are anointed, Sands's body is curved in a position that becomes the ascetic inversion of Man Ray's sensual photograph "Le Violon d'Ingres." The film's meditation on the agonies of death by starvation and its rapt attention on the details of physical decomposition, including the stains from various bodily fluids left on sheets, help to emphasize the uniqueness of Sands's protest, a singularity that is antithetical to the intent and organization of the protest, and one that is historically misleading given the frequency of hunger striking in Ireland. In this respect, McQueen's fascination with Sands's body precludes the possibility of understanding the 1981 hunger strike within a wider historical and political framework and turns his death into a martyrdom without a clear cause.[22] The film

---

22. While this focus on the physical closes avenues of comparison with other ways to protest against occupied Ireland, it invites comparisons between Sands's agonizing death and the death of people with AIDS, thus becoming political in a completely unexpected way.

cements its portrayal of Sands's sacrifice as both sacred and unique in its final scene. As he nears death, the film slowly dissolves from Sands's eye to a shot of him as a child. He is on a bus on his way to a cross-country meet. Uilleann pipes sound discordant notes as a young Bobby Sands runs through the woods in the Irish countryside, a shot of flying ravens against the moody gray sky implying the release of his soul from its mortal coil. In the final image of the film, Sands's body is wheeled out of the hospital, but the guards remain locked inside.

Although McQueen's version of Sands is more austere and ideologically severe than that of *Some Mother's Son*, the Bobby Sands of *Hunger* is no less Christ-like. In leaving out the community on the inside as well as outside the prison to which Sands constantly rearticulated himself, McQueen obscures the crucial communal dynamics of the H-Blocks protests. While his film might initially seem to correct the heroism portrayed in *Some Mother's Son*, it ultimately reinforces an idea of the Blanketman as nationalist martyr. The hunger-striker-as-martyr image had important tactical value at the time of the protests, especially in garnering support for the Provos outside of Northern Ireland. But this support is itself problematic in that the people funding PIRA activities from the United States and elsewhere did not have to live with the material consequences of their actions. In contemporary films that look back at the hunger strike as a historical moment, the discourse of martyrdom risks feeding the more heroic strains of Irish nationalism, which in turn enables amnesiac and nostalgic histories of Ireland. These histories, as I argued in the previous chapter, exclude women except as symbolic figures, and they also prevent a rethinking of Irish masculinity. By contrast, *H3* foregrounds the exposure of the prisoners' bodies to an array of potential threats. Unlike *Some Mother's Son*, the film refuses to grant "special category status" to any aspect of the male body.[23] If, as Peter Lehman has argued, to avoid full frontal nudity in representations of the male body is a way to maintain

---

23. I have stolen this metaphor from Laura Lyons, who uses it to describe how the women of Armagh saw their menstrual blood as material for political protest (Lyons 1996, 122).

phallic power (Lehman 1993, 4–10), then *H3* may actually relinquish that power in order to construct new forms that allow for the prisoners' terrifying vulnerability.

The Politics and Aesthetics of Vulnerability

> I felt the cold chamfered edges of the mirror being pushed between my legs. They were scrutinising my anus, using the mirror to afford them a view from every angle. A foreign hand probed and poked at my anus and, unsatisfied, they kicked the back of my knees, forcing me down into a squatting position where they again used the mirror and, to finish off, they rained more kicks and blows on my naked, burning body for good measure. I fell to the floor, which was wet and dirty from the melted snow carried into the hut on their boots.
> —Bobby Sands, "One Day in My Life" (1997, 60–61)

H3 begins silently, with a series of close-ups and extreme close-ups. After the title "H-Block Prison, January 1981," the film cuts to a close-up of a prisoner's face as he opens his eyes in the early morning light. From this confining shot, the film closes in on the infinitesimal with an extreme close-up of a maggot writhing on the cell's cold concrete floor.[24] A cut back from the maggot to its host reveals a thin, young, bearded Blanketman with long matted hair, wearing a gold cross around his neck. He sits up on his bare foam mattress and stretches his back in front of a wall coated in excrement. Another extreme close-up of the card outside his cell door reveals his identity: twenty-four-year-old RC (Roman Catholic) Seamus

---

24. The maggot can be seen as both a metonym for the Blanketmen and a shorthand reference to one of the more horrifying aspects of the dirt protest. Because of the rotting food thrown into the corners of the cells, thousands of maggots would hatch in the warmer weather. Prisoners describe having to learn to live with maggots burrowing under their mattresses, crawling into their hair and beards at night, crunching under their feet as they paced their cells (see, for example, Campbell, McKeown, O'Hagan 1998). The film uses this detail sparingly: one maggot wriggling on the floor is a reference to the conditions in the H-Blocks; one thousand maggots on the body of a prisoner as he wakes up, while more accurate, would be a horror film.

Scullion, incarcerated in 1977 for twenty-five years. A beefy hand reaches into the frame and snatches the card from its metal holder. The jarring scratch of the card scraping against metal shatters the film's silence and relative calm.

The screw's gesture, an audio close-up as well as a visual one, initiates the violence of a wing shift and mirror search. Suddenly, an army of screws in uniform, their faces obscured by crisp black hats, appear at the gates of H3. The gate is opened, and a low, mechanized, ominous hum accompanies the sound of their heavy black boots crushing the pavement as they cross the yard. Scullion watches them from his window and yells out a warning in Irish "jaillic"—the first words spoken in the film—that a wing shift is about to occur.[25] While orderlies steam clean the emptied dirty cells of another wing, the screws descend on the prisoners, pulling them out in groups of four. The Blanketmen stand naked in the corridor, and the film cuts to a shot from their point of view of the gang of screws lining the hall. The screws stand still, staring at the Blanketmen's pale and atrophied bodies, but their heavy presence communicates the constant threat of violence that characterized the H-Blocks. It also alludes to the power that the screws accessed by maintaining this constant state of anticipation. In another corridor, the foam-padded mirror rests on the floor surrounded by four screws who stand at ease, as if on a break from heavy labor, their uniform jackets discarded and their shirtsleeves rolled up—like *Hunger*, *H3* is aware of the physical labor involved in brutalizing prisoners. The Blanketmen are brought over the mirror one at a time, while those waiting are held between the double grille separating one wing of the prison from another. As Scullion is shoved through the gate, three burly screws press the faces of the remaining three Blanketmen into the hard brick wall. Waiting at the mirror, one of the screws, Morton, mockingly comments, "Here comes their big chief," as Scullion, shorter than everyone else, cautiously walks toward the mirror. He is ordered to squat over the

25. The word "jaillic" is prison slang for the bastardized version of self-taught Irish (Gaelic) that republican prisoners spoke in prison. As a less formal and less structured version of the Irish language, it was even less likely to be deciphered by the prison staff.

mirror and refuses. The search is rendered in a series of quick audio-visual close-ups: a towel is whipped off of Scullion's pale buttocks, which quiver in response. Two hands grab his ears, as four screws kick and force him down over the mirror. A close-up of Scullion over the mirror reveals his (or rather, the actor's) spread cheeks and anus. The screws jerk Scullion back up, hit him in the stomach, and fling him down the corridor.

Scullion stands helplessly watching between the next set of double-grille doors as Ciaran Doyle is brought over the mirror, and the violence of the search escalates. Two screws tightly hold Ciaran's arms out perpendicular to his body, while two more screws push and kick him into a squatting position, thrusting him down over the mirror. While holding Ciaran down, the screws beat him across his lower back. Morton yells, "UP!" and they jerk Ciaran up by the hair, still holding out his arms. As Morton continues to yell, "Get down! Up! Get down!" the screws jerk Ciaran up and down over the mirror, adding to his physical humiliation with predictably juvenile taunts like, "Didn't your ma teach you how to wash?" Morton orders Ciaran down over the mirror a third time. Ciaran is held in a squatting position while a screw shines a flashlight up his rectum, and Morton yells in his face, "You spread your legs, and you stay down!" The screw's command rather overtly mimics that of a male rapist to his female victim, bringing in the Blanketmen's affective experiences of the mirror search in particular as well as the general sense of defenselessness that accompanied their being constantly naked and subject to the brutality of uniformed screws, who had the government's at least tacit approval of their violent methods. To emphasize Ciaran's total helplessness, the film shoots him frontally, in a long shot, so that the actor's penis and testicles are exposed.

On one hand, it may be tempting to read this scenario as a moment in which Ciaran is feminized. That he is the object of Scullion's gaze—shown in a long shot so that his full body is in view—framed and partially obstructed by the prison bars, and objectified by the screws, might support such a reading. But like *Hunger*, *H3* offers a version of masculinity that complicates discussions on cinema and masculinity because of its blend of Catholic and Irish nationalist aesthetics, its depiction of state-sponsored torture, and its detailed rendering of the Blanketmen's elaborate prison culture. There is certainly a muted level of homosocial desire in the film, but to read *H3* as through it were a Neil Jordan film, in which repressed homoerotic elements constantly break through to the film's surface, or as a Western or war film, where the male body on display is a potent if abject one, risks reading the film outside of its political context, where the weakened and wounded male body portrayed was, at the time, more likely to be on display for the visual pleasure of torturers as proof of their power or for the purpose of fostering a sense of nationalist rage. The mirror search sequence has more in common with the torture sequence in *The Battle of Algiers*—in which the brutalized bodies of Algerian revolutionaries give rise to an outrage that reinforces nationalist sentiment—than with the films of, for example, Anthony Mann.[26] Ciaran's particularly brutal search initiates a series of circumstances that lead to his decision to conform to the prison regime; but rather than condemn him for this "weakness," the film links his departure to a desperate sense of isolation.

After the mirror search, the prison governor issues a restatement of policy, explaining that the government will not make any concessions to prisoners on protest. Morton struts down the wing, whistling "The Sash" as he slips the printed statements over the tops of the cell doors. The film cuts among the Blanketmen's reactions, all of whom shout, grumble, throw the paper back out onto the wing or bang on the door with their cellmates. In the final shot of this sequence, Ciaran crouches in the corner of his cell, gripping his head in despair. As a sparse piano motif drowns out the sounds of the Blanketmen's resistance, the film fades to black on Ciaran's face—the first of three such edits—before fading in to a nighttime aerial shot of the Maze prison compound. A siren wails over the H-Blocks, and as the film cuts back to the prison interior, the siren turns out to be the voice of Madra, one of the Blanketmen, calling all prisoners up to their doors for "some craic and some scéale" (fun and storytelling). Madra begins another installment of a hardboiled detective story, taking the Blanketmen from the cells of the H-Blocks to "the mean streets of the Big Apple." The film cuts away from Madra and Liam sitting at their cell door to the dim prison corridor as Madra's voice echoes through the

26. See Neale 1993, 13.

empty space, and then to a shot of Ciaran. Ciaran lies down in the back of his cell as Madra's voice drifts away, replaced by the same subjective piano motif, and the image fades from a close-up of Ciaran's face to blackness.

Like *Some Mother's Son*, *H3* portrays the strong sense of community that prevailed among the prisoners during the protests by cutting from the interior of one cell to the interior of another without reestablishing the prison's architectural divisions—cell doors, bars, the corridor. When the film quickly cuts among the cells, it is careful to establish the presence of two men in each, with the constant exception of Ciaran, whose isolation becomes increasingly unbearable. What *H3*, *Hunger*, and *Some Mother's Son* achieve through editing, the real Blanketmen achieved through sound. In the absence of a physical and visible community, the Blanketmen created a disembodied aural one, using the radio metaphor "on/off the air" to describe events happening on the wing. "Bears on the air" meant that screws were on the wing, but "off the air," could mean either departure from the wing or death, as when the Maze Prison governor Albert Miles was killed and the Blanketmen made up a song with which to taunt the screws, "Big Bear's off the air" (Feldman 1991, 207). When Madra's broadcast fails to reach Ciaran, it is because psychologically Ciaran is already "off the air."

In the H-Blocks (and Armagh), the "hegemony of the administrative 'eye' was countered with the sensory acumen of the 'ear.' In this process of sensory substitution and reversal, the prison regime and its violence were converted into auditory texts" (Feldman 1991, 206). If sound could play a role in resistance, it also became an instrument of torture and agonizing reembodiment in the hands of the screws. In many H-Block narratives, prisoners cite listening to their comrades being beaten as the single worst aspect of prison life.[27] The screws in the H-Blocks as well as in Armagh would administer beatings individually and sequentially. A crowd of screws would descend on one or two prisoners, beat them and then move on to the next cell. Unlike the torturer, who makes an

---

27. See, for example, Feldman 1991, 208; and Campbell, McKeown, and O'Hagan 1998, 84–106.

elaborate display of the instruments of torture to heighten the intensity of the victim's fear and to draw out the performance of his or her own power (Scarry 1985, 15–19), the screws could not visually display their mastery to any Blanketmen other than those whom they were beating. Instead, they used the sounds of pain—the unexpected jangle of keys, the thuds of blows, the cries of the prisoners—as a reification of their power. They also used sound to help break the morale of the prisoners whenever a Blanketman left the protest.

Every cell in the H-Blocks contained a panic button, which in ordinary circumstances would have been used to summon a guard in case of emergency. But during the protests, the button became a constant temptation, signaling to men who had not washed or used toilets in over three years that they could be taken out of the dank, reeking, maggot-infested protesting wings, away from starvation rations and daily physical and psychological torture with the push of a button. When prisoners did ring the bell, screws would come immediately with a fresh uniform and boots for the former Blanketman. After the prisoner put the uniform on, screws would march him down the hallway, making sure the rubber soles of his boots squeaked against the prison floor. A man who left the protest was given the derogatory nickname of "squeaky booter."[28] In *H3, a*fter a sequence in which the Blanketmen are serially beaten and dragged naked down the prison corridor with blood streaming from their noses, mouths, and heads, Ciaran is again alone in his cell. He stares at the panic button, which the film renders in an extreme close-up, making its presence all the more palpable. He summons the guard and is led down the hallway in silence; the telltale sign of the squeaky boots is absent from the soundtrack.

Shortly after Ciaran quits the protest, the hunger strike begins. Sands is taken to the hospital, he runs for parliament from his hospital bed, wins, and dies twenty-five days later. After Sands's death, the prisoners assemble for weekly Mass, and midway through the service, Ciaran enters the room. The assembled Blanketmen stare at him until Liam stands up and

---

28. See Campbell, McKeown, and O'Hagan 1998 for details about squeaky booters and the prisoners' attitudes toward them.

greets him, "Fáilte abhaile [welcome home] Ciaran; it takes a brave man to come back." Ciaran is welcomed back into the fold as prisoners stand up to embrace him. The film ends in a freeze frame, as Seamus clasps Ciaran in his arms and stares out at the camera. Closing titles list the names of the ten dead hunger strikers and explain: "within two years of ending the hunger strike the prisoners' demands were met. In July of 2000, the remaining political prisoners were released under the terms of the Peace Process."

The fact that Blanketmen left the protests is not often directly addressed in analyses or representations of the H-Blocks, which tend to emphasize the Blanketmen's success at functioning as a cohesive group and at fostering an unambivalent solidarity. For a former hunger striker (McKeown) not only to publicly acknowledge this other history, but to do so with such compassion for the character of Ciaran, is striking in its willingness to complicate heroic narratives of resistance. At the same time, Ciaran *must* return in fulfillment of Sands's scripture. As Sands states and Feldman demonstrates, the hunger strikers died not for five demands, but for the revival of the republican movement, to breathe life into their continuing anti-colonial struggle. This is the Gospel of Sands that *H3* emphasizes, in stark contrast to the hopeless death and destruction that the hunger strike brings to the characters of *Some Mother's Son*. It also helps to qualify the film's sacralization of Sands, which, like *Some Mother's Son*, casts aside historical accuracy in favor of a Christological rendering of this newest republican martyr.

When the hunger strike began, the Blanketmen came off the no-wash protest, showering and receiving haircuts; Sands had his hair cut on the fourth day of his hunger strike (Sands 1997, 222). In *H3*, as in *Some Mother's Son*, Sands retains his long hair and beard even on his deathbed. But *H3* rejects other Christological elements to the Sands death scene overwhelmingly present in *Some Mother's Son*. When Bobby leaves for the hospital in *H3*, he walks out to the yard in a prison uniform; he is not wheeled out cloaked in a blanket. The Blanketmen call out to him from their cells and, looking somewhat dazed from twenty days without food, Sands raises his right fist in salute to the disembodied voices and the revolutionary struggle. When Scullion visits Sands on the last day of his hunger strike, he is not shrouded in a white sheet and attended to by a priest and a praying crowd. Instead, he lies on a prison cot in a dimly lit room—a possible reference to the blindness that sets in after roughly fifty days without food—wearing the striped uniform pajamas of a prisoner. When the film cuts to a close-up of his face, his parchment-like skin and half-closed eyes and mouth are as much a grotesque rendering of agony as they are a mark of saintly reverence.

Like *Hunger*, *H3* remains rooted in the cruel physicality of the H-Block protests and embedded in the oppressive atmosphere of the prison; its characters remain incarcerated until the final image cuts to black. In restraining a heroic rendering of the Blanketmen, the film actually makes their protest all the more impressively innovative, since it was not easy or even immediately successful. The epilogue to *Some Mother's Son* asserts that the British government met all of the prisoners' demands shortly after the end of the hunger strike. This timing is quite different from *H3*'s assertion of two years, and it may stem from the filmmakers' divergent political agendas. While *Some Mother's Son* seems to use the hunger strike as a vehicle to explore maternal love under extraordinary pressures, *H3* functions more as a sketch of this turning point of the republican movement. In McKeown's written history of Long Kesh, he explains that key issues like segregation of republican and loyalist prisoners came slowly, over years, and only after continued protests in different forms (McKeown 2001, 87–98). It is possible that George's film, more focused on the symbols of resistance than actual resistance, missed the issue of segregation as a significant demand. Segregation of republicans according to paramilitary affiliation enables the type of political planning, historical discussion, and philosophical debates that help to keep a movement alive in prison.

The masculinity portrayed in *H3* offers a strong corrective to the dominant terrorist and freedom-fighter portraits of republican masculinity. The Blanketmen are not the callous "hard men" of *In the Name of the Father* and *Patriot Games*, nor are they the gentle gunmen exemplified by Fergus (whose name, incidentally, signifies masculine potency) in *The Crying Game*. They are not the saints of O'Malley's imagination or the sadistic terrorist criminals of Thatcher's fancy. Instead, *H3* takes Irish republican masculinity in a new direction, one that tries to allow for individual psychology as well as communal solidarity, and one that blends the transcendent and the material, the pious and the practical, revealing some of the ways in which republicanism has traditionally coded its revolutionary socialist politics in the language of Catholic apocalypse, Celtic legend, and romantic resistance, *tactically*, as means to gather as broad a support base as possible. In doing so, *H3* takes a step toward addressing the gap between the form of revolutionary visual language and its political content, and in this gap lies the potential to unthink nationalist as well as cinematic conceptions of gender and resistance.

3

Body Politics

Republican Women and Political Action

THE COVER OF LILY FITZSIMONS'S BOOKLET *Does Anybody Care?*
features a stylized image of a woman in a blanket. The woman's face is
drawn with stereotypically feminine features—a small nose, high cheekbones, a prominent mouth—and her loose dark hair flows past her shoulders, emphasizing her gender. The blanket she wears lends her body a
statuesque solidity that contrasts with the visual renderings of emaciated
Blanketmen from the same era. In her hand, the woman holds a poster
featuring an image of a man's face placed over the words "Long Kesh."
Fitzsimons's booklet documents her years as a member of the Relatives
Action Committee (RAC), a group of predominantly women activists who
organized in support of republican prisoners on protest in the H-Blocks
and Armagh Gaol. Like Fitzsimons, the woman on the cover of the booklet is also a member of the RAC; she is dressed in a blanket and holds a
representation of her own son. Placing herself on display, the RAC mother
functions as an emissary of her jailed son. She carries him symbolically so
that he may become visible to the wider nationalist community, in whose
name he suffers.

Nationalist women have used the authority ascribed to motherhood to
powerful ends, but the idealization of the "mother" as a national identity
has also been an obstacle for women who try to act as political subjects in
their own right or demand to be heard as political agents. When the 1921
treaty proposing partition and a twenty-six county Irish Free State was put
before the Dáil Éireann, Pádraig Pearse's mother shamed the deputies for
considering a settlement that would institute a deformed version of the

ideal nation for which her son and the other leaders of 1916 had died. She invoked her right as a mother to speak not on her own behalf as a *Teachta Dála* (TD) (a deputy of the Dáil), but for her son, who could not represent himself because five years earlier he had sacrificed his life to the cause of an Irish nation. At the same time, other women who spoke against the treaty as legislators were dismissed precisely because of their ties to the dead. When the treaty vote was put to the Dáil, all six women TDs vehemently opposed it, and Cumann na mBan (the Women's League) even tried to raise a union jack over the building "as a mordant comment on what was being proposed" (Kiberd 1995, 402).[1] Male deputies trivialized the women's opposition with the patronizingly sympathetic notion that "as bereaved relatives of national martyrs, they were allowing their hearts to rule their heads" (Kiberd 1995, 403). Women had actively participated in political meetings, military campaigns, and the construction of a national vision of Ireland that was decolonized, socialist, and anti-patriarchal, and although the six women deputies had their own political stakes in opposing the treaty, their relationships to slain male nationalists obscured this earthly motivation.

In the previous chapter, I addressed the prevalence of sacralizing imagery in representations of the Blanketmen who found a way out of the space of the exception by invoking the authority of an alternative set of laws. Republican prisoners were the objects of British sovereign power, but they became the subjects of a transcendental Irish national power. The Blanketmen used their *homo sacer* status as evidence of the illegitimacy of British rule. Their performance of and existence as men positioned outside the boundaries of British legality enabled them to reveal Britain's history of placing Irish people outside the law, a discursive practice often accompanied by physical displacement. The body of the Blanketman— naked, unshaven, covered in filth, starving, and jailed—evoked the historical mistreatment and dislocation of the Irish, from Cromwell's "to hell or

1. Partition was only one of several offenses in the treaty; in establishing an Irish free state and not a republic, the treaty required the Dáil to swear an oath of loyalty to Britain and to follow British foreign policy.

Connacht" policy, through the Famine and emigration, penal servitude in Australia and the Caribbean, and into the incarceration of twentieth-century political prisoners. They achieved this historical equation by deploying a potent mix of Irish nationalism and Catholicism. However, these discourses offered women a much tighter space in which to maneuver.[2] For the Blanketman, the filth, degradation, beatings, and starvation he underwent were consistent with the role of abjection and self-denial in Catholicism; it turned him into an ascetic and a martyr. Catholicism has its share of female saints who endured gruesome pain in the name of Christ, but the purity, self-sacrifice, and emotional agony of the Virgin Mother overshadows them all, especially within Irish Catholicism after the Famine.

The Blanketmen and the RAC successfully appropriated religious and nationalist imagery to motivate support for the Blanketmen, but the restrictive iconography of the mother-son dyad, especially when combined with important differences in the structure of the H-Blocks and Armagh protests, precluded the possibility of representing the women in Armagh. The RAC demonstrations used the cultural significance of motherhood tactically, in order to confront and publicly shame the British state through a performance of disempowerment that shares striking similarities to the protests of the Mothers of the Plaza de Mayo in Argentina (*Las madres*). Dressed only in blankets, RAC members blocked traffic, occupied tents in public places, and traveled to various European cities. The mothers of women in Armagh were equally vocal about their daughters, marching with posters of their names and faces, but because only H-Block prisoners wore blankets, the visual and allusive power of the blanket as a symbol of bare life and resistance to it could not extend to Armagh women.[3] In addition to the central place of mothers and sons in traditional Irish

2. This may be one reason for their omission from Feldman's analysis of the symbolism of the prison protests.

3. I doubt the RAC intended this marginalization or valued their daughters any less. But, like the hunger strike of 1981, the RAC protests involve a disjunction in meaning between their encoding by the protesters and their decoding by the public and filmmakers.

nationalism and Catholicism, other, more mundane factors also contributed to the disparity in visibility between the two groups of prisoners. The sheer difference in numbers of prisoners—roughly 350 to 400 men in the H-Blocks compared with 32 women in Armagh—strongly increased the likelihood that a mother in the RAC would have a son rather than a daughter in jail. The no-wash protest began in the H-Blocks three years before it did in Armagh, making men the central focus of activist work, as their situation was more severe at the time. Finally, although Armagh prisoners also began resisting criminal status in the 1970s, their protests took the much less spectacular form of a no-work strike.

In addition to their defiance of British law, the women in the RAC and in Armagh Gaol challenged ideals at the heart of feminism and Irish nationalism. Their connection to republicanism alienated some feminists in Ireland and Britain at the time, who saw republican women, particularly alleged members of the PIRA, as the dupes of a violent and patriarchal nationalism. At the same time, both the RAC and Armagh women developed gender-specific tactical resistance to Britain's emergency legislation that intersected with traditional feminine ideals in dynamic and challenging ways. Their protests relied heavily on the body's materiality and positioned that corporeality in dynamic tension with the transcendental elements of Irish nationalism and Catholicism, and film is often unable to maintain the dialectic between the corporeal and the transcendent. The tendency of Irish nationalism to render women as symbols and allegories means that women's political activism is frequently co-opted, denied, obscured, and rewritten within nationalist histories, a move addressed in Pat Murphy's *Maeve*. The marginalization and pathologization of politically active women in the vast majority of troubles films reveals the extensive reach of this tradition and speaks to the difficulty filmmakers have imagining Irish republican politics as existing beyond the exclusive purview of men. Even *Some Mother's Son*, which features a female republican activist in the character of Annie Higgins, ultimately favors a patriarchal version of motherhood that is transcendent, ahistorical, and decidedly apolitical. At the same time, *Silent Grace* (Maeve Murphy, 2001) "softens" its IRA leader by having her mother a juvenile delinquent while incarcerated in Armagh. The result of this inability to imagine and portray militant—or even simply non-maternal—women reinforces the exceptional status of female republican prisoners and contributes to nationalist historical amnesia. At the same time, dominant Irish (and British and US) cinema has consistently equated republicanism with violence and therefore dismissed it as irrational and inherently destructive. The RAC and Armagh women challenge this misconception; they have the potential to radically link republicanism and feminism in ways that cement women's liberation to national liberation and reveal the historicity of motherhood and gender as well as Catholic and Irish nationalist iconography.

This chapter considers questions of heroic memory and political film in relation to cinematic representations of the RAC protests in *Some Mother's Son* (1996) and of female political prisoners in *Silent Grace* (2001) and *Anne Devlin* (Pat Murphy, 1984). Addressing the ways these films reinforce or challenge stereotypical representations of Irish femininity in relation to nationalism, I argue that the films' potential as political cinema lies not simply in the extent to which they experiment with film form and narrative, but how they imagine gendered forms of resistance within Irish history. Ultimately, I find *Anne Devlin* to be the most compelling of the three films because in writing a feminist history of Emmet's 1803 uprising, Murphy articulates past and present in a way that challenges heroic ideals of resistance that fall along gendered lines. Recognizing the stakes in historiography, *Anne Devlin* answers Maeve's challenge in *Maeve* (Pat Murphy, 1981) to construct an Irish national history that includes her as an agent. By contrast, *Some Mother's Son* absorbs women's resistance into reassuring images of femininity that ultimately reinforce the gender ideology that has dominated nationalism for much of the history of the postcolonial republic, and the challenge *Silent Grace* poses to heroic visual language is compromised by the film's use of gender.

Some Mother's Son and *Silent Grace* make important efforts to put republican women on screen, and both films have as their project the admirable goal of humanizing political struggles. They challenge Margaret Thatcher's portrayal of the conflict in Northern Ireland as thuggish crime committed by "the men of violence" by depicting women who are politically active and historically aware. In addition, *Silent Grace* also challenges the heroic iconography and narratives of Irish nationalism by visualizing politically active women and addressing the marginalization of those women even within their own communities. However, while *Silent Grace* takes on the heroic framework of republicanism, it seems to share with *Some Mother's Son* an assumption that the political and the human are incompatible. Both films present republican politics as a set of lofty ideals and those who support them as fanatic in their willingness to sacrifice life for abstract principle. They do this by mobilizing gender stereotypes that conform to the maternal ideal of "woman" laid out in the Irish Republic's 1937 constitution. In these films, political ideology has little material relevance to everyday life, and as a result, it hardens women. Both films abandon historical-political analysis in favor of the spectacle of hunger and grief. Republican discourse itself has enabled some of this representation, but when films uncritically adapt these discourses of heroism and sacrifice into a conventional narrative structure, political nuance disappears, and emotional spectacle borders on the exploitative. Terry George and Maeve Murphy are clearly sympathetic to their characters. Their films offer important representations of Britain's declared state of emergency in the North in that each film marks state violence as violence rather than accepting it as the unavoidable collateral damage of maintaining law and order. However, their capacity to reveal the falseness of this state of emergency is hindered because the films present militant Irish republicanism as the only road available for opposition to the British state. In addition, George's film fails to consider republicanism outside of the language of fanaticism and martyrdom. By contrast, Pat Murphy's *Anne Devlin* steers clear of heroic portrayals of its main character, and in doing so, the film opens avenues for understanding the motives and stakes for women's participation in the contemporary republican movement, even though those very women are often marginalized within republicanism's various patriarchal organizations. Although *Anne Devlin* is set in 1803, I argue that it functions as an allegory for its contemporary moment—Ireland in the late 1970s to early 1980s—thereby engaging the question of republican and feminist resistance to British emergency measures in a way that also questions nationalist historiography.

"Do You Care?": The RAC and Blanket Maternity

A 1977 photo spread entitled "Resistance" in *An Phoblacht/Republican News* (AP/RN) features an image of three women dressed in blankets standing in front of the arches of what looks like a cathedral (AP/RN, 6). They hold signs stating, "My son is being beaten . . . ," "My son is lying in his own waste . . . ," and "My son is being kept locked up twenty-four hours a day. . . ." Each statement ends with the direct question, "Do you care?" The women were members of the Relatives Action Committee, formed on Easter Monday of 1976 (the sixtieth anniversary of the Rising) in order to organize protests against the criminalization policy instituted in March of the same year. Primarily comprised of the female relatives of republican prisoners, the RAC became a support system for anxious families as well as a means to address diverse issues pertaining to the prisons (Fitzsimons 1996, 18–21). The RAC achieved their highest degree of visibility through protests like the one shown in AP/RN, in which women relatives of prisoners (mostly mothers) dressed in blankets and performed acts of civil disobedience: they picketed, sat in makeshift cages, chained themselves to government buildings, obstructed pedestrian and automotive traffic, spent numerous days in tents without leaving or eating, and stood silently holding images of those on whose behalf they were demonstrating. These protests drew on the women's authority as the mothers of sons who had sacrificed their freedom—a symbolic death—for the cause of Ireland.

Like Allen Feldman, Begoña Aretxaga argues that religious or mythological readings of republican protests (in this case those of the RAC) are misinterpretations that take the religious rhetoric of republicanism at face value without considering the politics to which it is articulated. It was criminalization, Aretxaga reminds us, "not religious or nationalist mythology, [that] set the ground for the women's resistance" (1997, 116–17). Aretxaga approaches the protests from the position of the speaker and thus debunks meanings assigned to the RAC protests by journalists, focusing instead on the dialectic between emotion and activism that she places at the heart of women's political consciousness in the North. She distinguishes this politics of emotion from the interaction of politics and emotion within dominant (patriarchal) republican discourse. The republican movement,

Aretxaga argues, encouraged "empathetic identification with the grieving mother" in order to gain "ideological support." By contrast, the emotional distress of the RAC mothers "was not so much a rhetorical trope as the motivating force of a form of political action that departed considerably from the mythical paradigm of nationalist motherhood" (Aretxaga 1997, 117). Based on her extensive ethnographic research, Aretxaga points to the fact that involvement in the RAC often led women into deeper political activity that continued long after the prison protests ended: women went on to become elected officials, to organize community and women's centers, and to become active in Sinn Féin. In Belfast's republican communities, motherhood became an important and common route to politicization.[4]

Some Mother's Son reverses precisely the trajectory Aretxaga traces and reasserts patriarchal emotion at the expense of women's activism, though not to marshal support for Provisional Sinn Féin or the IRA. In its humanist attempt to appeal to what the film imagines to be the universal drama of maternal duty and love, it ultimately favors the state by violently rejecting the only anti-state discourse (militant republicanism) that it admits into the narrative. The film tells the story of two mothers—rural, republican Annie Higgins and middle-class, apolitical Kathleen Quigley—who have sons in the IRA: Frankie and Gerard, respectively. Their sons are arrested and sent to the H-Blocks, where they join protests for political status, including the no-wash protest and the hunger strike of 1981. While their sons are incarcerated, the two women begin to bond with and influence each other. Kathleen, who previously equated all republican politics with violence, learns to distinguish between the two: she becomes active in the campaign to elect Bobby Sands as a member of parliament, stands in a line protest, and travels with Annie to Westminster to petition her MPs. For her part, Annie is pulled out of what the film initially presents as her knee-jerk support of Sinn Féin and the IRA. But ultimately, the

---

4. Aretxaga's entire book makes this point convincingly, and women activists in the North have mentioned this themselves. See, for example, McAuley 1989, and *Mother Ireland*.

women drift back toward their original positions, and when they learn that as mothers of comatose hunger strikers they have the right to authorize medical intervention, Kathleen orders the end of Gerard's hunger strike, while Annie watches in agony as her son dies for his beliefs. By the film's end, Kathleen has terminated her flirtation with political activism and liberated herself from the prison of republican ideology, while the final shot of Annie, from Kathleen's point of view, leaves her in the prison corridor.

By linking and then separating two mothers who represent two different positions in relation to resistance to British occupation, *Some Mother's Son* suggests that motherhood is not a means to politicization; it is incompatible with politics. The film establishes a series of parallels between the two women, and like the "universal" similarities of everyday life in *Four Days in July*, the symmetry of Kathleen's and Annie's lives ultimately highlights their different class status and their divergent attitudes toward Irish nationalism. Both women have sons in the IRA—Frankie Higgins is a seasoned member wanted by the British and the RUC, while Gerard Quigley seems to be a new recruit not yet known to the security forces—but Kathleen is stunned when she learns of Gerard's activities, while Annie actively supports Frankie's involvement. Each woman also has a teenage daughter. Kathleen's daughter diets, wears makeup, works in a bank, and leaves for New York after her brother's arrest. Annie's daughter, distinguishable by her sturdy body and wild mass of red hair, stands in the path of British tanks, joins her mother in RAC protests, and ultimately becomes Annie's only living child. Kathleen has a younger son, Liam; Annie *had* a younger son, who was killed by the British Army. Neither woman's husband is relevant to the story: Kathleen's is dead, and Annie's husband seems to be near death—a couple of decades older than she, he sits silently in a chair, a cane by his side, his shoulders stooped from the burden of living in Ireland.

With a vocal republican woman as one of its main characters, *Some Mother's Son* initially seems to complicate what John Hill has identified as a longstanding trope in Irish drama "evident in the work of Sean O'Casey, for example—of contrasting the 'humanity' and 'commonsense' of women to the unyielding and destructive fanaticism of men" (1997, 46). As Martin McLoone points out, the Manichean split that figures women as humanist and men as fanatic is mitigated by the fact that the character of Annie offers "a different female engagement with male intransigence, one in which the political principle at stake is more important than the humanitarian issue of her son's life" (2000, 75–76). In addition, overshadowing the entire history of the hunger strike is the woman who came to embody British obstinacy: Margaret Thatcher, who assumes office as prime minister in the film's opening shot. George continues to make reference to Thatcher throughout the film, in media footage and in the form of British government agents who meet under dim light in front of large maps of Ireland, and who keep the Irish and each other under surveillance.

In the archival footage that opens the film, Thatcher prepares to enter No. 10 Downing Street for the first time. Surrounded by microphones, cameras, and policemen, she invokes St. Francis of Assisi, telling reporters, "Where there is discord may we bring harmony; where there is error, may we bring truth; where there is doubt, may we bring faith; and where there is despair, may we bring hope." On the word "discord," the film cuts from Thatcher's television image to a shot of a misty-gray sea and sky. The remainder of her prayer for enlightened rule continues over images of seagulls and a fishing boat, and the camera pans across a seaside cliff, keeping the boat in frame. As Thatcher finishes stating her noble aspirations, bodhráns, uilleann pipes, flutes, and guitars storm the soundtrack, accompanied by the mournful cawing of gulls, and the camera pans past a Martello tower. The film then cuts to a shot of a harbor as the boat pulls in. Two fishermen unload crates, pausing to look at British Army trucks and soldiers stationed atop a craggy cliff. For the lone spectator still oblivious to the setting after the barrage of audio-visual clues, the film offers an explanatory title: "Northern Ireland 1979."

Given Britain's history of extra-legal emergency measures in Northern Ireland, the film seems to use Thatcher's words with searing irony. She speaks with a calmness calibrated to support Britain's national self-image as a harbinger of enlightenment, progress, and justice, which stands in stark contrast to the discord, error, doubt, and despair that marked British rule in Northern Ireland. During the hunger strike, Thatcher became the embodiment of British cruelty and contempt for the Irish. Her global nickname, "the Iron Lady," was reiterated with scorn in the nationalist community, along with the less formal "Tin Knickers," both of which pit the steely coldness of armor against the warmth and softness imagined to be central characteristics of "normal" femininity. This armored aspect of her persona—strengthened in the TV shot by her suit, immovable coif, and the three sturdy policemen behind her—when grafted onto her gender evokes Britannia, the British Empire's decidedly *un*-maternal national allegory. Throughout the rest of the film, Thatcher is always mediated through TV or radio, and this technology functions as a type of armor, protecting and distancing her from the film's diegetic space. While McLoone argues that the unseen presence of Thatcher ties the question of fanaticism and an "unyielding attitude . . . to one particularly powerful woman" (2001, 75–76), *Some Mother's Son* complicates her gender through its choice to have her will enacted by Farnsworth, a diminutive wavy-haired male minion, whom George melodramatically lights from below and endows with the power of ubiquity.[5]

The cut from the media footage of Thatcher to a landscape image of Ireland uses the naturalness of the latter to construct the former as artificial. However, despite the early morning tranquility of this image, the film's narrative largely supports Thatcher's characterization of Ireland as an inscrutable land of violence. The romantic beauty of the Irish landscape is a familiar cliché of troubles films used to enforce the idea that violence takes its victims by surprise and to heighten the affective intensity of explosions and killings by contrasting the romantic beauty of the landscape with the brutality of destruction.[6] The constant threat of violence inherent in the terrain is echoed in the music, which lays the wailing pipes and wistful flute over a baseline of dread achieved by the somewhat

5. Hill notes that this character "persistently forc[es] the pace of events and manipulat[es] the prisoners' responses. Thus, he is seen in the 'war room' explaining the government's new strategy . . . ; in the prison when Frankie and Gerard arrive and when the dirty protest is initiated; at the Houses of Parliament when the two women go to visit MPs; in conversation with a government minister discussing tactics; and then in pursuit of the Foreign Office representative, Harrington, after he has negotiated a deal with the Sinn Féin leader" (Hill 1997, 45).

6. See, for example, *Shake Hands with the Devil, Cal, The Devil's Own, The Crying Game, Michael Collins.*

militant beat of the bodhrán. There is a sense here that Ireland, Herself Alone, is potentially natural, eternal, and maternal, while Ireland troubled by British rule—Ireland historicized and politicized—is a tragically deadly land of grief and danger perpetuated by the equally perverse mothers of British occupation and republican resistance. Sure enough, the morning calm is ruptured when British soldiers blow up a bridge across the water from Kathleen Quigley's home, while soon after, the IRA uses the landscape as cover when they retaliate by blowing up soldiers.

By privileging Kathleen's visual and political point of view, George sets up parallels between the destructive habits of the British and those of the IRA. At the sound of the bridge explosion, the members of the Quigley family run to the large glass door of their house, which overlooks the water. They witness the violence of the British state, but the thick, sturdy glass of their modern middle-class home protects them and distances them from it. However, in a later sequence that repeats this play with glass, distance, and violence, Kathleen is not so lucky. As she settles into her day teaching French, music, and Irish dance at a local Catholic girls' school, Gerard takes the family car and picks up Frankie and another man for an IRA operation. The film cuts back to Kathleen's classroom via a shot of the ankles and feet of girls practicing Irish dance. Their steps initiate the non-diegetic music that plays over the entire sequence as the film cuts back and forth several times between the dancers' movements and the IRA men, who run across a field and through bushes to get a clear shot of the soldiers. Once Frankie and his partner are in position, the film cuts to a slow-motion shot of the girls' feet and bare legs as they leap into the air in a neat line. As the fast-paced music continues, punctuated by the now-distorted thuds of the girls' steps, the film cuts to a shot of the British soldiers through the crosshairs of a bazooka, back to the dancers, and back to the soldiers, until the crack of the bazooka and the boom of the explosion burst into the soundtrack. Just as the sounds of violence disrupt the music, the force from the blast shatters the windows of Kathleen's classroom, hurtling the reality of IRA violence and republicanism into her world along with the flying shards of glass.

While McLoone is right to point out that George's film extends the quality of dogmatic adherence to nationalist principle to female characters, this inclusion is all it does. The use of parallel editing in this scene establishes as inevitable the intersection between the IRA's outdoor violence and the relatively safe interior space of the girls' school. Just as the state will later invade the homes of both women in the form of house raids and arrests, the violence of politics will find its way into all interior spaces in Northern Ireland. But while the crosscutting adds suspense and puts both lines of action on a collision course, it also links Irish culture and republican violence, gendering the former female and the latter male; women and girls become the symbolic embodiment of Irish national culture rather than the agents of nationalist action or political violence. While the dancers could be seen as a benign feminine counterpoint to the masculine realm of violence, they also signal the violence that is to come. It is their percussive steps that usher in the non-diegetic music that animates and connects the shots of this sequence, and their legs that switch to slow motion in anticipation of the explosion to come. Reduced to a uniform mass of anonymous bare legs, the girls function as an audio-visual chorus, supporting the actions of the militant nationalist men.

These two opening acts of violence establish a motif in the film whereby Kathleen is consistently pulled into politics by forces beyond her control. In contrast, Annie Higgins engages in an act of resistance from her first moment on screen, as she herds her cattle up an unapproved border road that British soldiers acting under RUC orders are preparing to block up. Whereas Kathleen is shown in her kitchen preparing breakfast for her family, Annie is introduced surrounded by the standard visual markers of rural Northern Ireland: livestock, winding roads, and overgrown shrubs that conceal British soldiers in green camouflage. She confronts the RUC officer in charge, who tells her the purpose of the barricade is "to prevent your son murdering people and running across the border down there," before continuing on her way with her daughter. As the mother of a key figure in the IRA, Annie is the seasoned republican insider who educates Kathleen about the political situation in Northern Ireland, so it is fitting that later in the film Kathleen's son is arrested on Annie's farm on Christmas Eve. Frankie and Gerard are tried, convicted, and taken to the H-Blocks, where they join the prison protests and refuse to take visits with their families. A vague amount of time passes, and Annie calls Kathleen with news that Gerard would like to see her. As Kathleen begins to ask questions about whether her son has come off the protest, Annie pleads ignorance and abruptly hangs up, implying that she knows something about the real purpose for the visit that would offend Kathleen's apolitical sensibilities. The women arrive at the prison, where Kathleen's dismayed reaction to the sight of a filthy and bearded Gerard again sets her apart from the more stoic Annie. After explaining to his mother the conditions of the dirt protest, Gerard leans close to her and whispers, "I've got to get a message out to Danny Boyle," forcing her to lean in to hear him. When she does, he grabs her by the back of her neck, presses his lips against hers, opens her mouth and pushes a communiqué (comm) into it with his tongue. Kathleen turns away, frozen with shock and fear. She says nothing to Annie until she leaves the prison, when she urgently pulls the polluting comm from her mouth.

In addition to raising public awareness about their sons, RAC women used their bodies to smuggle contraband and comms in and out of the prison. "The emotional link between mothers and sons, so elaborate in the political culture of Irish nationalism," Aretxaga observes, "assumed a corporeal dimension during the prison protest that gave it a chilling literalness" (1997, 113). But it is the *political* violation of her body as much as the breaking of oedipal taboos that shocks Kathleen. After she exits the prison and begins to drive away, Kathleen lashes into Annie, hissing, "How *dare* you? You *knew!*" She then defiantly declares, "I'll not be used as some stooge for violence!" Kathleen's outrage over her body's appropriation for republican politics and violence is so great that in order to reclaim control, she pulls the car over, gets out, and against Annie's fearful objections, opens the comm and reads it—an act explicitly forbidden with punitive consequences for those who recognize the command structure of the IRA. It turns out not to be a hit list, but an urgent plea from Bobby Sands, warning that a hunger strike is imminent. The reminder of their sons' mortality unites the two women again, and they go for a drink in the nearest bar, a unionist pub. As they settle into a booth, Annie refuses to sit under a painting of Queen Elizabeth, joking, "She'll sour the drink." Kathleen finds no humor in such republican fervor, and when Annie toasts, "*Tiocfaidh ár lá*," Kathleen impatiently asks, "And what does *that* mean?" Annie translates, "Our day will come," and Kathleen snaps, "and what day is that?" Annie explains, "The day the British go home," and Kathleen responds, "'The day the Brits go home,' that's all you people think about, isn't it? Well, my life won't change either way." Annie responds, "Well now, your life and my life are two different things missus, my son was shot dead by the British." Again, the specter of losing a child elicits Kathleen's sympathy; she changes her tone of voice and begins to talk to Annie as a mother and potential friend.

Throughout the film, Kathleen functions at the primary point of identification for the spectator, not only because she is played by the bigger star (Helen Mirren) and privileged with more close-ups, screen time, and point-of-view shots, but also because of her ignorance about Northern Ireland. *Tiocfaidh ár lá* appears in murals and graffiti throughout the North, and its literal and symbolic meaning are widely known, making Kathleen's exchange with Annie an educational device likely intended for non-Irish audiences. As the hunger strike progresses, Kathleen's friendship with Annie strengthens, and she becomes politically active, taking the spectator along with her. When Annie visits Kathleen to ask for her help in the campaign to elect Bobby Sands to Parliament, Kathleen, like the media, equates republicanism with violence, and reminds Annie, "I don't support violence, Annie. You *must* understand that." Annie allays Kathleen's fears (and possibly ours as well) by explaining, "This isn't about violence, Mrs. Quigley; it's about elections." In a series of exuberant shots, the two women energetically parade with bullhorns through towns, handing out leaflets, carrying posters of Sands, and urging, "Vote for Bobby Sands! Don't let him die!" Their slogan extends accountability for preserving Sands's life beyond the British government; the nationalist community must mobilize in order to save the life of its own. In shifting the responsibility for Sands's life onto disenfranchised nationalists, the election campaign shifts political agency. Like the question "Do you care?" the slogan reminds the republican interlocutor of the high stakes involved in state politics. Not to vote for Bobby Sands is to let him die. Not to stand with the republican movement is to support the British status quo. Yet not long after, the film depicts republicanism as a decimating force that binds the hands of those who support it. Sands is elected from his deathbed, and Father Daly, the prison chaplain, urges him to save his own life by ending the hunger strike, claiming, "You've won. You made your point." Sands refuses and soon dies. His death sparks a riot, after which Kathleen begins to extricate herself from politics altogether. The film is overshadowed with despair as Kathleen's feelings of helplessness about Gerard's condition lead to disillusionment with what the film presents as the intractable mind-set of Irish republicans.

Through artistic license that authorizes historical implausibility, Kathleen becomes a go-between for the Secretary of Northern Ireland (Harrington) and Sinn Féin president, Danny Boyle. She helps to broker a deal between the men that will grant the prisoners' demands as a *right*. In the meantime, Farnsworth has sabotaged Harrington's career and has struck his own deal with Fr. Daly: after the prisoners go off the protest, the government will grant their demands as a *privilege*. The film trivializes the difference between "right" and "privilege" as an exercise in semantics, but in the British prison system, privileges can be legally taken away for any reason at the discretion of the prison governor whereas rights cannot.[7] Kathleen, Boyle, and a Blanketman wait for Harrington in the prison hospital, but instead, the priest rushes in and triumphantly announces his deal, provoking outrage from Boyle and the Blanketman. As the screenplay describes it: "The men are screaming at each other now, a wall of sound, the words drowned out, each arguing the righteousness of his position as the seconds tick away on Gerard's life . . ." (George and Sheridan 1996, 150). Kathleen watches the two republicans shout down the priest, who pleads, "It's only a word!" As the camera pans around the room from her point of view, the men's voices fade away and are replaced

---

7. Although they broke countless other laws, British prison authorities actually adhered to this one during the protests in the H-Blocks and Armagh. Protesting prisoners were granted their minimal rights to one half-hour visit a month, one parcel a month (containing no food), censored mail, weekly Mass, and religious reading materials. Presumably, they did this to maintain an air of humanity in order to shield their gross violation of human rights from international scrutiny. Although Amnesty International condemned the treatment of Irish political prisoners, visitors from the Human Rights Commission and the Red Cross did not.

by a mechanical, discordant note—the "wall of sound" that is cinematic republicanism. Kathleen surveys the assembly of hunger strikers' relatives, who are paralyzed with anguish. In a slow-motion shot that echoes the earlier use of this technique in the IRA blast sequence, Kathleen turns her back on everyone in the room, and according to the screenplay, "she's out, broken free of the arguments" (George and Sheridan 1996, 150). She goes to her son's hospital bed, removes a clipboard from the wall, and signs the authorization for medical intervention. As orderlies come to take Gerard to an ambulance, Kathleen encounters Annie in the hall and confesses, "I took him off. I had to." Annie replies, "Somebody had to. You're lucky you had the choice." Kathleen follows Gerard to an ambulance, and attendants wheel in the crisp white sheet and cold metal gurney that will carry away Frankie's emaciated corpse, while Annie stands imprisoned and immobilized by grief, clutching her only remaining child. In the final shot, Kathleen stands at the edge of the harbor that opened the film, as a new day breaks on the horizon, suggesting a glimmer of hope for the future amid the uncertainty of the hunger strike. The film seems to support its own visual promise of better days ahead in its epilogue: "Ten men died on the hunger strike. . . . On October 3, 1981, [it] ended after several mothers intervened to save their sons. The British government granted all the prisoners' demands shortly after the hunger strike ended."

In crediting Kathleen with putting an end to British and Irish intransigence, *Some Mother's Son* redeems relatives who were seen at the time as having betrayed the prisoners' cause. Unfortunately, it does so at the expense of families who "let" their sons die.[8] Throughout the film, Kathleen demonstrates a levelheadedness that is contrasted with Annie's fiery passion, manifest in her red hair. Kathleen's clarity of vision is bolstered by the epilogue and reflected in the architecture of her home—a white house with floor-to-ceiling windows and a shrub-free lawn. When she confesses

8. I use quotation marks here because the situation families found themselves in was clearly untenable, and the language used in George's film seems to carry a value judgment and an unfair corollary: if parents intervened to "save" their children's lives, then parents who refused to intervene "let" their sons die. The use of the word "save" in the epilogue glosses over the profound difficulty of the families' dilemma.

to Annie that Sands's election is the first time she has ever voted, her exile from politics seems to have been a personal choice that stemmed from what she saw as the intransigence of "both" sides rather than the result of gerrymandering. Avoiding a direct analysis of the politics of economic marginalization and state exclusion, the film omits an important motivating force for Irish republicanism that would make it seem less romantically fatalistic and more rational, a politics that emerged in response to specific historical and material conditions. This separation is further enabled by the film's non-urban setting. Substituting a generic, small, seaside town for the specificity of working-class Belfast (where a majority of hunger strikers were from) or Derry, *Some Mother's Son* affords itself the luxury of ignoring the ways in which the state consistently and forcefully excluded working-class nationalists. Omitting the "besieging cartography"[9] of urban Northern Ireland—the heavy presence of surveillance technology and police and military personnel and the difficulty in moving through space (through checkpoints as well as partial strip searches and pat-downs on the street)—*Some Mother's Son* excises the daily violence of occupation. Kathleen can take Gerard off hunger strike, and the film can back her because the stakes of the protest remain limited to the five demands, without a sense of the wider significance of those demands. Finally, the epilogue is factually incorrect, unless "shortly after" can be understood to mean two years, which is how long it took for the administration to meet the demand for free association and segregation by political affiliation (McKeown 2001, 87–98).

Annie's commitment to republicanism enables her to stand back and honor her son's convictions despite personal anguish, partly because she has her own stakes in sustaining the republican movement. From her perspective, Frankie's death is both a personal loss and a deliberate step toward not just the abstract notion of an Irish nation but also the concrete goal of better daily conditions for the prisoners and an end to a sectarian police state outside of the prison. The film gestures toward the violence of

---

9. The phrase is Camille Mansour's in relation to Palestine. See Mansour 2001, 87.

British occupation in the house raid, in brief scenes featuring the characters' clashes with Northern Ireland's security forces, and in the mention of Annie's dead son. But its final image of Annie upholds cinematic clichés of the mournful Irish mother who has lost her sons to the melodrama of Irish fanaticism. While it might be argued that the experience of losing a child may have been Annie's impetus for joining the republican movement, the film suggests otherwise in its mise-en-scène. Annie's farmhouse speaks to generational ties to the land, and its landscape is consistent with historical representations that use the wild and moody land as a metaphor for the Irish.[10] Like earlier literary and cinematic republican women, Annie is also chained to the past: every year on Christmas, she sets a place at the dinner table for her dead son, whose presence is enshrined in the living room. Because the film offers *only* these two women in its oblique portrayal of the RAC, republicanism becomes a lethal ideology that leaves mothers who participate in it bereft of both children and hope. It achieves this portrayal also by establishing a sense of fatalism through the religious iconography that proliferates around the hunger strike. The film's Christological representations of Bobby Sands combined with its motif of grieving mothers give the protests a tragic tone: Irish republicans are condemned to suffer from their own ideological intractability, a stubbornness exemplified in Sands's refusal to end his protest after becoming an MP and in the argument in the prison waiting room over what the priest trivializes as "only words."

Recognizing that *Some Mother's Son* is problematic in many ways, Hill and McLoone also commend the film for paying tribute to the anguish that families of hunger strikers endured, positioned as they were between two impossible options: defy the wishes and negate the sacrifice of a loved one, and therefore negate any meaning in the preceding deaths of hunger strikers, or watch him die a gruesomely slow and excruciating death knowing they had the legal authority to intervene. Hill notes that as a proud member of "what he calls the 'sledgehammer school of

10. See Hill 1988 and Gibbons 1988.

filmmaking,'" George is not interested in complex political analysis (Hill 1997, 45).[11] George may not be concerned with using film to formulate a lucid political argument, but his film nonetheless functions politically in ways that are both innovative and regressive. On the one hand, by favoring Kathleen's decision to take Gerard off the hunger strike and crediting her with initiating a process that saved lives and granted the prisoners' demands, George undercuts heroic republican narratives of national martyrdom, which appear in abundance around the hunger strike, as even a cursory survey of contemporary republican murals reveals. Within that framework, the parents and one wife who intervened were imagined as the weak links in a republican chain, vulnerable to manipulation by priests into betraying their sons. *Some Mother's Son* recuperates as valid the opinions of those who disagreed with the strike to begin with, or who had a change of heart after the British government's high tolerance for Irish death became abundantly clear. But in place of heroic republican memory, George offers the heroics of maternal love.

My argument with George's film is less its portrayal of Irish republicans and more its insistence on a depoliticized image of motherhood. *Some Mother's Son* ultimately sides with a false ideal of motherhood as eternal and natural—a notion of motherhood that *Four Days in July* critiques, and one that naturalizes the postcolonial domestication of Irish women. But even so, Annie's experience carries with it the realization that "motherhood," as Anne McClintock argues, "is a political issue" (1995, 387). As a "social category under constant contest" (381), the role of mother is a useful one for challenging repressive regimes because of its imagined passivity. In 1977, seven women members of the RAC traveled to London to raise awareness about conditions in the prisons. Dressed only in blankets, one group of women chained themselves to the front gate at Downing Street, while another picketed on the steps of the British Labour Party headquarters, where they also handed in a letter from H-Block

11. Of course, if George is not interested in using film for complex political analysis, he could also avoid mining highly political situations for dramatic material (see *Hotel Rwanda* for another example).

prisoners. Police arrested and jailed the women at Downing Street, and the next morning they appeared in court, still in only their blankets. The judge released them with a warning and "ordered the women to return to Belfast and never set foot in the 'United Kingdom' again" (Fitzsimons 1996, 22), apparently missing the fact that by the logic of the very government whose discriminatory laws he upheld, the women already lived in the United Kingdom—in order for them to obey the judge's ruling, the goals of Irish nationalism would need to be fulfilled. The following day, a Labour MP invited one of the women to speak at a special meeting of the House of Commons; she compared the British penal system to an abusive parent: "What would happen to me if I were to lock my son or daughter in a small room for twenty-four hours a day and feed them on an almost non-existent diet? . . . I'll tell you what would happen. I'd be sent to prison accused of gross cruelty, and rightly so" (Fitzsimons 1996, 23). The emotional power and authority of this statement is rooted in the speaker's identity as a mother who literally laid the mistreatment of her children on the doorstep of the British government. Like *Las madres*, the RAC women "perform[ed] the social role of mother," contrasting their ability to nurture with the government's cruelty toward and neglect of its citizens, and like the Argentinian women, these mothers chose public spaces that figure prominently in national narratives.[12] The RAC protests intersect with familial models of governmentality such as those delineated by Foucault and challenged in *Four Days in July*. In comparing their own good mothering with the bad mothering of the state, they question the seamless ideological link between government and family, revealing that for the disempowered, the government does not keep the family safe, but destroys it.

Like the seemingly nonviolent body of the hunger striker, the bodies of these women became weapons to fire against the state, which were only cloaked (blanketed) in the mantle of passive suffering. By traveling

12. The phrase is from Holledge and Tompkins, who also write of *Las madres*, "They have always been very visible because of their choice of meeting place: the Plaza de Mayo, well known in Argentina for its patriotic and historical significance" and its location at the center of Buenos Aires (Holledge and Tompkins 2000, 47).

to major European cities, defying the Prevention of Terrorism Act, arriving at the threshold of the British government, and deliberately putting themselves in the path of pedestrian and automotive traffic, the RAC confronted state officials and civilians alike with the injustice done to their children. The refrain "Do you care?" expresses the frustration and despair that Aretxaga cites as a key factor in the women's politicization, and, just as important, it shames the interlocutor. The Blanketmen are ill clad, battered, lying in their own waste, deprived of sunlight and fresh air, and starved because the public is allowing it to happen.[13] Without the women's identity as mothers and not simply relatives or women activists, the question "Do you care?" would not carry as much weight. Mothers, after all, are the moral guardians of the nation. They have the culturally sanctioned authority to reprimand along the lines of ethics, responsibility, and morality. The role of suffering mother was a subject position the RAC could publicly and temporarily occupy in order to provoke a particular political response. Whereas, as Aretxaga argues, the women experienced their suffering as suffering and not as allegory, their tactics functioned as a poaching of national allegory and Catholic iconography.

The protests of the RAC provoke fissures in the logic of gender, state, and nationalist history. The physical bodies of mothers who had been pregnant, borne sons, and metaphorically "carried" them once again to symbolically release them from prison become contested sites where discourses of state, family, home, and gender compete for recognition. The blanketed bodies of the RAC mothers can be seen as articulations in Stuart Hall's sense of the word—bringing together its double significacion as connection and utterance. Like Soviet montage, an articulation joins two "distinct elements" within a specific context; the connection between the two ideas is "not necessary, determined, absolute and essential for all time. . . . So the so-called 'unity' of a discourse is really the articulation of different distinct elements which can be rearticulated in

13. One of the women from the 1977 Downing Street group directly implored the British public to look at what the state was doing to Irish men and women in their name (Fitzsimmons 1996, 22).

different ways because they have no necessary belongingness" (Stuart Hall 1986 interview quoted in Lyons 1996, 115). Hall's concept opens an avenue to see how nationalism naturalizes and essentializes the relationship between its various components through the deployment of key signs. In her analysis of the Armagh protests, Laura Lyons argues that Mother Ireland is such an articulation. Her attributes may change over time, but "one notices that while she may be 'named' or 'articulated' through different means . . . vestiges of the Virgin, the sorrowful mother, are retained" (Lyons 1996, 115).

In the body of the blanketed mother are joined and expressed a nationally valorized form of femininity and a specific mode of suffering based in oppositional politics. The stoic mother figure is fused to poverty, disenfranchisement, and state violence in the body of the blanketed RAC woman as a sign of the radical dispossession of the Irish under British rule and therefore the need for republican insurgency. Like the Blanketman, the blanketed mother evokes Britain's history of attempting to reduce the Irish to bare life, and like both the H-Block and Armagh prisoners, the RAC mother transforms the signifiers of bare life into a language of resistance. Far from being the fanatic mother who urges her sons to go out and die, or the helpless *mater dolorosa* of slain martyrs, the RAC mother speaks to the logic of republican discourse and its radical potential. That this happens through the appropriation of symbolic national maternal suffering is problematic for the time after the revolution, as is disastrously exemplified in the Irish Republic, but quite useful for the revolution itself. But Hall's concept might even lead to a way out of this post-independence trap. Reading motherhood as an articulation makes visible its historicity— it is not an immutable concept over time, but something to be snatched and deployed by multiple groups for diverse ideological ends at critical moments in a national history.

The "Girls in Armagh"

> I was suddenly pinned to the bed by a shield and the weight of a male screw on top of me. Then my shoes were dragged off my feet. . . . I was just bodily assaulted—thumped, trailed and brutally kicked. . . . I was

then trailed out of my cell, and during the course of my being dragged and hauled from the wing, both my breasts were exposed to the jeering and mocking eyes of all the screws (male and female). . . . While being carried, I was also abused with punches to the back of my head and stomach.

The whole episode for me was totally embarassing [sic] and degrading. I was eventually carried into the governor—my breasts were still exposed. While I was held by the screws the governor carried out the adjudication and I was then trailed back and thrown into the cell (WAI 1980, 22).

In a comic strip by the Irish prisoner Cormac, the aging figure of British Justice stalks the Irish landscape. In the next frame, a man enumerates the injustices British Justice has brought to Ireland: the Diplock courts, the H-Blocks, and now Armagh Gaol. When another character, shocked, asks him, "Do you mean to say that women in Armagh are forced to live in the same abominable conditions as. . . ." The first man quips, "Believe me, Jimmy, when it comes to the degradation of human beings, British Justice is a real force for sexual equality" (Cormac 1982, 16). The joke acknowledges that state brutality against suspect communities spares no one on the basis of sex, age, or health. However, being equally cruel to men and women is not the same thing as being gender blind. As the above statement by Rosemary Callaghan demonstrates, a central aspect of the physical and psychological torture of female prisoners involved the screws' calling attention to their bodies as specifically female ones. Women under interrogation at Castlereagh recall threats of rape, incidents of fondling, and verbal sexual harassment, in addition to more gender-neutral forms of violence such as punches, kicks, and being held down. As in the H-Blocks, prisoners in Armagh responded to the physical and psychological violence they had suffered since their arrests with a noxiously confrontational form of protest that made the work environment for their warders miserable. But at the same time, the gender of each group of prisoners affected interpretation and representation of their protests in ways that seem to have made it more difficult to make the women of Armagh visible without resorting to biological essentialism or national-feminine imagery.

If the couple of Jesus and Mary, martyr and mother, proved to be a powerful image for republican appropriation in order to galvanize support for male prisoners and their faithful relatives on the outside, it also precluded the possibility of representing people who were neither sons nor mothers of sons. A critical problem that arises with representing Armagh prisoners is the symbolic function of the female body in Irish nationalism. Even murals that depict male and female prisoners have a tendency to portray women as ancillary or symbolic. One such example is a stunning mural of Raymond McCartney by the Bogside Artists, a Derry-based mural collective, whose work frequently uses a grayscale color scheme reminiscent of the black-and-white media images that have played such a disproportionate role in the visual construction of Northern Ireland.

In the mural (fig. 4), McCartney's emaciated, blanketed body and bearded face rise up from the ground in front of a red, aerial rendering of an H-Block. Above the H and behind McCartney's Christ-like visage is a wind-swept sky, implying what the artists understand to be a gathering political storm, which, following the eschatological intent of the H-Block protests, would also herald the hunger striker's liberation through republican ideology and protest. McCartney, who participated in the first hunger strike and suffered permanent damage to his eyesight as a result, is rendered in medium close-up and occupies more than half the frame of the mural. To his left and behind his shoulder, in front of the stone wall and barred window iconic of Armagh Gaol, stands a woman hunger striker, portrayed in the equivalent of film's medium-long shot. McCartney looks off to an undefined point to the right of the frame, while the woman, whose face is not that of a specific Armagh prisoner, confronts the viewer with a steadfast gaze. She too is dressed in a blanket, which simultaneously renders her as a visual echo—or even disciple—of McCartney and also evokes the RAC mothers. Here, brought together in a mural tribute to the courage and determination of Irish hunger strikers, is a specific historical man, who is now a local politician and well known in his community, and a symbolic woman, whose non-specific facial features and blanket transform her from a 1980 Armagh hunger strike into an icon of Irish womanhood, history, and the spirit of nationalist resistance. The woman's non-specificity reiterates in visual form the tendency, which historians of

4. Derry Bogside Artists, hunger striker Raymond McCartney with a blanketed woman behind him. Courtesy of the artists.

the Armagh protests as well as the prisoners themselves have noted, to understand Armagh prisoners as supporters of the H-Blocks protest rather than protesters in their own right.[14]

14. To be fair to the Bogside Artists, whose talent and dedication to preserving history I don't mean to disparage: Raymond McCartney is a Derry resident, which is the

In 1976, when the British government revoked political status, it did so for all prisoners, male and female, but the issue of the prison uniform pertained only to men. Prior to 1972, Armagh did have a uniform consisting of a polka-dot blouse and a skirt (Murray 1998, 10). While Feldman reads the (men's) uniform on its symbolic level as a signifier of serialized (male) bodies broken by the state, in Armagh before 1972, the uniform helped to break women prisoners on a material level as well. For political prisoners, the uniform became a source of demoralization and discomfort: republican women were issued skirts that were three sizes too big and had to be wrapped sarong-like around their hips in order to stay on; they were given mismatched socks and sometimes boots of two different sizes; blouses and sweaters were stained and torn and offered little protection against the cold. Even prison-issued underwear was tattered and old. Women were given bras that not only were the wrong size but had often been patched and re-sewn with two different cup sizes, making them impossible for anyone to wear comfortably (McCafferty 1981, 17–18). In a culture already marked by shame about the body, particularly the female body (a sentiment shared by both sides of the political divide and certainly not limited to Ireland), ill-fitting bras, in addition to being physically uncomfortable, can adversely affect a prisoner's relationship to her own body in specifically gendered terms. Using the outward signs of their sexuality against the prisoners, the prison authorities shared punitive measures with the Catholic nuns who ran Ireland's Magdalene laundries and would force their female inmates to bind their breasts with calico. Both institutions exploit an aspect of culture already present and use it to further alienate women from themselves, facilitating their institutionalization. However, a key difference between

---

principal reason for his specific portrayal. Another important mural in Derry depicts the civil rights activist Bernadette Devlin McAliskey. I am not suggesting that the Bogside Artists have omitted women from Irish history or that they routinely use women as symbols. I only mean to point out the tendency, even today, to position the Armagh protests as secondary to those of the Blocks. There are many reasons for this positioning, and it cannot be simply blamed on sexism. At the same time, the ancillary role of Armagh prisoners has become commonsense in representations of the H-Blocks, which speaks to the persistent need for feminist historiography.

these two groups of inmates is that the Armagh women may have been marginalized within Irish nationalism, but the victims of the Magdalene system were ejected from the national family entirely.

The uniform was abolished for women prisoners regardless of the nature of their offenses in 1972 when the British government first granted special category status to paramilitary prisoners. It was never reinstated for women, even after the implementation of the criminalization policy. Therefore, when republican women joined the protest for political status in 1977, they retained the right to wear their own clothes. With this new policy and the justification that it was found to have a "rehabilitative effect" on women prisoners, the government skirted the possible public relations disaster of Blanketwomen.[15] Without the spectacle and symbolism accompanying the blanket, the Armagh protest was largely obscured by the H-Blocks, even for the women themselves. In *Mother Ireland*, Mairéad Farrell, who was OC for A-wing of Armagh during the protests, explains that initially, the women saw themselves in a supportive role as "the girls in Armagh," but eventually they realized that they were protesting for their own political status "as women" (Lyons 1996, 123).

The dirt protest began on February 7, 1980, when the women were locked in their cells for twenty-four hours and denied access to toilets. The lockup came as punishment for a riot, which was initiated by a search of the prisoners' cells for the contraband black clothing they used to identify themselves as members of the PIRA. According to Nell McCafferty, the search seemed designed primarily to instigate a riot. Before noon, "all social workers, education officers and religious ministers were cleared off the premises of Armagh jail. All prisoners, other than those on protest, were locked into their cells" (1981, 26). Once all the protesting prisoners had assembled for lunch, a group of about thirty-five male guards entered the wing and encircled the women. Their chief officer informed the prisoners that there would be a search of their cells. The women were not

---

15. I am purely speculating. There is no evidence that women prisoners would have gone on a blanket protest had the uniform been an issue.

allowed to leave the floor of the wing, and were forced into the association rooms (common areas on the wing) while the cells were searched. As Farrell explained in a letter smuggled out to her parents:

> The male officers never gave us a chance. They immediately jumped us and started beating all round them. One male officer just picked Anne Marie Quinn up and threw her across the wing where she landed on her head. Another one had Peggy Friel's right arm up her back and was punching her. . . . Anne Bateson was punched in the face by a male officer. Una Nellis was held by male officers while being punched and kicked. . . . Eventually we were able to calm the girls down a bit and pull them out of reach of the male officers. All were in a state of panic and jumped to a defensive position by throwing dinner plates at male officers (WAI 1980, 23).

Once the women were returned to their cells in the late afternoon, male and female screws in full riot gear burst into each cell in order to bring the women individually before the governor for adjudication concerning their participation in the riot. As in the H-Blocks, the screws carried out this action methodically and sequentially in order to maximize the women's sense of dread; as each woman was battered individually, the others could hear her screams. They were powerless to help and uncertain as to who would be attacked next. Aside from being taken to and from adjudication with the governor, the women were kept locked up for twenty-four hours without access to washing or toilet facilities. With nowhere to empty their chamber pots, they began a dirt strike.

When the journalist Tim Pat Coogan visited the protesting wings of Armagh in 1980 after having toured the H-Blocks, he found the "smell of the girls' cells far worse than that at Long Kesh and several times found myself having to control feelings of nausea" (Lyons 1996, 120). Although he does not account for his perceived difference in smell, it haunts his inventory of the waste lying in the prison corridor: "Tissue, slops consisting of tea and urine, some faeces and clots of blood—obviously the detritus of menstruation" (Lyons 1996, 120). In a critique of Coogan's patronizing and squeamish account of Armagh, Lyons questions whether "his assertion is not, in fact, based on a common Western cultural assumption that equates women and their sexuality with various odors" (1996, 121). Coogan's observation is also interesting for its disproportionate emphasis on menstrual blood. As Aretxaga shrewdly asks, "What can make thirty dirty women more revolting than four hundred dirty men if not the exposure of menstrual blood? An element that cannot contribute much to the fetid odors of urine and feces but can turn the stomach" (1997, 137). Coogan's response is almost a textbook illustration of Julia Kristeva's discussion of the affective power of the abject, but the primal importance he gives to menstrual blood is common in representations of Armagh, although the ways in which feminist writers and activists have discussed it are at the opposite end of the political spectrum from Coogan's. The prisoners reported the lack of sanitary towels and tampons to their families, communities, comrades in the H-Blocks, and to interested feminists including McCafferty and the members of Women against Imperialism (WAI). These women, who were sympathetic to the republican movement or came from republican communities themselves, used the fact of menstrual blood on the walls of Armagh as a rallying point to garner support from other women's organizations in the United Kingdom and Ireland.

In republican communities, support for the prisoners often marginalized gender as a concern. Noting the prevalence in 1980 of the noun "girl" over that of "woman" in pamphlets and articles in support of the Armagh protesters, Aretxaga foregrounds the question of gender in the gaol. She writes that women who joined the Irish nationalist military campaign in the 1970s did so as members of the Provisional IRA, and not as members of Cumann na mBan; in fact, they had fought with the army council specifically for the right to join the PIRA as female combatants (1997, 138). In rejecting Cumann na mBan for the Provos, the women "consciously rejected gender as a differential factor in political militancy" (Aretxaga 1997, 138). Once inside prison, women had tried to join the dirt protest before February 7, 1980, but were barred from doing so by the Provo Army Council. When they were finally able to join in the wake of the twenty-four-hour lockup, they saw their dirt protest as "no different from that of the men; it was the same struggle undertaken by equal comrades for political recognition" (Aretxaga 1997, 138). This position, Aretxaga argues, should be seen as a stance taken in response to the ways in which their gender had obscured women's participation in the prison protests (since 1977, the Armagh republicans had been on a no-work protest). In order to become visible as *prisoners*, the women had to strip themselves of their specific gender identity (Aretxaga 1997, 139). This was a tactical maneuver against their double oppression as republicans and as women.

But the presence of menstrual blood, Aretxaga argues, "negated this negation" by calling attention to sexual difference. Aretxaga imagines the blood as a return of what the women had repressed in order to mark themselves as political prisoners; it "became a symbol through which gender identity was reflected, pushing to the surface what had been otherwise erased" (1997, 139). In resurfacing, menstrual blood pushed the meaning of the dirt protest beyond the confines of the republican struggle, Aretxaga and Leila Neti argue; it became a protest against the repression of female sexuality and the strictures placed on women by a Catholic, patriarchal society (Aretxaga 1997, 139–42; Neti 2003, 82–84).[16] While it is possible to see the women prisoners as deploying an extreme form of defilement to counter the extreme form of purity at the heart of Catholicism, Lyons argues such a reading risks "'abstracting' these women's actions from their dirt. The Armagh women's *immediate* struggle was not against a myth; rather, they were engaged in a specific historical and political confrontation" (Lyons 1996, 121). Like McCafferty, Aretxaga, and Neti, Lyons must deal with the fact that the addition of blood marks the Armagh dirt protest as different from that of the H-Blocks, but she observes that the Armagh women insistently placed blood in the same category as excrement and urine, as "just another bodily material . . . on which their protest [could] be built" (Lyons 1996, 122).

16. Aretxaga and Leila Neti both blame the women's sense of shame about menstruating on Catholicism and what they seem to see as an inherently patriarchal republican community. Laura Lyons, on the other hand, has recognized that taboos of feminine purity are at the center of Protestant culture as well. To construct the republican community as uniquely patriarchal because of its ties to Catholicism is to inadvertently support unionist and British hegemony, which repeatedly position themselves as enlightened, modern discourses in opposition to an atavistic Irish culture.

Menstrual blood takes on heroic significance in feminist readings of the protest. Aretxaga asserts that the menstrual blood in Armagh gendered the prisoners female against their will, and that such gendering had a positive function in that it allowed issues pertaining specifically to women to break to the surface. It may be true that men in the IRA could not even bring themselves to say the word "period" in any context other than a grammatical one (Aretxaga 1997, 127). But to argue, as Neti does, that "it is precisely this sort of forced coming to terms with shame and embarrassment . . . that has opened a dialogue of feminist politics surrounding the issue of Armagh" (Neti 2003, 83), is to ignore the more mundane (and more common) ways in which feminism entered into dialogue with republicanism: through the presence in Armagh of WAI activists Margaretta D'Arcy and Liz Lagrua, through the campaign of McCafferty and WAI to raise awareness of the situation in Armagh, and even before that, through the growing consciousness and community organization of Catholic women, who were exposed to and interested in the women's movement in the North during the 1970s.

I agree with Aretxaga, Lyons, and Neti that it is impossible to discuss Armagh without addressing the presence of blood, that the blood became a forceful symbol of sexual and gender difference, and that it added a dimension of horror, making the Armagh protest somehow "dirtier" than that of the H-Blocks. At the same time, I heed Lyons's caution to bear in mind the protest's historical, material, and political specificity. Neti's interpretation of menstrual blood as empowering and her portrayal of the protest as a "counter-modern" strategy that provokes crises in the modernizing apparatus of the British penal system are provocative but problematic. The addition of menstrual blood to Armagh transformed the meaning of the dirt protest, Neti states, because it "explicitly sexualized" the women's protest, signaling not only pain and suffering but also "birth potential" (2003, 80). Because of the blood's multiple symbolic functions, Britain's reaction against the protest was more than simply "a reaction against dirt and filth. With the addition of menstrual blood, the British now seemed to be condemning the sexualized bodies of Irish women" (Neti 2003, 80). Neti constructs a misleading portrayal of the women's dirt protest as more successful than the men's in upsetting the rationality of the penal system.

Citing comms from Mairéad Farrell that imply that the number of guards in Armagh had dwindled over the course of the dirt protest, Neti concludes, "It follows then, if complete control could not be asserted over the bodies of the prisoners at all times, there could possibly arise a new threat of resistance at every level of discipline. In this manner, the fear of primitive symbols of disorder translated into a corresponding fear regarding the efficacy of the modern British prison. On a fundamental level, the prisoners forced the British penal system into a state of powerlessness" (2003, 86). Like Feldman, Neti is aware of the potential of the protests to rebuff the controlling gaze of the penal system and thus throw its logic into crisis. But this victory, while important, is also a predominantly discursive one. The prison system—manifest in Armagh Gaol—remained quite powerful, as the emaciated body of Pauline McLaughlin forcefully attests.

The dirt protest undermined the effectiveness of surveillance, but as in the H-Blocks, the prison system found other ways to inscribe its power onto the bodies of the Armagh women. By controlling access to nutrition, doctors, and medical supplies, the authorities maintained their physical and institutional dominance. Pauline McLaughlin, who weighed approximately 133 pounds (9.5 stone) when she entered Armagh as a teenager is only the most extreme example of how food and medicine became contested sites of struggle. While in prison, McLaughlin developed a stomach condition, and when the dirt protest started and the prison authorities changed the women's diet in the hopes of coercing them off the protest, she had trouble digesting the poorly prepared food. The punitive starvation rations that accompanied the protest, when combined with McLaughlin's stomach problems, accelerated her weight loss, and doctors who tended to her at the prison hospital recommended she be placed on a special diet immediately. The prison authorities offered her this medically prescribed diet if she agreed to end her protest. She refused, and her weight plummeted to dangerous levels. The prison system began a cycle of restoring McLaughlin to health and letting her deteriorate, using her own body as an instrument of torture; her weight would drop to dangerous levels, she would be placed in the prison hospital and fed properly until she recovered and then placed back on the prison diet until her weight dramatically dropped again (WAI 1980, 18).

Against the rest of the prisoners, the prison system used sanitary towels and tampons as a uniquely gendered form of abuse. At the beginning of the dirt protest, women were issued these supplies whenever they needed them, and they were given as many sanitary towels and tampons as they wanted. However, as the protest endured and showed no signs of ending, the prison authorities announced that sanitary towels and tampons would be given out at the beginning of each month, that prisoners would have to choose between the two forms of feminine hygiene, and that only a limited number of each would be given out. The prisoners were not given bags in which to store these supplies, and so they sat out in the open, exposed to the patina of shit on the cell walls and ceilings until the women needed them. In addition, belts were not given out with the sanitary towels, so prisoners who chose to use them had to deal with the awkwardness of trying to keep the towels in place whenever they moved (D'Arcy 1981, 80). Like the issue of weight, the prison authorities' use of feminine hygiene products as a mode of degradation became a rallying point to garner support for the Armagh women among feminists; it fell into the category of women's sovereignty over their own bodies.

The Armagh prisoners' "refusal to grant menstrual blood, the sign of women's potential to reproduce, 'special status'—forcefully raises the question of whether or not women can be recognized as political beings both inside and outside of the prison" (Lyons 1996, 122). *Silent Grace*, set in Armagh's A-wing during the dirt protest and the 1980 hunger strike, engages with this question as it sets out to readmit Armagh women into republican history as *women*. For feminist Armagh activists, marking the gender of the prisoners as female was an important step in making them visible to people outside of the republican community, particularly women's groups in Ireland and Britain. This use of gender differs radically from that of Coogan, whose reaction to menstruation implies that for him, the real horror is the aggression behind the Armagh women's seizure of their own bodily functions as material for protest (Lyons 1996, 122). However, the ways in which feminists gendered the Armagh women differs from how *Silent Grace* constructs the gender of its characters. Like *Some Mother's Son*, *Silent Grace* challenges traditional nationalism by imagining characters that cling to it as rigidly dogmatic. But also like *Some*

Mother's Son, Maeve Murphy's film shares with George's an emphasis on maternal images of Irish women. By "softening" Eileen as she learns to mother Áine, contrasting Eileen's open-mindedness and friendliness with Margaret's hostility, and representing Eileen's hunger strike in imagery steeped in national allegory, *Silent Grace*, even as it tries to appropriate that iconography for women, seems to suggest the answer to Lyons's question is "No."

The only film to even acknowledge the women in Armagh Gaol, let alone portray them on screen, *Silent Grace* challenges the existing cinematic language for representing political violence and resistance in the North. The film reverses the gender dynamics of films about the prison protests, placing women at the center of the story and in the middle of the frame, while marginalizing men on both a visual and narrative level. It also makes a clear attempt to appropriate the heroic images of suffering Blanketmen for women prisoners, most explicitly through shots of the Armagh women wrapped in blankets (fig. 5).

At the core of the film is a maternal love story between a republican prisoner and the apolitical juvenile delinquent whom she takes under her

5. Áine wrapped in a blanket. From *Silent Grace* (Maeve Murphy, 2001). Courtesy of Maeve Murphy.

wing. Like *Some Mother's Son*, *Silent Grace* opens with the quintessential bad mother of the British Isles, as Margaret Thatcher's voice competes with a mechanical hum, which could be radio interference but is amplified to provoke a sense of foreboding. Voiced over a black screen, she reiterates her stand on political prisoners, "There can be no question of political status for someone who is serving a sentence for crime." The broadcast is cut off by a woman with a northern accent (Eileen) ordering, "And march!" Thatcher's mediated voice and Eileen's unaltered voice interrupt each other in audio crosscutting, "Crime is crime is crime; it is not political it is crime," "About turn! At ease," before the film cuts to an image of women stylishly dressed all in black: V-neck sweaters, tailored shirts, neckties, skirts, stockings, pumps, and berets. Two women carry makeshift Irish tricolors and two others wear green camouflage netting over their faces (fig. 6).

The women dressed in IRA uniforms are parading in Armagh's prison yard, under the direction of their OC, Eileen (modeled loosely after Mairéad Farrell). Their military discipline contradicts Thatcher's characterization of republican prisoners as base criminals, and their gender implicitly challenges assumptions about PIRA members as exclusively male. By

6. Political prisoners of Armagh. From *Silent Grace* (Maeve Murphy, 2001). Courtesy of Maeve Murphy.

opening with a conflict between the voice of the Iron Lady and that of a female OC drilling her cadres, Maeve Murphy's film immediately rejects the polarization that aligns men with war and women with peace and the home in troubles narratives. In the shots that follow, cinema's standard gendering of vision and power as male are subverted when Eileen looks up defiantly at the prison governor who stands at a window surveying the scene in the yard. Startled by her gaze, he turns away, and the film cuts to the story of its other lead character, the Catholic Belfast teenager Áine Quinn.

Áine is arrested after drinking, huffing spray-paint fumes, and then joyriding through a British Army checkpoint. At her trial, to spite her worried mother, Áine declares herself a political prisoner. Although Áine is not so far off—when military checkpoints dot the city streets, even riding in a stolen car can intersect with the politics of occupation—her statement is used to foreground her willful ignorance of Northern politics. The film links her political superficiality to the boisterous energy of youthful rebellion. It sets Áine's wildness against Eileen's mature and sober political convictions when it crosscuts between Áine's arraignment and arrival in jail and Eileen's negotiations with the governor in the wake of the February 7 riot. Áine's transport van arrives at Armagh, and the Clash's "I Fought the Law (and the Law Won)" blares over jerky hand-held shots of Áine as she descends from the van and enters the prison. The helter-skelter style of this sequence contrasts starkly with the static shots of Eileen's formal meeting with the prison governor, and the stylistic disparity emphasizes Eileen's self-control, affirming her identity as a political prisoner through an aura of resolute calm. Not realizing the seriousness of her decision, Áine reiterates her political status and refuses to be jailed with the ODCs. Thinking he's found a way to break the dirt protest, the governor decides to grant Áine her wish, and puts her on A-wing in a cell with Geraldine, a teenager whose brother is also on protest in the H-Blocks. Áine and Geraldine quickly bond over boys, bands, and lipstick, and when he sees that the two young women are getting along, the governor transfers Áine to Eileen's cell, moving Margaret in with Geraldine. Rather than smashing the disciplined unity of the POWs, Áine becomes increasingly politicized along republican lines. Eileen assigns essays by James Connolly for Áine to read, lectures her on Irish history and politics, and drills her on what she's learned. As the two women bond, Áine matures, and Eileen relaxes, sharing details about her personal life, including the fact that her boyfriend is on protest in the H-Blocks (where Farrell's fiancé was imprisoned).

Silent Grace places women at the center of the struggle for political status, but its sympathetic women—Eileen, Geraldine, and Áine—are feminized along heteronormative lines. In addition, the film retains the masculine embodiment of nationalist fanaticism typical of troubles films through Margaret, Eileen's cellmate prior to Áine's arrival. Blonde, perpetually scowling, and dressed in lumpy, shapeless sweaters, Margaret recalls Jude's rural terrorist incarnation in *The Crying Game*. Margaret is also the "butch" character of women's prison films, the woman who has managed quite well to adapt to the psychological tortures of prison, but whose success at survival is presented as having come at the expense of her femininity and possibly her heterosexuality too. In terms of troubles narratives, Margaret is the republican hard-liner whose politics have isolated her from her family, barred her from the natural role of mother, and are so strongly fused with personal rage that they even alienate her own political community. In fact, Margaret is so hardened that she will not even accept the new mattresses ordered by the governor for the protesting prisoners. As Eileen becomes a surrogate mother to Áine, Margaret's republicanism impedes her function as an actual mother. Her two-year-old daughter is being raised by Margaret's sister, and at one half-hour visit a month, she no longer recognizes Margaret as her mother. Margaret is instantly suspicious of Áine, fearing that she may be a British spy sent in to infiltrate the IRA. She raises this concern a few times in the film, only to have it dismissed as excessive by Eileen. In an account of her own incarceration in Armagh, D'Arcy (who deliberately had herself imprisoned on A-wing for three months) describes being self-conscious about the kinds of questions she could and could not ask in order to allay the women's fears of espionage (D'Arcy 1981, 88–95). But the film anchors Margaret's suspicions to her jealousy of the growing bond between Áine and Eileen. It also contrasts Margaret's hardness with the cautiously friendly welcome Áine receives from the other women. As the story progresses, Geraldine and Eileen gravitate to Áine at the expense of their solidarity with Margaret.

The contrast between heterosexual, giggly Áine and dogmatic, grim Margaret becomes most salient in a crosscutting sequence where Áine and Eileen discuss boyfriends. Áine asks Eileen what Conor's favorite sexual position is, and the Clash's "I Fought the Law" starts up on the soundtrack as Eileen smiles and Áine commences a carnivalesque performance of Conor having sex. Áine holds her hands wide apart and walks with her knees and hips bent to accommodate a giant imaginary erection, and the film cuts to a shot of a woman's hand writing a comm on a tiny piece of paper balanced on her knee. The camera tilts up a dark blue sweater and turtleneck, a gold cross on a chain, and Margaret's angry face. Back in Eileen's cell, Áine sinks down on the bed and, still holding her imaginary penis, starts thrusting her hips, yelling, "Ireland unfree will never be at peace!" The film cuts back to Margaret, who gripes, "she should be isolated; she's not one of us," and back to Áine, who finishes her performance as she and Eileen roar and cackle with laughter. The Clash continues to play, and the film cuts back to Margaret and Geraldine's cell, which is considerably darker, as the two women finish their dull military tasks: writing comms and listening to the news on the contraband radio smuggled into the prison, most likely through someone's vagina.

In addition to Áine's desire for heterosexual sex, *Silent Grace* uses the trappings of beauty to confer traditional gender identities on the prisoners. Played by the radiant Orla Brady, Eileen's beauty is accented by makeup, earrings, a delicate gold necklace, and form-fitting V-neck sweaters. Eileen is the only one of the three republican characters to have a boyfriend, and her clear heterosexuality facilitates her bonding with Áine, who as a "normal" (that is, heterosexual and politically apathetic) teenager is somewhat boy crazy. Eileen's beauty, consistent with Western narrative traditions, is a manifestation of her exceptionality and her natural place as a leader. The fact that she is fair of face reflects her fair-mindedness, which in turn enables her to embrace Áine into the prison community without suspicion or judgment. The film's emphasis on Eileen's attractiveness at the expense of historical accuracy (prisoners were not allowed jewelry and cosmetics; they did not even have soap) and its assertion of her heterosexuality thus undermine the potentially explosive meaning of women's participation in dirt protests and hunger strikes. *Silent Grace* seems to foster sympathy for its characters almost in spite of their politics because, under the dirt of their protest and except for Margaret, they are just ordinary women with the "universal" human dreams of (heterosexual) romance, peace, family love, and freedom.

If the Armagh dirt strike has gotten only limited attention, Armagh's contribution to the 1980 hunger strike has been almost invisible, even within republican discourse and feminist texts on women's political activism, including work specifically on Armagh. Several factors contributed to this absence. The Armagh women did not join the 1981 hunger strike, but they did join the failed group hunger strike of 1980 that ended in a swindle, which in turn refocused attention on the H-Blocks, given that civilian-style clothes—rather than civilian clothes—replaced the prison uniform. In histories of the H-Blocks, this hunger strike is treated as an object lesson for the more strategically organized one that followed it. But given the centrality of the Famine to national narratives of colonial suffering and the tendency to allegorize famine as an emaciated woman, the specter of women starving and willing to die for a republican movement dominated by men may have been too great an inversion of traditional gender roles. In *Mother Ireland*, Farrell explains the Army Council's opposition to women's participation in the dirt protest. Despite the presence of IRA female combatants in prison, there remained an attitude that women were ancillary to the armed struggle. Most men in the republican movement believed that "women weren't supposed to be politically active, that they ought to be taken care of, looked after and certainly not participating in a no-wash protest" (Lyons 1996, 123). Finally, the death of women on hunger strike in 1981 would have given more fodder to opponents of Sinn Féin and the PIRA, potentially shifting blame away from Thatcher and back onto "the men of violence."

In *Silent Grace*, Eileen expresses to Áine in feminist terms her determination to get the Army Council's consent for her participation in the hunger strike. She argues that the hunger strike in Armagh is about women's equality within the republican movement. The Armagh hunger strike, like the Armagh dirt protest, is about political status for women as women as much as it is about political status in the United Kingdom as republicans. In other words: here "woman" is a political identity. But the film soon loses these debates in the melodrama of a woman's decision to travel alone to the brink of starvation. Eileen begins her hunger strike in her cell, sitting on her bed and reading beneath votive candles and an image of the Virgin while her meal grows cold on the floor. The film returns to the printed image of Mary hanging on the excrement- and blood-covered walls several times, and this image of the Virgin becomes fraught with ambivalence. The print seems to evoke Mary as an intercessor for the women ("Holy Mary, Mother of God, pray for us sinners, now and at the hour of our death"), a role that is initially strengthened when Eileen leads them in reciting the "Hail Mary" while screws beat Geraldine offscreen, in her cell.[17] However, while the prayer calms the women down, it is powerless against the violence of the prison system, and the sounds of the brutal beating compete with the voices of the women praying on the soundtrack. When Eileen goes on hunger strike, the film's cuts to the image of the Virgin seem to signify Eileen's own impending transcendence; her body is removed from the earthly needs of food, which means she will no longer produce waste with which to "decorate" her cell, and eventually, she will also stop menstruating, freeing herself from the final sign (or stigma?) of corporeal femininity.[18]

The passing of time during Eileen's hunger strike is rendered in a series of dissolves, which are accompanied by the mournful strains of a violin and lend a compelling vagueness to the film's temporality, suggesting the amorphousness of prison time. The cinematic image dissolves from one space to another, and Eileen fades in and out of that space before the next spatial dissolve. Against a shot of a cell wall, Eileen fades in and disappears, then again in front of the cell window, then pacing in her cell and finally crouching by a window. Through these shots, the film positions

17. Along with Finoula Gheraty and Caroline Seymour, Maeve Murphy co-wrote the play on which *Silent Grace* is based, entitled *Now and at the Hour of Our Death* (Cambridge: Trouble and Strife Theatre Group, 1988).

18. This is not to say that I agree with the notion that menstruation is an essential aspect of being female or of female sexuality. To do so is to fall into the trap of reproductive determinism and to imply that women who have had hysterectomies or who do not ovulate are somehow not "really" female.

her on an inevitable path toward death. Her fading in and out of spaces recalls Gabriel Conroy's inner monologue at the end of *The Dead*, when he mourns the fact that "one by one" the people he knows "are all becoming shades." These shots also speak to the permanence of the prison; it pre-dates Eileen and will endure after her death or release. The days drag on, and eventually Eileen collapses. Áine drags her out to the corridor and several guards lift her corpse-like body and slowly dissolve out of the frame, leaving only the empty corridor and a large cathedral window. Eileen's final evaporation from the frame evokes the assumption of the Virgin—the idea that Mary did not die but, as the only person possessing corporeal and spiritual purity, was assumed bodily into heaven. Eileen becomes iconic; these dissolves anticipate her fusion with the Virgin and with Ireland herself in a later sequence depicting Eileen's near death on hunger strike.

After accompanying Eileen to the hospital and tearfully imploring the governor to do something to help her, Áine is sent back to her cell. The film cuts from her point of view to a low angle shot of the image of the Virgin framed in excrement, which has spread from the wall onto the paper and is now anointing the top of her head, as if to comment on her impotence in protecting the prisoners from the brutal conditions of their everyday lives in jail. Áine has now taken Eileen's place, pacing the cell wrapped in a blanket. The film cuts back to an extreme close-up of Eileen's face in the prison hospital. Her head lies in the center of a pillow, and her long wavy black hair radiates neatly in all directions, recalling John Everett Millais's painting of Ophelia drowned (1851–52). A fiddle plays the dirge-like tones of an Irish song as the film dissolves from a tight close-up of Eileen's dormant face, now anointed with holy oil as part of extreme unction, to a shot of a beach in winter. A bird flies through the gray sky, over the gray-blue water and muted sand-colored shore. The camera slowly tilts up to follow the gull (Eileen's spirit broken free from her body?), and the image dissolves from the seagull to a low-angle shot of weedy dunes set against a steel-gray sky. Two figures, a man and a woman, dissolve into the frame. The violin continues as the film cuts from the dunes to a shot of the governor on the phone and back to the beach where the figures have crossed to the other side of the frame. Eileen's face appears superimposed over the shot of the beach, and the seascape fades away.

Placed between two close-ups of Eileen's face, the scene on the beach is clearly a dream, a wish, or a memory of a walk on the beach with Conor, but not from Eileen's conscious mind. The slow dissolves from her face to the landscape and back to her face align her with the land. The shadows cast by her features evoke visual renderings of Éire, whose high cheekbones and deep-set eyes are a prominent visual element (fig. 7).

The choice of a wintry-gray beach at sunset with a seagull cawing in the sky also pulls this image out of its narrative context and places it in the tradition of romantic cinematic representations of the wind-swept West of Ireland. In this sequence in a film by a woman director about women political prisoners who came to feminism during their incarceration, Eileen is no longer a politically active woman *in* Ireland; she has become Ireland herself. This moment in *Silent Grace* attests to the power of nationalist iconography to displace women engaged in nationalist politics. In this respect, *Silent Grace* is consistent with images of Armagh hunger strikers in murals such as the one in Derry of Raymond McCartney.

In the character of Eileen, *Silent Grace* offers an individual and exceptional hero for Irish women. Her beauty, her uncanny resemblance to Éire herself, her patience, political savvy, kindness, and concern for the welfare

7. A starving Eileen bears a striking resemblance to Éire. From *Silent Grace* (Maeve Murphy, 2001). Courtesy of Maeve Murphy.

of her comrades are unmatched by any of the other women in the film, who struggle alongside Eileen's ability not only to endure prison but to transcend it as well. Just as *Hunger* intercuts Bobby Sands's protracted death in the prison hospital with flashbacks and fantasy shots of him running cross-country alone in the Irish landscape, *Silent Grace* imagines a lone hunger striker willing to sacrifice her body for the salvation of the community. However, also like *Hunger*, the film fails to incorporate that very community and is ambivalent about portraying its political ideology. As Eileen is on the brink of death, Áine hears a news report that the H-Block strike is over. She rushes to the prison's hospital wing to tell the governor the news, but Margaret refuses to acknowledge this information since it has not come through official PIRA channels. Margaret's position is portrayed as callously bureaucratic; her concern about British propaganda is refigured as blind obedience to the Provos. In fact, the three Armagh hunger strikers did spend an extra day on the protest because that was the time it took to get official word from the H-Blocks to Armagh. However, the prison governor steps in and orders Eileen off hunger strike because—at the Catholic prison chaplain's suggestion—he is releasing her under the "cat and mouse act" established in the early 1900s to deal with hunger-striking suffragettes. Eileen's life is saved thanks to state and church intervention, and the dirt protest ends.

Toward the end of the film, Áine takes a hot, vigorous shower, and filth pours off her body and into the drain, raising the question of whether she has also scrubbed off the republican politics she might have acquired in prison. On her last night in Armagh, she and Geraldine link arms and dance. Both of them are wearing fresh clothes, and Geraldine's curly auburn hair bounces as she moves, glimmering with its newfound cleanliness and suggesting a restoration of her femininity with the end of the no-wash protest. Finally, Áine is released into the loving embrace of her mother, and the two of them run down the street away from the wrought-iron prison gates. Like Kathleen in *Some Mother's Son*, Áine is liberated from the prison of nationalist ideology, and the film is resolved with her moving forward while her former cellmates remain in jail. The film offers a historical epilogue: "Armagh Prison was closed in 1988, and all the women were moved to Maghaberry Prison. The women won most of their demands but were never granted political status. A female prisoner was released under the 'cat and mouse act.' She was never rearrested." *Silent Grace* clearly wishes to pay tribute to the Armagh women by telling their story in a marketable narrative format, and it provocatively severs the women's protests from the men's by omitting the 1981 hunger strike. But the film also omits the fact that the situation for women in Armagh and in Maghaberry (to which women were transferred beginning in 1984) actually worsened after the protests. In 1982, on the heels of the H-Block hunger strike, the British government introduced excessive strip searching in Armagh Gaol for remand and convicted prisoners as a means of harassing and intimidating republican women.[19] While the dirt protest may have been successful in obtaining political status for the identity "woman," it was considerably less successful in improving the situation for those women as republicans in British prisons. In the context of the often-contested relationship between nationalist and feminist historiographies, it is not enough to make a film about women prisoners; the very means by which to represent them must be challenged. In *Anne Devlin*, Pat Murphy takes the story of a woman celebrated for her silent loyalty to a nationalist hero and restores her voice. Murphy's project is a cinematic work of feminist historiography, and in telling the story of Anne Devlin, she generates another story: an allegorical history of women's contemporary participation in nationalist politics.

Anne Devlin and Political Allegory

> "The very idea of heroism is horrible."
> —Trinh T. Minh-ha, *Surname Viêt Given Name Nam*

Pat Murphy's *Anne Devlin* answers the challenge in *Maeve* to find a way of remembering Irish history that includes stories of women as agents rather than symbols and that avoids the pitfalls of heroism. In *Mother Ireland*, Murphy explains that in making the film, she sought to expand the

---

19. What constitutes excessive? Remand prisoners who had to appear in court could be fully strip searched up to thirty times on that single day.

discussion of women's presence and participation in nationalist history beyond romantic images of Constance Markievicz, who led a battalion of men against the British on Stephen's Green during the Rising, thus earning a place in history as a heroic nationalist who happened to be female but was able to overcome that handicap. Murphy's objection is not to Markievicz herself, but to her imagined uniqueness in the canon of Irish nationalism at the expense of women who acted in less dashingly dramatic ways. *Anne Devlin* functions as a feminist intervention not only in its subject matter but also in its very structure. Murphy places Anne Devlin at the center of the narrative, but she does not place her at the center of history, and she rarely places her at the center of the cinematic frame. As Gibbons writes, *Anne Devlin* offers a view of history "from the wings, the view, incidentally, which exposes the artifice of spectacle, the contrived nature of dramatic action" (Gibbons 1996, 110). The film is clearly focused through one woman's perspective, but that woman has limited access to the central planning of events; she travels along the margins of history only to be jailed for her political convictions. Through Anne, the film addresses the power dynamics of a centralizing colonial authority but also the problematic ideology of a nationalism that seeks to replace that authority with a patriarchal republic.

Like Markievicz, Anne Devlin has an important place in the heroic memory of Irish nationalist mythology. But unlike Markievicz, who is celebrated for exhibiting stereotypically masculine qualities like leadership and bravery in the face of battle, Devlin is remembered and revered for exuding the feminine virtues of loyalty, self-effacement, and silence. In the standard Anne Devlin narrative, she is loyal to nationalism *through* Emmet; she is the typical faceless servant (or wife) whose consciousness is given freely to her master along with her labor. Anne Devlin is a model not only for women but also for the working classes within the paradigms of patriarchal bourgeois nationalism. She exists in popular memory as "the woman who refused to speak, the faithful servant of Robert Emmet, who, despite protracted torture and maltreatment at the hands of her British captors [she was stabbed and hanged to near death repeatedly over several hours], would not betray her master or the nationalist cause to which he was devoted" (Gibbons 1996, 107). Gibbons locates the construction of this version of Anne Devlin within the context of the newly constructed feminine ideals that emerge in post-Famine Ireland, pointing out that her "virtues of loyalty, fortitude and forbearance, combined with an unlimited capacity to endure suffering, are all too easily reconciled with the domestic ideals of womanhood fostered by the 'devotional revolution'" that swept through Ireland in the decades following the Famine (1996, 107). Modeled on the purity and quiet fortitude of the Virgin Mary, these Catholic ideals "in effect, helped to disenfranchise women from participating in public affairs," and they reached an apotheosis in the apparition at Knock in 1879, which, significantly, was marked by Mary's silence (Gibbons 1996, 108).

In the nationalist framework Gibbons describes, Anne Devlin's heroism is also rooted in her ability to recognize the value of Emmet's life and the expendability of her own. In order to reinscribe this passive, self-abrogating form of silence with a feminist politics of agency, Murphy must smash the links in the chain of events that constitute nationalist history, which, although littered with the debris of failed uprisings, repeatedly recuperates those failures into a heroic narrative. Thus, the United Irishmen's rebellion of 1798 paved the way for Emmet's uprising in 1803, which sparked the flames of the 1916 Easter Rising, which led to a full-blown war of independence in 1918, which ended in 1921 with the liberation of (three-quarters of) the nation (after a bloody civil war). Choosing a failed rebellion and telling its story from the perspective of a woman whose life was actually worse after it, Murphy undercuts the heroism of this historical chain and denies Irish history—and her film's audience—of a comforting sense of liberation. In this regard, *Anne Devlin* crosses the border between histories of the North and those of the republic, simultaneously addressing both. From the outset of the film, Anne is politicized along Irish nationalist lines. Over the course of the narrative, she becomes aligned with those excluded by class or gender from Emmet's vision of an independent Ireland, and in these concerns, the film offers its strongest critique of anticolonial and postcolonial nationalism. *Anne Devlin* acquires different meanings on either side of the Irish border, especially in its historical context of 1984. It serves as a rebuke, a warning, and a tribute. South of the border, at a time when Irish feminism was dismantling conservative, Catholic, middle-class gender ideals, the film reproaches hegemonic Irish nationalism for its patriarchal and middle-class concerns and the historiography that arises out of such a focus, which foregrounds the noble attempts and thwarted dreams of male martyrs. In the North, it offers a warning about the blind spots of a nationalism still in struggle against an occupying power. On both sides of the border, the film pays tribute to the women who fought for Irish independence, who continue to do so, and who are active in other areas of politics as well.

Deconstructing history as it writes a new one, the film works against "the contrived nature" of cinematic spectacle and of a cinematic historiography that positions the spectator as an omniscient observer, watching history unfold before his or her eyes. The film belongs to what has become almost a "golden age" of Irish cinema: the late 1970s and early 1980s, when films took on politically charged subject matter that deconstructed nationalist history and mythology and did so in a style that was clearly in dialogue with the dynamic approaches to the politics of form that flourished in France, Italy, Cuba, Brazil, Germany, Senegal, and the United States in the 1960s and 1970s.[20] Murphy's preference for shots of longer duration, her frequent use of long takes, and her willingness to allow the camera to remain on a space after characters have exited or before they have entered the frame contribute to this self-reflexive treatment of theatricality. Just as important are her visual quotations of European masters such as Vermeer and De Hooch,[21] whose paintings often convey a sense of intrusion on domestic space. In Vermeer's art and Murphy's film, we witness private moments, which are often framed through a doorway, window, or other architectural element, a visual device that works against suture, making us aware of our own spectator presence. Thaddeus O'Sullivan's saturated cinematography becomes almost burdensome in its beauty, whereas the film's sparse soundtrack uses non-diegetic sound minimally and emphasizes the

---

20. For excellent historical analyses of this moment in Irish filmmaking, see McLoone 2000 and Pettitt 2000.

21. Farley also mentions Vermeer as an inspiration as well as Caravaggio and Jacques-Louis David (2000, 33).

sounds of everyday life: the thud of wooden heels on hardwood floors, the rustling of the heavy clothing of the period, the clatter of horses and carts on cobblestone streets, the squeak of a broken water well. The film's silence mimics Anne's political silence, and it also heightens the terror accompanying the moments of violence, since those are the rare instances when the soundtrack becomes crowded with noise.

Reconsidering resistance and questioning historiography from its initial moments, *Anne Devlin* opens in 1798 with a sequence that evokes Walter Benjamin's claim that "to articulate the past historically . . . means to seize hold of a memory as it flashes up at a moment of danger" (Benjamin 1969, 255). In a dark field lit only by their lanterns, a group of women remove a coffin from a wagon, pull the dead body of a United Irishman from a roadside ditch, and place the corpse into the coffin in order to carry him to a proper burial. This action establishes the film's essential project, which, as Gibbons notes, is "an exercise in retrieval" (Gibbons 1996, 110). The women's efforts also add a grim literalness to Benjamin's warning that the danger facing memory "affects both the content of the tradition and its receivers. The same threat hangs over both: that of becoming a tool of the ruling classes. In every era, the attempt must be made anew to wrest tradition away from a conformism that is about to overpower it. . . . Only that historian will have the gift of fanning the spark of hope in the past who is firmly convinced that *even the dead* will not be safe from the enemy if he wins. And this enemy has not ceased to be victorious" (Benjamin 1969, 255).

The dead rebel becomes a symbol of the tradition of resistance in Irish culture, and the film sets up Anne and the other women as historians, rescuing corpses, understanding the pervasive power of the colonizer's grasp. From the perspective of 1984 (and even more recently), it is not only the British who threaten Irish corpses. The dead are vulnerable to ideological appropriation by patriarchal Irish nationalism and its aides in the Catholic clergy. Therefore, the women on-screen are metaphorically performing the work of the woman behind the camera: just as they rescue the corpses of the slain from desecration and oblivion, Murphy's film pulls Anne Devlin from the distortions of heroic nationalist memory. But it is not only Anne Devlin that Murphy wrests from the hands of conservative nationalism; by opening the film in 1798, she resurrects the memory of the 1798 rebellion, which crossed sectarian and class divides. At the end of the film is a dedication to "the women forgotten by history: the women who worked for freedom and are imprisoned for their beliefs," adding another dimension to her project of excavation and restoration. Her choice to dedicate the film to the women who *are* imprisoned for their beliefs and not the women who *were* imprisoned is significant, given the prison protests that immediately preceded the film's creation and that failed to liberate women prisoners from their oppressive conditions, as evidenced in the sharp increase of strip searches for women prisoners exclusively, beginning in 1982.

Based on Devlin's journals (housed at the National Library in Dublin), Murphy's film depicts an educated, well-read woman from a middle-class republican family who literally stands up for her beliefs in the opening sequence. After they load the corpse onto the wagon, the women drive away with Anne at the reins. At dawn, they are stopped at a crossroads by a group of yeomen, whose white-banded red coats stand out against the cool dark tones of the group of women and the rich indigo of the early morning sky. With women walking or sitting on either side of them, Anne and her sister Julia stand up, their heavy skirts and loose long hair blowing in the wind. The women's bodies in this shot have an earthly solidity that, when paired with the haunting and recurring violin motif on the soundtrack, produces a formidable, awe-inspiring sight, one that procures its power through specifically feminine traits. Silently, they stand above the Redcoats, looking down on them, their bodies speaking an unmistakable language of resistance as they barricade the soldiers' view of the contents of the cart.[22] The yeomen step aside and let the women pass. In the next shot, a large group of girls in white dresses run, cheering, to greet the women and the cart, the ribbons in their hair and hands fluttering festively in the breeze. The all-female presence in this shot establishes the

---

22. Gibbons writes, "The female body here offers resistance to vision, just as the obvious contrivance of the image points to the refractory, allusive nature of any visual medium which seeks to address itself to female experience" (1996, 116).

film's gender focus, and it also alludes to the absence of men in the wake of the United Irishmen's rebellion, the failure of which crowded English jails with Irish political prisoners and roadside ditches with the corpses of United Irishmen. In that sense, 1798 has a parallel in Belfast and Derry of the 1970s after the introduction of internment without trial, which led to the removal of thousands of Catholic men from their communities, pushing women to organize politically and fend for themselves.

The film travels with the Devlin family from Rathdrum, County Wicklow, in 1798 to Dublin in 1803, where they run a dairy. Knowing the family's politics, Robert Emmet arrives to ask for their help in constructing an appearance of normalcy for his house on Butterfield Lane, which he has turned into the strategic headquarters for another rebellion. Anne's father agrees to give him chickens for the yard and a horse to keep in the stables, and Emmet asks for a housekeeper as well, "someone to run the house and make it look like the house of an ordinary businessman." Despite her parents' hesitation, Anne volunteers. Although her parents are worried about her safety, their hesitation also stems from concerns over class and gender propriety. Anne's mother reminds Emmet of their class standing, "Mr. Emmet, no one in our family has ever been in service." Emmet explains that Anne will not really be in service, as there is "no house to keep" adding, "Besides, servants get paid for their work." As a volunteer, Emmet later assures Anne, she is an equal to the rebels, "no one's servant." However, as other authors have noted, this declaration of equality is immediately undermined by a cut to the following scene in which one of the strategists behind the rebellion asks Anne to fetch him some hot water and a dry towel (Gibbons 1996, 110; Sullivan 1999, 90). As a *female* volunteer, Anne is not quite the servant of no one: she is the servant of no one in particular, subordinate to the entire movement.

Murphy's film argues for an acknowledgement of the importance of these subordinate tasks. The women in *Anne Devlin* primarily remain within their assigned gender roles, taking care of the details of everyday life. But as Fidelma Farley notes, these actions and tasks are also political ones (2000, 14). In the context of an anticolonial struggle, traditionally female roles can function like the veil in *The Battle of Algiers*: their external appearance can ensure a specific reading from the colonizer in order to hide insurgency within. Femininity in *Anne Devlin* is "denaturalized and made strange," it becomes "a strategy that consciously draws on the 'normality' of gender roles, presenting a surface appearance which bears no relation to the real purpose of the role" (Farley 2000, 21). As one salient example, both Gibbons and Farley cite the moment when Julia sits on the gate at the farm in Rathdrum and brushes out her long black hair, signaling to the rebels that it is safe to come in from hiding. In this moment, Gibbons argues, "the body does not transmit a signal, it *is* a signal" (1996, 114). But Farley makes the vital point that although femininity is used to disguise anticolonial politics, "the masquerade itself can be naturalised, reducing its threat to gender conventions," which "is exactly what happened in the subsequent renarrativization of Anne Devlin's role in the 1803 rebellion" (2000, 22). Such a naturalization of silence, servitude, and fidelity as feminine traits facilitated the exclusion of Irish women from full access to the rights of citizens in the postcolonial nation. This dynamic is also at work in interpretations of the RAC protests, as I argued in my critique of *Some Mother's Son.*

But where Farley sees strategies and Gibbons reads signals, I would argue for an understanding of these actions and performances as tactics in Michel de Certeau's sense outlined in the previous chapter. Anne and Julia, like the mothers of the RAC, are poaching in the realm of femininity. Their actions are politicized in terms of gender in addition to containing anticolonial politics. The women perform femininity not only to hide republican insurgency from the British under a patina of normality, but also because such a performance allows them to participate in the national struggle, a struggle in which they have their own stakes. Murphy pays tribute to these women, and in feminist fashion, she alters the definition of what constitutes political action or contribution to historical events. This shift, in addition to raising questions about how femininity signifies, allows Murphy to explore what the trappings of femininity and the norms of gender behavior might mean to women themselves. Pat Murphy thus opens the door to a critique of middle-class feminism, since women's investment in traditional gender roles does not necessarily mean mere patriarchal servitude in all contexts. Farley addresses this multivalent aspect of gender roles when she points out that in a colonial context, the family is not always the originating site of oppression, as it has been addressed in middle-class Western feminism (2000, 22). Tactically, the women in *Anne Devlin* take the roles they can get and use them to fight the colonial power and to influence the revolution. It is in her performed role as housekeeper to Emmet—a role similar to that of wife—that Anne advises him on practical matters when sentimentality clouds his vision.

In the women's performances of feminine tasks, there is no easy relationship between action and intention. Actions and appearances cannot be taken for granted in their meanings, just as the role of language as a clear system of communication cannot be assumed. Unlike Maeve, whom Murphy defined by her discursiveness, Anne Devlin moves increasingly toward silence. Gibbons argues that language breaks down in the film as an effective and egalitarian means of communication; as the narrative progresses, speech becomes aligned with patriarchal power. He concludes, "it is hardly surprising, that faced with this attenuation of language and its identification with both male domination and imperial domination, Anne should have recourse to silence, to the mute condition of her own body, as a site of resistance" (1996, 112). Gibbons implicitly ties this breakdown in language to the theatrical trappings of insurgency as well as colonial power, linked through the visually similar uniforms worn by both groups of men. In a scene shortly before the rebellion, Anne comes across Emmet's green rebel uniform in his study. She holds it up to her body and looks into a full-length mirror. Emmet comes into the room and, seeing her with the uniform, asks what she thinks of it. She protests against the uniform, calling it a "green version of the redcoats." "We are ourselves," Anne protests, "we should rebel as ourselves." Emmet responds by sharing his vision, "Anne, it will be like a green wave, like the land itself rising up." To which Anne pragmatically points out the uselessness of uniforms for guerilla war: "But the fighting will be in the streets. You will be seen a mile off. How will the men get away?" For Gibbons, Anne's act of holding the uniform against her body in Emmet's mirror is "the nearest she comes to having access to the male symbolic order" (1996, 112), which in true Lacanian fashion occurs in front of a mirror. However, Anne does not mistake this mirror image for an idealized or whole self and does not identify with this figure, masculinized through the uniform. Instead, she rejects it outright.[23]

Murphy provides an additional critique of Emmet's impractical romanticism in the characters of James and Rose Hope. A veteran of 1798, James Hope chastises Emmet for his departure from the United Irishmen's ideals. As Farley argues, Emmet's romantic attachment to the uniform illustrates his passion for the cosmetics of revolution and testifies to Hope's view that the 1803 uprising is essentially a bourgeois one (Farley 2000, 26). As Sullivan points out, Hope's character brings a more radical, socialist discourse into the film, particularly when he chastises Emmet for emphasizing Catholic emancipation (which will benefit and thereby ensure the support of middle-class Catholics) over the needs of the poor—whether they are Catholic or Protestant (Sullivan 1999, 88). His contemporary relevance is strengthened by his northern accent and the fact that he and his wife are from Belfast. As Presbyterians invested in the ideal of economic equality, the Hopes speak to a non-sectarian history of Irish nationalism, a history repressed in Northern nationalist narratives and ejected entirely from unionist ones. Anne quickly befriends the Hopes, and they share their ideals with her. Rose tells Anne that what happened in 1798, with Wolfe Tone's United Irishmen, was "a real rebellion," explaining, "there's a difference when the Revolution is for everyone." Their statement resonates with utopian recollections of the early phases of the Northern civil rights movement, which initially found allies in working-class Protestants, before the unionist state successfully imparted a sectarian divide. The Hopes' argument for the inclusion of all classes in the new state is echoed in Anne's assertion that Emmet's uniforms are just "a green version of the redcoats,"—an Irish version of the middle-class colonial state (Sullivan 1999, 87). According to Declan Kiberd, that was indeed the outcome of decolonization. Writing about the new postcolonial state, he uses the "insignia of the British monarch [that remained visible] under a light coating of green paint" as a metaphor for a "state apparatus [that went] largely

---

23. As a colonized female character, perhaps Anne is used to being a fragmented, imperfect self.

unmodified" (Kiberd 1995, 265). When Anne asserts, "We are ourselves. We should rebel as ourselves," she evokes the two standard translations of *Sinn Féin*: *We Ourselves* and *Ourselves Alone*. Given this context, Anne's reference could be seen as a memorial to the hope lost with the postcolonial silencing of republicanism's class politics in the republic, but it also serves as a caution to a Sinn Féin still embattled in the North.

Anne Devlin is built around the instability of not just verbal language but also visual language. The film's reflexivity and its resonance with contemporary Irish republicanism encourage an allegorical reading of *Anne Devlin* as a representation of "the women forgotten by history: those who fought for freedom and are imprisoned for their beliefs." Murphy's film is flooded with self-reflexivity. Many scenes are shot frontally and framed as if under a proscenium. The haunting and melodramatic violin motif swells at moments of silence and stillness in the image, calling attention to the frame's staticness even as it animates the image. When Anne enters Emmet's study for the first time, the contents of his desk sit idly as if laid out for a still-life painting or left on stage after the actors have departed. Anne opens the shutters of Emmet's study, literally shedding light on his notes. As she explores his desk, smelling the gunpowder, surveying his journal, touching the implements of war, the violin motif returns, lending a significance to her actions, making it clear that she is exploring out of her own intellectual curiosity and not mindlessly tidying up. When Emmet bursts into the room, his presence is enough to stop the music, and as he puts his plans back into obscurity by closing the shutters, he physically displaces Anne, who retreats to the back of the room, enveloped in darkness so that only her face is visible. The composition of the shot echoes that of the hunger strike mural but in a self-conscious way that turns the shot into an illustration of how Irish history is remembered. Emmet's action extends beyond the moment of his exchange with Anne, symbolizing a tendency in nationalist historiography to bar women from the center of the stage and consign them to the wings, that is, when they are admitted into the story at all.

Ultimately, by foregrounding the contrivances of cinematic representation, *Anne Devlin* reveals the theatrical nature of not only Emmet's rebellion but also of the state of emergency. If Emmet is caught up in the theater of resistance, the colonial administration is equally invested in the artifice of the state as a rational institution and the prison as a means of maintaining law and order, and in these moments depicting British violence, the film's resonances with its contemporary historical and political context are most clear. The raid on the Butterfield Lane house after the failure of the rebellion has all the terrifying violence characteristic of descriptions of house raids, arrests, and interrogation in the working-class areas of Belfast in the 1970s. Emmet and his men escape into the darkness, and Anne stays behind to burn evidence that might be used against the revolutionaries. Her youngest sister stays with her. Yeomen burst into the house, and Anne scoops up the little girl and tries to run away through the underground passages built for servants. The yeomen chase and grab Anne and the child. In the next shot, the little girl's nose and mouth are covered with blood, as if she had been hit with the butt of a bayonet. Anne clutches her close to protect her, and the soldiers yank them apart. Anne tries to resist and screams in terror as the soldiers wheel a cart into the yard and tie a rope to its crossbar. They drag Anne out to the yard, tie the rope around her neck and repeatedly hang and release her, demanding that she talk. While Anne is being hanged, the film cuts to a shot of her sister, still bloodied, watching this scene of torture, an insertion reminiscent of the two young girls on swings who watch as British soldiers humiliate Maeve and Roisín in *Maeve*. The fact that there is a witness to Anne's torture brings the sequence into dialogue with Elaine Scarry's insight that its real aim is not intelligence gathering but the transformation of the body of the victim into a surface for the display of state power (1985, 27). For the British army and RUC, house raids and internment were as much a means to terrorize the Catholic population as they were strategies of counterinsurgency. When Anne's family is arrested later in the film, the yeomen follow the pattern of British Army predawn raids on households, arriving at four in the morning and ordering the entire family—small children included—out of bed to stand before them for interrogation (Sullivan 1999, 92). The yeomen arrest the Devlin family, including Anne's terminally ill eight-year-old brother, and take them away. However, they miss the little girl, and she wanders out alone into the rubble of the yard, her white nightgown illuminated by the moon against the deep blue of the night. Her long white gown visually recalls the girls' dresses in the energetic Wicklow sequence, heightening her terrifying isolation in this shot.

Anne is presented before the members of a tribunal, who offer her the opportunity to save her life by giving a full confession, although they do not say what it is she must confess to. She points out the illegality of her internment by indicating that she has not been charged with anything when she asks, "What am I supposed to have done?" Frustrated by her awareness of the contrived conditions of her imprisonment, one of the tribunal members declares, "You are dead to the noble feelings that adorn the character of a woman. You will hang for it." His sentence is the only official statement of a reason for Anne's internment. She will hang not for a charge of treason against Britain, but for her treason against gender norms (Sullivan 1999, 97; Farley 2000, 16). As a woman involved with republican politics, Anne is seen as even more subversive than the upper-class gentlemen rebels who enjoy a less arduous prison sentence, as the jailers have decided to give male prisoners amenities based on their "former stations in life." Anne's anomalous position is reflected in the conditions of her incarceration. As a political prisoner, she is segregated from the women of the general prison population, and as a woman, she is also isolated from the other political prisoners. Once Anne is in Kilmainham, the film enforces her isolation by maintaining the strong sense of her subjectivity established in the earlier sequences.

Major Sirr interrogates Anne in a six-minute-long take that conveys how the threat of violence is enough to provoke feelings of powerlessness in a prisoner; it does not need to be carried out. When he receives no information from her, he tells her she is being transferred to Kilmainham, where she will be under the "care" of Dr. Trevor. Her gender provokes a particularly vitriolic response from the serpentine Dr. Trevor, who speaks to her in the slow, measured tones of a gentleman and a concerned physician. But like the prison doctors in Armagh, this performance of medical professionalism goes no deeper than its surface appearance. In fact, Dr. Trevor uses his methodical tones to ensure that Anne experiences the full violence of his words. When Anne stands at a window in Trevor's office, overlooking the gallows, Trevor informs her, "I have only seen one woman hanged in my time, and I would not like to see such again." But lest Anne think this chivalrous aversion to the sight of a woman hanged pertains to her, Trevor adds, "And yet I would travel any distance to see you hanged," and as he closes his hand around her throat adds, "I would feel pleasure in pulling the rope myself."[24] In the shot, Anne is positioned between the physician's death grip and the scaffold beyond the prison window, both presented as a means of negating her existence.

In Murphy's film, the primary agent of Anne's oppression is Dr. Trevor, not Major Sirr or even the Kilmainham warden, Mr. Dunne. Dr. Trevor performs the role of a physician but actively seeks to undermine Anne's health and welfare. His actions resemble those of the state under emergency measures, which enacts a performance of legality. Arrests, trials, and incarceration maintain the appearance of the rule of law even as the state transforms the judicial and penal systems into branches of occupation. In her memoir of Armagh, under the chapter heading "Control of Bodies," Margaretta D'Arcy addresses the place of medicine in the structures of dominance and repression in Armagh. The chapter heading itself has a double meaning: it alludes to the feminist slogan about women's rights to control their own bodies, and it references how access to the bodies of women prisoners became a way for the authorities to control them. In the Northern Ireland judicial and penal systems, medicine became just another technology aiding counterinsurgency. D'Arcy cites several instances where the medical staff of the prison held the prisoners' health hostage, hoping this would provoke women who needed medical attention to come off the protest. In addition to the case of McLaughlin, D'Arcy cites the well-documented circumstances of one prisoner with special category status who suffered from ulcers while in jail and had an emergency operation upon her release. While she was out of prison, she was arrested again, but this time in 1980. Given her medical condition,

---

24. Sullivan astutely notes that frequently in the film, Dr. Trevor not only lets Anne know that he has complete authority over her body and can therefore "touch her whenever he so desires," but he also does so "in a sexual manner" (98). She argues that this motif calls attention to Anne's gendered status (98), and I would add it resonates with the sexualized violence Armagh prisoners describe to activist groups like WAI and Manchester Women for Ireland, among others.

doctors on the outside stated that she required a special diet, but because she had joined the dirt protest upon her reincarceration, she was denied this medical attention. It took a full two years of petitioning, ulcers, and general bad health before the Northern Ireland Office granted her doctor's request (D'Arcy 1981, 84).

The authorities in Armagh deflected responsibility for the prisoners' welfare by telling women that they had the power to improve their health by coming off the protest, a perspective echoed by the Human Rights Commission. Similarly, in *Anne Devlin*, Dr. Trevor coolly informs Anne, "If you had given the information that was required, you would not be in this position with only a few days left to live." Anne counters this attempt to shift responsibility onto her by throwing the illegality of her situation—as a prisoner facing the death sentence for an undeclared crime—back at her captors, when she reiterates, "I've not been charged with anything." For Anne, Kilmainham is a space of the exception: facing the death penalty for an unnamed crime, she must confess to what her captors refuse to tell her she has done in order to save her own life. The film explicitly presents the absurdity of her situation, foregrounding the theatricality of the state of emergency—in *Anne Devlin*, the patriarchal, colonial law suspends itself in order to make a spectacle of Anne's traitorous body, by torture and possibly hanging. When Anne confronts him with the illegality of her condition, Trevor changes the subject by feigning medical interest in Anne's health. He tells Mrs. Dunne (the warden's wife) that Anne requires fresh air and exercise since she does not look well. The film conveys Anne's wise distrust of Trevor's motives by cutting from a close-up of Anne's face in the prison corridor to the darkened stairwell that Trevor tells her to descend. Although no violence awaits her in the courtyard, Trevor's motives become clear: Emmet stands in the yard, hitting a ball against its wall. Trevor watches from above, hoping for Anne and Emmet to betray a sign of recognition, but Anne and Robert Emmet counter one form of artifice with another by perfectly performing their roles as unknown prisoners taking exercise.

When Anne does need medical attention, it is denied to her. During one of her many lonely nights in the darkened cell, she stands up and pounds on the heavy iron door for Mr. Dunne. Blood is visible on her

hand either from pounding on the door or as evidence that she is menstruating. When Dunne arrives and she yells through the door that she needs
his wife, he tells her that Dr. Trevor has forbidden it. Anne sinks down in
her cell and tears a strip of cloth from her petticoat. In the next shot, when
Mrs. Dunne brings her food hours later, she finds Anne collapsed on the
floor of her cell and takes her up to her quarters to rest, wash, and have a
bit of company. When Trevor discovers the potential solidarity building
between the two women, both of whom are, to varying degrees, trapped
in the prison, he reprimands Mrs. Dunne.[25] She responds that it isn't right
to keep Anne locked up in darkness all day, completely isolated from any
human contact. Dr. Trevor slithers back into medical mode, and in his
dulcet tones asks, "So you're lonely, Anne? Why didn't you say so? I can
arrange company for you." Again, he uses this tone of mock concern to
impress on Anne the fact that he has absolute power over her body; her
physical existence continues at his sufferance. In the next scene, Anne is
moved into the large, crowded, straw-lined room where the general population is incarcerated, and among the lost souls is her sickly brother.

Although Anne is allowed to take her brother back to her cell, their
time together is cut short by his death, which the film represents in a
Pietà-like shot. Anne sits in the corner of her cell, in the only weak shaft
of light to break the darkness. She stares offscreen, at nothing, her face
frozen, cradling the corpse of her young brother. The film cuts from this
still shot to another in Anne's cell, where she lies across the bottom of
the frame, her belly lit by the moonlight that breaks into her cell, but not
strongly enough to counter the heavy darkness that looms above her. In
voice-over she remarks, "I used to know time was passing by my body.
Every month I knew. Now, even that part of me had stopped. Because of
the darkness maybe." Gibbons links these two shots as a unit that presents
Anne's incarceration as "a form of confinement from which there appears
to be no issue or delivery" (1996, 113). The Pietà is part of the film's use of
artifice; he argues, "The 'natural' role of mother is offset by the deliberately

---

25. As Farley notes, the film portrays "the social positioning of women . . . but not at
the cost of obliterating [class and power] differences between women" (2000, 16).

posed and 'artificial' character of the shot; so far from depicting woman as nature, it points to woman as *representation*, the coded, tableau-like composition constituting what is virtually a direct, iconographic quotation from the history of art" (1996, 113). The falseness of this image of motherhood for Anne is confirmed in the following shot in which Anne's period has stopped, "as if displaying the symptoms (or rather the signs) of an imaginary pregnancy" (Gibbons 1996, 113).

Given the centrality of menstruation to the Armagh dirt protest, it is difficult to hear Anne's statement that her period had stopped without thinking of Armagh. Anne does not lament the loss of her period in relation to the future possibility of having a child, but rather in relation to the practical function menstruation held for her as an internal way to mark the passage of time in a situation where she was denied access to any other way to measuring the duration of her incarceration. That the film keeps her in prison longer than the men is consistent with history (Trevor had her briefly transferred to another jail so that her name would not appear on the list of prisoners to be released by the declaration of amnesty), and it also corresponds to the fact that the dirt protest and hunger strike in Armagh both lasted after the men's protests had ended. Because of the women's isolation from the "regenerating center" of the republican movement (as Feldman has characterized the Blocks) there was a time delay in getting information to Armagh. In the case of the hunger strike, this delay could have killed one of the female hunger strikers, and it has also become something of a badge of honor and a symbol of the greater obstacles women face owing to their double oppression. To end the film without depicting Anne's release is to end with her story unresolved and to end with her still incarcerated—one of the women who *are* imprisoned for their beliefs. This brings Anne into the present, into solidarity with contemporary women POWs, into the temporality of the women to whom the film is dedicated.

The film ends with Anne incarcerated in body, and although her voice-over speaks of her release, that release seems to have brought little liberation. She explains, "After my liberation at the end of 1806, I met with some former state prisoners in the street. They passed on without seeming to recognize me, but something like an inward agitation was visible on their faces. And though I was homeless and friendless, I never troubled any of them with my distress, although I'd held the life of more than fifty of them in my hands." This is Anne's last act of silence—not asking her fellow former prisoners for help. Like her earlier silence—her refusal to inform—this act is for herself, for the freedom not to be beholden to the gender restrictions that would inevitably arise had she allowed one of these men to "rescue" her from her poverty and loneliness.

4

Washed Away

Ireland's Magdalene Laundries
and Religious Incarceration

IN 1940, CHRISTINA MULCAHY gave birth at a home for single mothers run by Catholic nuns. She had gotten pregnant by her boyfriend and would have married him, but the nuns intercepted the couple's communication. After the birth, Mulcahy tried to return home, but her father barred her from entering the property and sent his daughter—who at age twenty-two was an adult by legal standards—to the Sisters of Mercy Magdalene laundry in Galway. There, Mulcahy became a "penitent," paying for her transgression under an austere regime of prayer, hard labor, and physical and psychological deprivation. Mulcahy eventually escaped, finding shelter at the home of a nearby friend, who had had no idea that she had been shut away "in that madhouse up the road." Fearing she would be caught and returned to the laundry if she stayed in the country, Mulcahy fled across the border to Northern Ireland. Safely out of reach from her family, the Church, and the agents of the state who enforced their will—such as An Garda Síochána (the Irish police force)—Mulcahy became a nurse, married someone else, and raised a family. She remained silent about the past for over fifty years, finally telling her story to her family shortly before her death from cancer in 1997 (*Sex in a Cold Climate* 1998).

Roughly fifty years after Mulcahy's ordeal, another young woman was detained by the state in what became known as the X Case. In 1992, a fourteen-year-old girl was raped by the father of one of her classmates and became pregnant. With her parents by her side, she traveled to England to seek an abortion. But, because her father had asked the gardaí if the

DNA from the fetal tissue could be used to identify his daughter's rapist, the attorney general learned of the family's intentions, and while they were in England, the parents received an injunction preventing their daughter from having an abortion. They returned home, "where the Irish High Court ruled that the young woman could not leave the country for nine months" (Conrad 2004, 102). News of her detention provoked national outrage against the government, which was seen as hypocritical in its willingness to sacrifice the welfare of an assaulted child in order to maintain the official national fiction that Irish women do not have abortions (Smyth 2005, 92). Eventually, after repeatedly threatening suicide, the young woman was allowed to terminate the pregnancy.

Mulcahy's search for asylum took her from south to north, from the Irish Republic to the (British) province of Northern Ireland, reversing the trajectory typical of nationalists fleeing incarceration and disturbing the Irish nationalist dichotomy that imagines the North to be the "fourth green field" that remains in "bondage" while the rest of Ireland is free. In Mulcahy's story, the Irish Republic is a space of internment and detention, a zone of exclusion where the civil rights of women and girls are routinely suspended for the greater good of a pious nation whose very existence is imagined to be under constant threat by rampant female sexuality. As Martyn Turner's 1992 cartoon for the *Irish Times* indicates, the X Case also raised unpleasant similarities between the Irish Republic and the repressive state to its north. In it, a little girl holding a teddy bear stands inside the borders of the Irish Republic, which are secured by fencing and barbed wire. The text accompanying the drawing reads, "17th February, 1992. The introduction of internment in Ireland—for 14-year-old girls" (reprinted in Conrad 2004, 108).

But, as Mulcahy's earlier story demonstrates, Turner's choice of inaugural date is far too recent. Seventy years before the X Case, almost twenty years before Mulcahy's, and half a century before the North had men behind the wire (as the Long Kesh internees were known), Ireland had begun interning women behind convent walls. From 1922 to 1996, the Catholic Church ran detention centers for women who failed to meet a national standard of femininity that demanded either virginity or married motherhood (or ideally, both). Often rejected by their families and a wider

Irish society, these women were effaced from the image of the nation and placed in a Magdalene laundry. The detention of women without trial for "crimes" committed against a nationalist ideal of female purity collapses any moral distinction between North and South in relation to state of emergency discourses. Furthermore, as spaces of the exception, the Magdalene laundries undermine the historical position of Irish nationalism as a righteous opponent to British colonialism. No longer a heroic nationalism defending Ireland from the excesses of a brutal occupying force, Irish nationalism is now the occupier, bypassing due process in the name of national purity.

This chapter addresses representations of Magdalene laundries in two films released in 2002: *The Magdalene Sisters* (Peter Mullan) and *Sinners* (Aisling Walsh). Both films represent the Catholic Church as a postcolonial occupying power whose control stretches to the police and the family and whose extensive reach as an Irish institution privileged by the state and society complicates the Manichean dichotomy between English colonizer and Irish anticolonial hero. Set almost entirely within the confines of a Magdalene laundry, each film addresses the exceptional status conferred on women whom the Church and family with the state's support labeled as sexually transgressive and therefore a threat to the moral security of the nation. Using the conventions of the prison movie as their narrative blueprints, the films shift the locus of incarceration away from British injustice to a context wherein the prison was predicated on the extra-legal discourses of nationalism and religion, wherein women's agency was circumscribed by a constitution that imagined the patriarchal nuclear family as the principal national unit, and wherein the state accorded "primacy of policing" (to borrow a phrase from British policy in Northern Ireland) to the Catholic Church. In doing so, the films present women for whom the Irish Republic is a zone of total abandonment where religious, civil, and paternal law suspends itself. As James Smith has revealed, whereas a percentage of inmates had been remanded to the laundries after being convicted of a crime, it was more likely that women found themselves in a laundry without having broken any state laws. Furthermore, even the convicted felons placed into the nuns' custody were not given the benefit of a set sentence or parole schedule (Smith 2007, 54–72).

The Magdalene laundries were institutions for "fallen" women—sexually active, unmarried women; victims of rape, incest, and abuse; and women convicted of infanticide or concealment of a birth—as well as women considered to be at risk for a moral fall because they were too pretty, mentally disabled or ill, or the children of fallen or destitute women.[1] Initially established by Protestant reformers in colonized Ireland as halfway houses for prostitutes, Magdalene asylums were taken over by the Catholic Church after the formation of the Saorstát Éireann (Irish Free State), when they became commercial laundries, becoming a source of revenue for the orders that ran them. The institutions existed in Dublin, Galway, Cork, Dun Laoghaire, Waterford, and New Ross, and they were run by four Catholic orders of nuns: the Sisters of Mercy, the Sisters of the Good Shepherd, the Sisters of Charity, and the Sisters of Our Lady of Charity of Refuge (Smith 2007, 28–30). The laundry regime revolved around taxing, monotonous, and symbolic labor: for ten hours a day, six days a week, the women would wash away their sins by hand-washing (without gloves) soiled sheets, clothing, and clerical vestments. They cranked wet clothing though cast-iron wringers, used heavy irons to press clothes, and coated dirty laundry with toxic lye. They varied in age from teenagers as young as fourteen to elderly women who had been institutionalized for life. They were deprived of any luxury as well as fresh air, recreation, and education.

---

1. The reasons for incarceration vary greatly, and although I use the term "women" here, inmates could be as young as fourteen (one woman survivor was incarcerated at the age of twelve). The *Report of the Inter-Departmental Committee to Establish the Facts of State Involvement with the Magdalen Laundries* (also referred to as the McAleese Report) lists the following routes into the institutions as among the most common: women remanded by the court in connection with a crime, minors released from industrial schools, referrals from social services and other institutions at a time when women's shelters and facilities for people with disabilities did not exist, "young girls who had been boarded out and were rejected by their former foster parents when maintenance payment from the authorities ceased," placement in the laundries by family members, and voluntary entry in the absence of homeless shelters and other safety nets for impoverished women (2013, II–III). For excellent and thorough histories of the laundries, see Finnegan 2004 and Smith 2007. Smith's study in particular dispenses with the pretext of moral reform and addresses these institutions as what they were: prisons.

Friendships were forbidden, and to minimize the risk of solidarity or simply mutual tenderness, the nuns had them pray aloud while working. If, as Allen Feldman has argued, the goal of cellular incarceration in the North was a recoding of the prisoner's existence from freedom fighter to common criminal, the goal of the Magdalene laundries seems to have been a recoding of the women's existence from "woman" or "girl" to offender against the family, the Church, and therefore the Irish nation. In other words: the existence of the laundries criminalized female sexuality.

Although nuns ran the laundries and the Church profited from the unpaid labor of the inmates, they could not have existed without the collusion of the family and the postcolonial Irish state, as Smith effectively demonstrates in his groundbreaking study of the laundries. Smith argues that the laundries were embedded in what he calls Ireland's "architecture of containment," a set of laws and institutions that "empowered the decolonizing nation-state to confine aberrant citizens, rendering invisible women and children who fell foul of society's moral prescriptions. In this way . . . the state regulated its national imaginary" (2007, 47). Although officially women went into the Magdalene laundries "voluntarily," Smith reveals that the state "repeatedly sought ways to funnel diverse populations of women into the nuns' care" and "provided the religious orders with direct and indirect financial support" (2007, 47–48). Many of the women were unaware of the fact that they had the legal right to leave, partly because any attempts at escape were severely punished (Finnegan 2004, 45). But even if they managed to escape, as Mulcahy did, they usually had nowhere to go and no financial means of survival. Without a respectable job on the outside or a male relative coming to claim them, women could remain institutionalized indefinitely. Unpaid, undereducated, and branded as immoral, Irish women in the laundries were utterly devoid of economic, cultural, or social capital. As much as they may have despised the conditions of the laundry, they were also dependent on it for survival.

Looking at the Magdalene laundries within the context of "occupied Ireland," I see the state of emergency that enabled them to thrive as part of a wider carceral dynamic in all of Ireland. Understanding confinement in a laundry as an injustice on par with internment in Long Kesh illuminates the ways that the national imaginary of a postcolonial Ireland remains dependent on an image of the Irish nation as embattled and innocent, thus sidestepping the issue of women's oppression. Representations of the Magdalene laundries structured around the prison genre reveal the dangers of Irish nationalism's holy alliance with Catholicism, and although they are set in the past, both *Sinners* and *The Magdalene Sisters* have the potential to raise uncomfortable questions about women's rights after the 1960s as well. One of the many values of Smith's book is his commitment to link the history of the laundries to the trauma of present-day victims and survivors of Catholic institutional abuse. But his history of the laundries also has implications for a wider understanding of where "woman" as a political identity fits into Irish nationalism, past and present, North and South. The laundries fall at the extreme end of a postcolonial nationalist continuum that sought to replace revolutionary women—including suffragists and Irish republican women—with symbolic domestic ideals. As Kathryn Conrad argues, "the marital trope of Britain as the colonial 'husband' of the unruly Irish family echoes in the subtext of Irish nationalist discourse wherein the Irish man [after independence] was expected to control both family cell and nation." The existence of politically active women, she explains, threatened this construction of Irish postcolonial masculinity, which replaced historical women with allegorical and symbolic ones. Images of Mother Ireland and celebrations of the rebel's mother "simultaneously idealized women's place in the private sphere and attempted to limit their public appearances to the merely inspirational and iconographic" (Conrad 2004, 12). Through these figures, Irish nationalism enacted a form of historical amnesia. The clause in the 1937 constitution that imagined domestic motherhood as "woman's" national duty was retroactively legitimated through a rewriting of Irish nationalist history.

The experiences of women in Magdalene laundries at times resemble those of political prisoners in Northern Ireland from the introduction of internment (1971) through the era of excessive strip searches in Armagh and Maghaberry prisons (early 1980s). The incarcerating institutions tried to appropriate the prisoner's body and recode it as one that posed an immediate threat to national security (political in one case, moral in the other) and that was in dire need of rigorous punishment and reform.

Like prisoners, Magdalene inmates were issued uniforms designed to strip their identity, make them physically uncomfortable, and recode them as deviant; underwear became especially important in this project because the uniform included a tight bodice of calico designed to flatten their breasts. In the jails of Northern Ireland and in the laundries, the body of the inmate became a highly charged signifier because of its stubborn materiality. The violence unleashed on the prisoners in both contexts was a means of control and a display of power for its own sake. In order to break the inmates, prison guards and clergy placed the body of the prisoner at the center of different scenes of physical and psychological torture. Maureen O'Sullivan's experience of the nuns at the Good Shepherd laundry in New Ross, County Wexford, was one of constant surveillance and humiliation: "Undressing, you were watched; dressing, you were—you couldn't go in to wash your teeth, wash your hands, but they were watching you, passing terrible remarks on you. Degrading you all the time" (Coleman 2009). O'Sullivan's treatment bears a striking resemblance to the use of strip searching as a gender-specific form of discipline in Armagh and Maghaberry prisons, where female prisoners were strip searched multiple times a day and guards would typically jeer at the women's bodies. Female prisoners frequently discussed feeling humiliated, degraded, embarrassed, and ashamed (McAuley 1989, 72–74; Republican POWs 1991, 10). In both contexts, those with power over the inmates exploited prevailing cultural attitudes about modesty, shame, and sex in order to reconfigure the prisoner's body as a betrayer.

Even though their conditions of incarceration share key similarities, the exceptional status conferred on the "penitents" differs from that placed on men and women nationalists in the North. The orders established a severe regime for the internees that put the British prison system to shame in terms of its success at breaking inmates and maintaining near-total surveillance. This efficiency was due in large part to the extensive role Catholicism played in the homes, schools, and public life of Ireland. Political prisoners in Northern Ireland were able to alter their position as *homines sacri* by invoking the higher authorities of Irish nationalism and Catholicism. Because they refused to recognize the legality or legitimacy of the state that held them captive, any abuse or degradation the prisoners suffered became fodder for a discourse of national martyrdom. Although this symbolic language was more readily available to men, male and female republican prisoners saw themselves as part of a proud and long history of Irish national resistance, a self-image that was typically supported within the communities and publicly affirmed in republican murals, street protests, demonstrations, pamphlets, and journals. In contrast, the laundries were sanctioned by a postcolonial state that was supposed to have cast out its oppressor. As such, the women's jailers were no longer external to Irish culture or opposed to Irish nationalism; instead, it was the prisoner herself who was an enemy of not just the state but also the nation. In her failure to adhere to the strict Catholic ideals that distinguished the Irish from their debauched British and Protestant oppressors, she had betrayed the cross-border, ideal Irish nation. The women's jailers were representatives of an institution that had been a fundamental part of Irish identity at least since the penal laws of the eighteenth century politicized Catholicism by criminalizing it.[2]

Sinners and *The Magdalene Sisters* share important narrative elements that enable them to cover a broad scope of horrors associated with the laundries. Nuns mercilessly beat their charges; families fully support the Church's authority; the surrounding community is well aware of the laundry's existence. Each film has a character who is sexually assaulted by a priest and dragged off to an insane asylum when she dares to speak up about the violation. Women try to escape in each film and are brought back to the laundry by family or local residents. Each film also depicts the Garda Síochána as a Church security force rather than a civic one. In *The Magdalene Sisters*, gardaí flank a parade of Magdalenes on a religious procession through the local streets, while in *Sinners*, the police search the

---

2. Furthermore, the Catholic Church had begun to consolidate power over Ireland long before Irish independence, when, to more effectively control the Irish, Britain gradually legalized Catholicism and expanded the Church's power, especially in the realm of education. Of course, this collusion with British colonialism was also edited out of amnesiac nationalist histories. For an in-depth explanation of Catholicism's opportunistic ties to Irish nationalism and British colonialism, see Inglis (1998) and McLoone (2000, 9–32).

surrounding town for an escapee.³ Both films allow their main characters to exit the laundry in the end, although they are both careful to resist presenting physical escape from the laundry as liberation for the characters; in this way, release from the laundry offers little emotional release for the spectator.

The question of release and escape is relevant not only to the stories of these films, but also to each film's understanding of Irish history and the contours of occupation in Ireland. Like Patricia Burke Brogan's play *Eclipsed* (also about a Magdalene institution), *The Magdalene Sisters* and *Sinners* are set in the mythical decade of national modernization, the moment when Ireland was supposed to have broken with its poverty-stricken, religious past and sped toward technological advancement and membership (by 1973) in the European Economic Community (EEC). Even the presidential election of John F. Kennedy seemed to vindicate Ireland's relevance to world events, and his smiling visage graces the mise-en-scène of both *The Magdalene Sisters* and *Sinners*. But whereas the choice to set these films in this particular decade reinforces a separation between a patriarchal, parochial past and an enlightened European present, the films also undermine a sense of escape both in their final images and in their critique of the patriarchal nuclear family's place at the center of Irish national identity. In *The Magdalene Sisters* and to a lesser degree in *Sinners*, the family functions as another institution of oppression that works in tandem with the Church to maintain national female chastity.⁴

3. Smith argues that through the presence of the gardaí at the religious procession, *The Magdalene Sisters* takes the Irish state to task for its collusion with the Church: the police stand on either side of the penitents, clearly contradicting the notion that the women were there voluntarily (2007, 139). But it is also possible to read this image as imagining even the state security forces to be under direct orders from the Church. Thus, if there is a critique of the state, the state remains subordinate to the Church in controlling Irish people rather than a civil, secular entity that facilitated and encouraged Catholic postcolonial occupation.

4. For example, Smith argues that the film takes to task the Church, the family, patriarchal society, and the state. Fintan O'Toole (2003) notes the film's critique of the Irish family and its centrality to society, and Jonathan Murray (2004) also points this out. I agree that the family is a central point of focus in the film; I am less inclined to agree with Smith over the inclusion of state culpability.

Families in these films are not ahistorical sources of refuge, nor are they horrifically dysfunctional groups presided over by tyrants. By imagining the family as a site of exclusion and an institution invested in maintaining its own power by reinforcing hegemonic conceptions of gender and sexuality at the expense of its own members if necessary, the films implicitly connect past to present and Ireland to the world beyond, owing to the many countries (including, of course, the United States) that persist in imagining the "family" and its "values" to be in constant, dire peril.

Despite their similarities, *Sinners* and *The Magdalene Sisters* diverge in their narrative structure and audio-visual style, which in turn affects how each film imagines the Catholic Church as a postcolonial occupier. Some of these differences stem from the circumstances surrounding each film's production and distribution. Mullan's film circulated at international festivals and won several awards (including the Golden Lion at Venice) before being picked up for global distribution by Miramax. In contrast, Walsh's film was made for television, aired on RTÉ and BBC, and has not circulated beyond the borders of Ireland and Britain. But as a made-for-TV movie, *Sinners* has the advantage of being broadcast directly into the home, the inner sanctum of both Catholicism and Irish nationalism. Thus, while the film is a straightforward, character-driven television drama that relies on exposition and narrative events to tell a story of Church oppression, this alone is not enough to immediately disqualify it from the category of political film. The problem with Walsh's film has to do with the ways that *Sinners* often seems to posit the Church as an external occupying power, one that secured a hold over Irish people almost against their will. Furthermore, like *Silent Grace*, the film uses gender clichés to make its characters more sympathetic, and in doing so imagines patriarchy as a thing apart from femininity. Just as *Some Mother's Son* contrasted the steely coldness of Margaret Thatcher with what it imagined to be women's essential maternal impulse, *Sinners* encourages identification with characters along the lines of heteronormative femininity, making the nuns the antithesis of "natural" feminine warmth.

Mullan's film presents the Church as a far more insidious occupier, one that secured power through commonsense notions that failed to question the historical link between Catholicism and Irish identity. Over the course of Mullan's film, details accumulate that silently convey the pervasiveness of Catholicism in Irish life. From the first shot on screen of a *bodhrán* embellished with a scene from the Passion, the trappings of Catholicism are ubiquitous and often ironic: rosary beads hang from a chair next to a glass of whiskey; the words "God is Just," carved on a beam in the laundry dormitory, appear when characters whisper about the injustice of their incarceration at night; a statue of Jesus with arms outstretched in benediction is mounted high in a corner of Sister Bridget's office and is often visible when she beats the inmates. Each of the nuns wears a large metal crucifix around her neck, while more crucifixes and crosses hang throughout the laundry room and hallways of the compound. Crispina wears a Saint Christopher medal and holds it to her lips to commune with her child, whom her sister brings regularly to the laundry gates to wave at his mother. Even the burlap sacks that the women put clean laundry into contain a cross and quatrefoil design. It is this omnipresence of the Church in the mise-en-scène that allows Mullan to mobilize a potent and eloquent critique of an institution that repeatedly violated its own tenets in the context of the laundries, through labor exploitation, sexual abuse, physical violence, and profit. Through such detailed observations as well as the film's broader narrative events, *The Magdalene Sisters* offers a more complex understanding of Catholic occupation than *Sinners*, one that extends to Irish nationalism.

Guests of the (Postcolonial) Nation

Mullan has candidly stated his use of the prison genre in *The Magdalene Sisters*, naming both *The Shawshank Redemption* and Milos Forman's *One Flew over the Cuckoo's Nest* as central influences (Murray 2004, 154). The presence of the genre's narrative outline elucidates the carceral nature of the laundries even though it also offers emotional catharsis in the form of escape.[5] While critics have characterized Mullan's choice as fulfilling

---

5. In his review of *The Magdalene Sisters*, Fintan O'Toole writes, "If you have seen *The Shawshank Redemption*, you know the broad shape of *The Magdalene Sisters*: unjust

the economic needs of commercial cinema and thus sensationalizing the story, through his reworking of the genre within a gendered and religious framework, the film reveals the extent to which resistance is limited when the prisoner is jailed by her own body. The prison movie approaches the penal system from a position of radical exclusion and physical displacement. Guilty or innocent, justly or wrongfully convicted, the characters in prison movies as diverse as *Carandirú*, *Cool Hand Luke*, and *The Mansfield 12* are subject to punishments that far exceed their crimes and reveal the noble aim of rehabilitation to be a lie. In the prison genre, the state—represented by corrupt wardens, crooked politicians, and sadistic or kind-but-ineffective guards—assumes a violent, brutalizing form. Because it generally pulls audience sympathy away from the forces of law and order and toward convicts—who are otherwise invisible in society—the genre is also useful for representations of the Magdalene laundries that seek to contradict the history of idealized cinematic images of clergy and Catholic faith that dominate such Hollywood films as *The Song of Bernadette*, *The Sound of Music*, *Boys Town*, *Going My Way*, *The Quiet Man*, and *The Bells of Saint Mary's*, which Mullan quotes in *The Magdalene Sisters*.

The audio-visual style and editing of *The Magdalene Sisters* further emphasize the confinement, surveillance, and deprivation central to incarceration, and these formal elements impart a visceral sense of confinement. Mullan limits his color palette to the black and white of the nuns' habits and institutional browns, grays, greens, and creams. He uses a tightly restrained field of vision, cutting among medium shots, close-ups, and extreme close-ups. This intense editing pattern persists throughout the film, and it establishes a frustrating experience of restriction—the visual equivalent of being bound in a straitjacket—that enhances the narrative violence unleashed on

---

incarceration, sadistic cruelty, heroic endurance and eventual escape." Elaborating on O'Toole's observation, Murray writes, "Sister Bridget is initially presented as the sadistic Head Warden, taunting the central trio with the punitive terms of their sentence; victims are institutionally stripped of their names and personal histories . . . minor characters quickly instigate the standard prison movie's generic subplots, themes and character types such as the difficulty but necessity of escape . . . and the decrepit or psychically broken collaborator" (Murray 2004, 154).

the spectator from the very first moments of the film. With the exception of one shot, *The Magdalene Sisters* restricts its range of story information to its four main incarcerated characters. We do not leave the laundry until the last of these women do. In fact, in the sequences before Margaret, Bernadette, and Rose enter the laundry, each young woman is shot in a way that signifies her condemnation to confinement. Margaret's voice is taken from her, Bernadette is cloistered in the yard of her industrial school, and Rose is framed within the narrow confines of a hospital corridor.

The Magdalene Sisters divides its focus across four main characters: Margaret, Bernadette, Rose, and Crispina. Each woman is in the laundry for a different "crime": Margaret was raped and had the audacity to tell someone rather than suffer in quiet shame; Bernadette grew up in an industrial school and had the bad luck to beautiful, which put her at risk for a moral fall; Rose got pregnant; and Crispina (whose back story is not shown) had the misfortune of being mildly developmentally disabled and becoming pregnant. Each of the young women responds differently to her incarceration, and as in the prison film, the way each character handles the conflict between individual survival and a shared experience of incarceration within an institution that forces conformity at the expense of personal history and identity is a central part of her development. Margaret survives by remaining compassionate; her care for Crispina becomes an act of conscious resistance in a context designed to shatter the subjectivity and humanity of its inmates. Bernadette remains defiant until the end; her wrongful conviction even by the narrow standards of Catholic morality— she points out, "I've never been with any lads, ever"—enables her to see the injustice of the institution for what it is. Rose and Crispina, who seem to be more religious, have a harder time resisting the institution, which is partly symbolized in the fact that both women are renamed by the nuns. Rose becomes Patricia, and Crispina, who has pin-straight, bobbed hair, explains that the nuns changed her name from Harriet to Crispina, which means "girl with the curly hair."[6]

6. While this moment offers a note of humor at what appears to be the nun's complete indifference to how they assign names, in a "game" of sexual humiliation where

After the pre-title sequences explaining how Margaret, Bernadette, and Rose came to be incarcerated, the film depicts the three new inmates being inducted into the system together. Dressed in shapeless, rough, brown shirtdresses, the young women enter Sister Bridget's office. With her back to the camera, so that only the shape of her black habit is visible, Sister Bridget is the outline of a nun, a generic stand-in for all nuns. The portrait of JFK—who was assassinated in the previous year—that rests on her desk is both an Irish Catholic stereotype and a *memento mori* to the dead president and the progressive, youthful hope he symbolized. Sister Bridget explains the mission and rules of the laundry to the young women in a monotone, as if by rote, "The philosophy at Magdalene is a simple one. Through the powers of prayer, cleanliness, and hard work, the fallen may find their way back to Jesus Christ, Our Lord and Savior." As she speaks, the camera cuts to a close-up of the large metal crucifix around her neck and tilts down to her hands, which are busy counting, rolling, and organizing Irish punt (pound) notes, the laundry's profits. Without pausing in her mechanical counting, Sister Bridget continues in voice-over, and the film offers a series of shots of women at work in the laundry, "Mary Magdalene, patron saint of the Magdalene convents, was herself a sinner of the worst kind. . . . Salvation came only by paying penance for her sins, denying herself all pleasures of the flesh, including food and sleep, and working beyond all human endurance so that she might offer up her soul to God and so walk through the gates of Heaven." When Sister Bridget mentions the gates of Heaven, the film cuts to a shot taken through a windowpane in the laundry of women hanging sheets on a clothesline. Sister Bridget explains that the soiled sheets and clothing the women will be washing for ten hours a day "are the earthly means to cleanse your very souls, to remove the stains of the sins you have committed. Here, you may redeem yourself and, God willing, save yourself from eternal damnation. Breakfast is at six; prayer is at half-past six. . . ."

Sister Clementine judges which women have the largest and smallest breasts and buttocks, Crispina "wins" for most pubic hair, a moment that raises the possibility that the assignment of "Crispina" to Harriet is a sexual joke at her expense.

Throughout Sister Bridget's orientation, the film presents shots of anonymous women working. Dressed in the same brown dresses and muted blue aprons, they fold starched collars into towels, press heavy irons onto wet clothes, crank large sheets through cast-iron wringers, and mark on a chalkboard the type and number of clothing items the laundry takes in and returns. The women's actions are efficient; they work in utter silence. The only sounds to coexist with the nun's voice-over are those that belong to the women's tedious labor and the ubiquitous rustle of the paper notes Sister Bridget continues to count throughout her introduction, implying that the women are the unseen workers whose grueling labor produces the profit that Sister Bridget holds so dear. When she explains that working in the laundry is not punitive labor but an opportunity for redemption, the film cuts to a close-up of her black dividend book and pans across a pile of loose punts, a box full of money, and banknotes tightly rolled and stacked in a cookie tin. Finally, the camera tilts up and pulls focus to reveal a small wooden cross that sits on the nun's desk amid her sea of profit.

Mullan's focus on Sister Bridget's concern with money risks transforming the nun into a villainous caricature, a profiteer whose greed stands as a moral lesson to the audience. However, the film's aesthetics work to contain such melodramatic excess. The use of close-ups in the nun's office constricts our field of vision to the minuscule. The film forces its audience to focus on the tedious and mundane things that consume Sister Bridget and the women in her care. The penitents' existence has been reduced to dirty clothes, priests' collars, lye, starch, clothespins, and irons—a nightmarish extension of the cult of domesticity that expects women to perform such labor for free within the home. For Sister Bridget, obedience to the Church and aid in its wealth make up her world. Crucifix, money, dividend book, and cross are presented in a stream of information about the nun before we even see her face; if dirty clothes are the earthly means for the penitents to cleanse their souls, then money becomes the earthy means through which Sister Bridget may serve God. For both penitents and nun, the Church's exploitation of unpaid laborers is reimagined and sanctified as a mission of redemption. The juxtaposition of religious and capitalist iconography functions ironically to make a comment on the corruption of spiritual ideals. At the same time, crosscutting between a nun's hands counting money and an exploited labor pool yanks the Catholic Church firmly back down to earth and insinuates that the laundries lasted as commercial enterprises for decades *because they were profitable*; it remained in the Church's economic interests to run them.[7] The convergence of God and money in this sequence is not a melodramatic cliché; it is a Marxist cliché, but one that works well in this context as a cinematic trope ensuring that Mullan's film begins from a critical analytical position that discredits the Church's alibi of redemption and presents the women as exploited workers in a commercial enterprise. Sister Bridget may be head warden but she is also middle management, concerned with the company's bottom line. Mullan's economic argument is directed at the middle-class values that became a central part of the postcolonial state's identity and thus facilitated and worked in tandem with conservative Catholic hegemony.

Sinners adheres even more closely to the conventions of the prison genre, establishing a clear main character in Anne-Marie, who is psychologically stronger than the others and thus better able to resist institutionalization. Like many prison films, *Sinners* introduces its audience to the institution's power structure by depicting the new inmate's induction into the prison system. Allen Feldman has characterized the moments essential to this process—when prisoners are stripped, washed, examined, assigned a prison number, and given a uniform—as "identity fixing events for both the inmate and his [sic] keepers" (1991, 155). Such events rob prisoners of

---

7. The McAleese Report refutes this characterization, stating, "The results of the financial analysis carried out tends to support a view that the Magdalen Laundries were operated on a subsistence or close to break-even basis rather than on a commercial or highly profitable basis" (993), a claim that suggests Mullan's portrayal is factually misleading. But as I argue, the film's style undermines what critics have sometimes taken for its commitment to realism. The insinuation that the Church made a fortune off the backs of Irish women may be inaccurate, but it allows the film's critique of religious exploitation to extend beyond the borders of Ireland, and beyond Catholicism, to raise questions about the implications of the economic, political, and social power that religious institutions wield in ostensibly secular states. In this wider project, the film is relevant to the contemporary United States as well.

their individuality and re-socialize them as members of a deviant collective whose bodies and minds must be reformed according to the laws of the institution. After her social-climbing aunt and guardian discovers that Anne-Marie is pregnant from a consensual incestuous relationship with her brother, Eamonn, she signs her into the local laundry. Once inside the laundry walls, Anne-Marie is taken to a room and told by a nun to strip. When she hesitates out of modesty, the nun snaps at her, "You've nothing we haven't seen before," trivializing her sense of embarrassment. Anne-Marie's clothes are taken away; a nurse examines her; a nun cuts off her long wavy hair and tightly wraps a piece of elasticized cloth around her breasts. She is told that to protect the privacy of the penitents while they're on the inside, no personal information is allowed, including names. Anne-Marie is thus stripped of the last vestige of her identity on the outside, and she becomes Theresa the penitent. Like the internees in *The Magdalene Sisters*, Anne-Marie is thrown immediately into the laundry's work regime. Before she has a chance to process what has just happened to her, Anne-Marie is brought to a large washtub. A nun tells her to get to work; as she stands somewhat dazed and helpless, an inmate hands her a bar of soap. The characters repeat this action several times in the film, and while it conveys the serialization of bodies that come through the laundry, the gesture also functions as a quiet one of sympathy and shared oppression.

Secondary characters in *Sinners* also follow the genre's typology. Rita functions as the hardened convict who hides her vulnerability under a shell of swagger. Niamh shares with Kate in *The Magdalene Sisters* the role of the institutionalized older inmate—the bleak future that awaits those broken by the system. Kitty is the mature convict who tries to get by without making waves, and who educates the newly incarcerated Anne-Marie, while Angela is the weakling singled out for extra abuse by the clergy screws. Like Crispina in *The Magdalene Sisters*, Angela is raped by a priest, and like Crispina, when she talks about it she is permanently removed to a psychiatric facility. The Magdalene laundry in *Sinners* has a resident medical expert, Nuala, who lives in the compound but as a lay employee has the freedom to come and go as she pleases. Nuala obeys the mother superior warden, but she is also kind to the women, consistently furrowing her brow in concern for their well-being and speaking to them as a friend and peer. Visually, she stands out from the nuns in her colorful, feminine clothes. Her dresses are cinched at the waist to reveal an hourglass figure, and the knee-length hemlines show off her calves, enhanced by the heels of her stylish pumps. Unlike Nuala, Walsh's nuns are black, formless entities visually indistinguishable from one another. They recall anonymous uniformed prison guards or Tom Inglis's memories of priests as "dark, distant, unapproachable . . . figures of power who instilled fear" (1998, 2). Their cruelty places them in opposition with what the film imagines to be the essentially warm nature of women, which it conveys through its portrayal of the inmates and Nuala. If the nuns function as sadistic screws who savagely beat the women until their faces are swollen and bruised, Nuala is the kind prison guard who worries about the prisoners' welfare without realizing that the entire institution is designed to weaken their physical and mental health, and that she herself is compromised.

In *Sinners*, genre and gender interact to present the nuns as deviant and the incarcerated women as healthy and ordinary. In order to achieve this play with femininity, the film parts ways with strict historical accuracy. The character of Nuala, as a lay employee with living quarters on the laundry premises and the freedom to come and go as she pleases, seems highly improbable, and the film presents her as a modern career woman whose medical training puts her at odds with the archaic realm of the female religious. Kitty and Anne-Marie have an equally unlikely friendship. They hug, chat in bed together at night, and refer to each other as best friends. When Anne-Marie discovers Kitty's affair with the garda officer Patrick, Kitty reassures Anne-Marie with the explanation that they plan to get married so that she can keep her baby and liberate Anne-Marie from the laundry as well. Their sisterly intimacy seems unhindered by the strict surveillance and grueling routine of the laundry. Whereas Mullan's film is relentless in its cycle of work, prayer, food, and sleep, *Sinners* frequently returns to an association room, where the women gather for recreation, a chance to listen to the latest pop hits on the radio, and dance. They share laundry gossip, knit, write letters, and discuss their hopes for the future. In one scene, several of the women even congregate in Nuala's room to help her get ready for a date. They sit or lie on her bed, select which purse she should take, and giggle when Rita reminds her to tell them all the details, including "how many times he kisses you." Niamh reminds Rita that marriage can be its own kind of trap, but she remains a minor character throughout the movie, marginalized among the women who live vicariously through Nuala's heterosexual adventures. Like *Silent Grace*, which uses talk of sex and boyfriends to soften its political prisoners, *Sinners* uses the desire for heterosexual romance as a universal longing that unites all "normal" women.

The romantic aspirations of Nuala, Rita, Kitty, and Anne-Marie (whose relationship with Eamonn is rewritten as a story of lovers torn apart by cruel circumstance) distinguish them from the asexual nuns. *Sinners* uses romance just as the prison film demarcates its hero's heterosexuality from other forms of sex—consensual or not—that it lumps together as perverse. In its attempt to remove the stigma of shame from sexuality, *Sinners* constructs the nuns' celibacy as decidedly unnatural, which in turn mobilizes the cliché that their sadism stems from sexual frustration—a trope of troubles films seeking to explain the excesses of the IRA as well.[8] In one scene, Kitty glides through a maze of sheets hung up to dry in the laundry, searching for Patrick, whom she usually meets there for sex. She whispers his name and pulls back a white sheet. A discordant note sounds as Kitty reveals Sister Bernadette waiting behind the sheet, clutching a rubber truncheon. The film cuts to a shot of the women scrubbing clothes; over the splashing of water, they hear Kitty's screams from off-screen. When she resumes her place by the women, Kitty has welts on her arms, and blood trickles from her forehead, nose, and mouth.

Instead of challenging a social structure that imagined "woman" as merely a synonym for "mother," the film uses the women's motherhood to make them sympathetic characters. Walsh's film features many pregnant characters—including Kitty, Rita, and Anne-Marie—who give birth in the laundry and are allowed to take breaks from work in order to nurse their babies before they are adopted by Catholic couples abroad. As Smith points out, *Sinners* fuses together "the Magdalene asylum, mother and

8. See John Hill, "Images of Violence," discussed in the introduction of this book.

baby homes, and other residential institutions." While the film portrays its characters giving birth on the grounds of the Magdalene asylum, "historically, there is no evidence to corroborate such representation" (Smith 2007, 224n12). Fiction film often elides historical fact for narrative simplicity, but here the inclusion of pregnant women and nursing mothers enables Walsh to present her characters as caring mothers who cradle and coo at their babies, nurse them, and boast of their health and beauty. This choice performs an important historical intervention that establishes the Magdalene women as the rightful mothers of children who were stolen from them, but it also promotes a dominant national ideal of the grieving mother. The young mothers' gentleness is juxtaposed with repeated shots from the nursery window of Nuala handing a swaddled baby off to an anonymous figure in a car who then drives offscreen, signifying the historical fact that once their babies were taken away, most women never saw them again and never learned what happened to them.

The way *Sinners* approaches the task of exonerating the Magdalene internees might clear them of immorality charges, but it leaves dominant constructions of Irish femininity—in which motherhood is the primary role for women and reproduction is the female body's most valuable asset—largely unquestioned. While the film portrays what was probably a heartbreaking moment for at least some of the women forced to give up their babies, it also precludes the possibility that women and teenage girls who had gotten pregnant might not want to be forced to carry a pregnancy to term or keep their babies afterward. In this way, *Sinners* successfully quarantines the history of Magdalene laundries from other women's issues, past and present, including access to abortion. The story of the Magdalene laundries literally hits home through the film's televised broadcast, and adding to how the film troubles the domestic sphere is the fact that Anne-Marie and Eamonn's incestuous relationship is explicitly presented as consensual, which portrays the family as a dysfunctional, perverse unit and suggests that by repressing sexuality and withholding sexual education in the name of the national family, Ireland is destroying itself from within. But *Sinners* weakens the subversive force of this infiltration by displacing a critique of the family onto the Church. The Church's cruelty stems in large part from its callous disregard for the mother-child bond, a bond idealized by the national family. In fact, the film expressly goes out of its way to present Irish women as maternal. Until she gives birth, Anne-Marie repeatedly expresses resentment over her pregnancy and wishes her fetus would die. She understands her pregnancy as a condition imposed on her, a "confinement" that caused her incarceration, stands as evidence of her "guilt" while her brother remains free, and makes her a hostage to her womb. After she gives birth, Nuala tries to get her to hold the baby, but she refuses. However, when Nuala places the helpless baby boy next to Anne-Marie, she melts and falls in love with her baby. From that point on, Anne-Marie is focused on figuring out a way to keep her son; her interest in her own escape and survival is sparked by her maternal drive to protect her baby. Through Anne-Marie's transformation, the film presents unwanted pregnancies as babies that women did not even realize they wanted until they had them; motherhood is thus stripped of historicity and naturalized as the fulfillment of a woman's biological and emotional potential.

The inmates' identities as mothers becomes central to how the film imagines the essence of women as maternal and enthusiastically heterosexual. Such a construction of "normal" or "healthy" femininity contrasts with the pathological nature of the celibate, shapeless nuns. The film positions the inmates' gender identity as the opposite of the brusque nuns who demonstrate the same depraved detachment whether they are delivering babies, battering women, or removing infants from the nursery. My argument is not with the portrayal of the nuns as callous, it is with the film's portrayal of callousness as inherently opposed to a loving female nature. In this respect, *Sinners* neatly separates what it constructs as real women from the masculinized Irish state and church. The nuns exist as something other than women, and they alone are the agents of patriarchal power. Against this alien power, *Sinners* posits the true sisterly bonds as existing among the inmates. The women's oppression at the hands of the nuns fosters a sense of solidarity (albeit a tenuous one) that is reinforced by their shared experiences of romance, pregnancy, birth, and the loss of a child. Even as it makes an impassioned claim for the legitimacy of pregnancies outside of marriage, *Sinners* stops short of challenging the centrality of motherhood to female and Irish national identity.

The Magdalene Sisters refuses to install a comforting border between women and patriarchy or between femininity and the ability to victimize. The women who run the laundry are simultaneously the agents of patriarchy and its victims. Their power is maintained through a combination of psychological coercion, brutal force, and collusion with the Church hierarchy. The women under their care are clearly victims of a patriarchal institution, but that does not make them incapable of oppressing other women or of looking to benefit from the patriarchal structure of the Catholic Church by acquiescing to its rules. Mullan's characters are sympathetic not because they are virtuous or create a sisterly space of resistance, but because they are trapped in an institution that has total authority over their lives. They exist in a zone of abandonment, where state law is suspended and the sovereign power of the Church and the family is applied arbitrarily. The women in the laundry live in a state of bare life, and in response to this condition, some inmates are completely broken whereas others snatch at opportunities for survival. In letting the laundry have total power over the women, *The Magdalene Sisters* shifts expectations of what constitutes resistance. Unable to heroically stand up to the system, Margaret, Rose, Bernadette, and Crispina find other ways to resist their own institutional erasure, even if that sense of agency comes at another inmate's expense, as when Bernadette finds but withholds the Saint Christopher medal Crispina lost. Her explanation for this gratuitous act of cruelty is simply, "She hasn't suffered enough. We're supposed to be penitents, remember?"

By spreading the narrative across several characters, Mullan presents a range of responses to the laundry as a carceral institution, including three escape attempts that only lead to deeper incarceration. After learning that one of the young women, Una O'Connor, had escaped in the night, Margaret decides to try it for herself. As she approaches the door, she hears screams and thundering footsteps. Margaret dashes back under the covers, and Una's father (played by Mullan) crashes through the door, dragging his sobbing, pleading daughter behind him. He throws her on her bed and walks away. But when she screams, "I just wanted to come home, Da!" he turns around, storms back toward her, and begins thrashing her with his heavy leather belt. Sister Bridget watches with a look of extreme discomfort on her face, as if she would like to intervene but is restraining herself out of respect for the sovereignty of the family patriarch. After the beating, Una's father grabs her hair and growls at her, "You've got no father; you've got no mother. You killed us, you little slut! You run away again, and I swear I'll cripple ye." When the women are left alone in the darkened dormitory again, Una and Margaret exchange silent glances as they put on their nightgowns—Una's failed escape and abandonment to the nuns reveals what Margaret's fate would have been had she escaped and made it home.

This scene is the last one in which Una speaks. The following day, Sister Bridget cuts Una's hair to the scalp, finishing just in time to take a switch to the thighs of Crispina and Bernadette. In the next shot, a physically battered and psychologically defeated Una returns to her sink at the laundry. Silently, she picks up her soap and begins vigorously scrubbing, her battered face twisted in mental and physical pain. Some time later, when her hair is chin length (one of the few ways of measuring time's passage in the film), Una stands before the women at mass, wearing the modest black dress of a consecrated penitent. After being disowned by her father, Una has traded the false hope of eventual liberation for the guaranteed security of slightly better treatment within the institution. Over a close-up of Una's face, Sister Bridget announces that Una has decided to "give herself to the convent." In the following shot, the two women stand on either side of the chapel's wooden altarpiece; their stiff postures and shapeless black garments make Una a weaker visual echo of the nun. As Una stares blankly ahead, Sister Bridget explains the significance of Una's sacrifice. "As most of you know, this is one of the greatest commitments a young penitent can make to our order. She has turned her back on the evils and temptations of the world and will face the light of the Lord with us here in this convent until the day she dies." Sister Bridget thanks her, and Una takes her seat in the front row with the other consecrated penitents, whose cropped gray hair and aging faces reveal the bleak future Una has "chosen" for herself. Furthermore, the fact that Sister Bridget speaks for her in this sequence and is visually paired with Una alludes to the limited range of options for women in postcolonial Ireland that likely played a role in the nun's own choice of the convent for life.

Una's escape attempt leads nowhere but back to the laundry, and the fallout from her rebellion enables the institution to secure a tighter hold on her. The same seems to be true of Bernadette after her first escape attempt. She convinces Brendan, a local teenager who works for the laundry delivery service and therefore has access to the compound's keys, to elope with her. But while waiting for her by the laundry door, he loses his nerve. Bernadette arrives in time to hear Brendan lock the back door. As she tries to break the lock, Sisters Bridget, Clementine, and Jude arrive, followed by Kate. In the scene that follows, Sister Bridget cuts Bernadette's hair as punishment with a level of violence reminiscent of the forced haircuts, shavings, and baths that Bobby Sands and other H-Block prisoners describe in their accounts of the no-wash protest. The sequence alternates between hand-held tight close-ups of Bernadette's contorted face and medium close-ups of a determined Sister Bridget. Sister Jude and Sister Clementine restrain Bernadette in a chair. She thrashes in defiance, while Sister Bridget snatches at clumps of her hair, cutting her scalp in the process. As blood begins to trickle down Bernadette's face, her resistance subsides.

Bernadette's punishment initiates a montage sequence that conveys the consolidation of the laundry's power over its increasingly defeated inmates. The film dissolves from Bernadette's face to an anonymous female hand turning the crank on an iron wringer. A sparse cello and piano motif begins, and the image dissolves to a tighter close-up of the gears turning, suggesting the passage of time. The turning of the gears is rhymed visually with the turning of a screw; in the shot that follows, a nun tests a new bolt lock on the dormitory door, revealing the tightening of control in response to the security breaches of Una's and Bernadette's escape attempts. Over the course of the montage sequence, shots of work and prayer dissolve into each other, and Bernadette's hair gradually grows back. With cropped hair, Bernadette stirs a pile of clothes covered in lye, as dust from the poison coats her face and hair. An anonymous group of women scrub the convent corridor. Women kneel in prayer at the foot of their beds (in a shot that evokes and subverts the comforting images of "twelve little girls in two straight lines" that recur in the homey Catholic boarding school of Hans Bemelmann's *Madeline* books), and the film cuts to a close-up of Bernadette staring at the ceiling.

With the women subdued, the film turns to the laundry's profits, again bringing the sacred back down to earth through its intimate ties to lucre. Brendan picks up sacks of clean clothes emblazoned with the laundry's holy logo and loads them into the van. His boss hands Sister Clementine a stack of money, and the nun smiles broadly. In the next shot, Sister Bridget piles rolls of notes into a cookie tin, gently caressing them into place before securing the lid with tape, and Father Fitzroy's voice begins a blessing, "In nomine Patris . . . ," that bridges a transition from this shot to a close-up of the priest's hand shaking a glass sprinkler of holy water. He finishes the blessing—"et Filii et Spiritus Sanctus. Amen"— with the nuns and laundry women assembled behind him. Sister Bridget leads a round of applause, and the film finally cuts to the recipient of the clergy's good wishes: three industrial-strength dryers that will increase productivity without easing the women's labor. Mullan shoots the trinity of dryers from a low position, with a wide-angle lens so that they loom on the screen, distorted. He hammers home the grotesque confluence of God and Mammon with a note of irony: a crucifix hangs high on the wall next to a dryer, while another one is reflected in its round, bulging glass door (fig. 8).

8. Commercial dryers and Catholicism. From *The Magdalene Sisters* (directed by Peter Mullan, produced by Frances Higson, 2002). Courtesy of Frances Higson.

Banished Children of Eve?

After watching *The Magdalene Sisters*, Mary Norris, who survived the Good Shepherd laundry in Cork, mused, "Wasn't Our Lady lucky? If she was in Ireland, she'd have been put in a Magdalene laundry, and Jesus would have been adopted" (McGarry 2002, 51). Norris's sardonic observation slyly questions the structure of the Holy Family, which consists of a stepfather, a mother who got pregnant before her wedding, and a child whose paternity is in doubt. But any concerns parishioners might harbor about Mary's virtue are handled through the narrative device of divine intervention, in the form of an angel's announcement (and in some versions of the story, just in case the word of the Almighty wasn't quite enough, the enduring presence of Mary's hymen after the birth of Jesus). In contrast, not even virginity was sufficient to exonerate Mary Norris after she sneaked out of the house where she was employed in order to see *My Wild Irish Rose*. Norris worked for the sister of one of the nuns who ran the orphanage where Norris grew up after she was taken from her mother. Her employer informed on her, and the nun sent her to a doctor for an invasive gynecological exam. Despite the doctor's affirmation of her purity—"this young woman is intact"—Norris was sent to Cork, renamed Myra, and effectively disappeared from Irish society until a nun decided she could be trusted to live among decent Irish people again. Norris's act of seeing a movie was legal, but she had challenged the family's law by asserting her will, and such a transgression was enough to mark her as criminal. But in the eyes of the clergy, Norris was already predisposed to immoral behavior because her widowed mother had also challenged the family structure by allowing a man to spend the night from time to time. Therefore, her children were removed from her care and placed into different Catholic orphanages (McGarry 2002).

Women sent to the Magdalene laundries had committed imagined crimes against the family and were therefore no longer allowed the privilege of its safety. The family is granted a primary place in Article 41 of the 1937 constitution, which in some ways is simply an official recognition of the centrality of family to much nationalist discourse, regardless of the specific country involved. Irish nationalism, for its part, has relied on the family as both a symbolic articulation of national belonging—as in the image of Mother Ireland and her faithful sons—and a practical means of resistance. Under colonialism, the family functioned as a safe space for anti-state sentiment, insurgents, and weapons caches; and it was also politicized and made public through house raids, searches, and arrests. The home and the family were therefore zones of struggle, which in turn meant that women figured into Irish nationalism as both symbolic figures and participants in the fight for national liberation. However, women's political agency was sanctioned by the needs of anti-colonial nationalism. After the nation was formed, Conrad argues, "without a change in the limited nationalist vision of the family cell, the current system merely reproduces power relations . . . and those in charge of the new nation-state find it necessary to police the private sphere in the name of national security" (2004, 15). After independence, the family's importance to nationalism was codified in the constitution, which placed it above the law, proclaiming, "the State recognises the Family as the natural primary and fundamental unit group of Society, and as a moral institution possessing inalienable and imprescriptible rights, antecedent and superior to all positive law. The State, therefore, guarantees to protect the Family in its constitution and authority, as the necessary basis of social order and as indispensable to the welfare of the Nation and the State" (Bunreacht na hÉireann 1937).

Crucial for the biological and ideological reproduction of Ireland, the family became a sovereign power within the new nation. The primacy of "the family"—defined implicitly in the constitution as the patriarchal nuclear family—has often meant that its privacy was protected at the expense of its individual members. If the patriarchal nuclear family has absolute autonomy (except for when, as in the X Case, the family has decided to contravene the laws of the Vatican), then respect for family sovereignty can enable the destruction of its most vulnerable members, as Nell McCafferty reveals was the case with Ann Lovett, the fifteen-year-old girl who died alone in childbirth at a grotto of the Virgin Mary in 1984. McCafferty writes, "Ann Lovett's welfare was the inviolate responsibility of her parents. . . . So as long as the Family kept silent, the community honored the unwritten code of non-interference with the basic unit of society"

(McCafferty 1984, 48). But the family's privacy, which is predicated on the Western humanist split that limits the family and the individual to the private realm while constructing the public realm as the space of politics, is based on a fallacy. As feminists have consistently argued, the split between a public sphere of politics and a private one of family is "illusory, a fact that must be acknowledged if there is hope for a vital public sphere" (Conrad 2004, 12). That the Irish state would intervene in the family lives of single parents, placing their children in Catholic "orphanages" if they transgressed the codes of social decency—even if, as in the case of Mary Norris, there was no neglect or abuse in the home—demonstrates the illegitimacy of the concept of family privacy. As the foundational unit of society and the measure of an individual's standing in the community, the family is a highly public institution.[9]

The Magdalene Sisters begins with three pre-credit sequences depicting the precariousness of women's freedom, two of which establish the family as an important site for the reproduction of Church power. In these stories, the family and the clergy work together to eradicate young women who threaten the illusion of a gendered national chastity. Mullan's film conveys the abrupt violence of this regulation of the national imaginary by eliminating expository shots of the women being told their fate or entering the laundry. Margaret, Bernadette, and Rose are simply disappeared from their former lives. After a title orienting us in time and place—County Dublin, Ireland, 1964—the film cuts to an extreme close-up of a *bodhrán* decorated with an image from Christ's Passion that depicts the moment acted out yearly at Palm Sunday Mass, when, given the choice between saving the life of Christ or that of Barabbas, the crowd chooses the thief. This image visually and metaphorically places humanity in opposition with the divine, hinting at the combative position from which the Church views its congregants, before the film has even properly begun. This perspective is strengthened when the film reveals that the drum belongs to a priest, who begins to sing "The Well below the Valley" at a country

9. For excellent histories and analyses of the family in Ireland, see Conrad (2004), Inglis (1998), McLoone (2000), and Smith (2007).

wedding. The film cuts to a close-up of a bride, a shot of her hand in her groom's hand, back to the priest, and then to a series of shots exclusively focused on women and girls of various ages who are assembled at the wedding. The film cuts back again to the priest, who, upon finishing the song, hunches over the drum, presses his lips against its rim, and begins to beat it vigorously. The tempo races, and the film continues to cut in close-up and extreme close-up among the priest's hands playing the drum, his face glistening with sweat, and three teenagers whispering among themselves and laughing. The priest's body shakes, lurches, and rocks against the *bodhrán* in time with the ever-increasing tempo until, in a tight close-up, he raises his eyebrows, sighs in relief, and finishes playing.

The uncomfortable display of the priest's displaced sexual desire raises questions about the practicality of celibacy, questions that cannot help but invoke the sex-abuse scandals that began to emerge in Ireland and the United States in the 1990s and that have yet to be thoroughly addressed or resolved. The stereotypical markers of rural Ireland that open the film—a priest, a rustic dancehall, traditional music, glasses of whiskey and beer— seem initially to do little more than hammer home the idea that yes, this is indeed the claustrophobic Ireland of the past. However, this sequence differs from such accounts in that it not only establishes cultural attitudes about sexuality and sin, but through the series of shots of women and girls, it also overtly expresses that the burden of national and religious chastity rested exclusively on Irish women. Unlike movies about the past that focus on sexual repression by presenting men and women as equally frustrated by the Church's expectations, Mullan turns away from sexual *repression* toward sexual *oppression*. It may have been a sin for men to engage in premarital sex, but, the film suggests throughout, it was virtually a crime for women to do so, even when they themselves were the victims of real crimes like rape, incest, and other forms of assault.

Even before Margaret is raped, the film conveys the hypocrisy of patriarchal constructions of sexuality through the opening ballad, which is loosely based on the story of Christ and the Woman of Samaria (Murray 2004, 158), but with a gruesome twist involving incest and infanticide, in which a woman learns from a stranger that she has given birth to six children: two by her uncle, two by her brother, and two by her father. She asks the stranger the fate of these children, and the man tells her that all six are dead and buried near the well. She then asks her own fate and is told, "You'll be seven years a ringin' a bell and seven years a burnin' in Hell," but she responds with faith, "I'll be seven years a ringin' a bell but the Lord above may save me soul from burnin' in Hell." Mullan's use of the ballad establishes a culture of blame, wherein, strangely unaware of what has happened to her own body and her children, the woman is completely dependent on the male stranger's version of events. Murray connects Margaret's situation to the ballad, writing that the story in the song "is precisely the native cultural discourse that legitimates the barbarism of Margaret's immediate ostracization and incarceration and the communal acquiescence in this" (2004, 158). Like the women in the laundries, the woman cannot testify on her own behalf and is the only one to face punishment because only her body bears the evidence of sexual transgression. In this construction, the supposed sin of sex is less severe than the stigma of corporeal evidence.[10] The concern is not with what has happened, but with how it looks to others. Just as "The Well below the Valley" makes no mention of what happens to the woman's rapist relatives, in *The Magdalene Sisters*, Margaret is the one incarcerated, not her cousin who committed the actual crime.

Margaret is criminalized not because she "allowed" her cousin to violate her, but because she chose to speak out, to reveal the private violence underneath the public veneer of family love. As Smith notes, what worries Margaret's family is less the fact that she has been raped and more the fear of "the potential for public awareness and scandal" (2007, 144). In fact, being sent to the laundry is the second time Margaret is punished for speaking; the first is the rape itself. After the priest's song, Margaret naïvely follows her cousin Kevin upstairs to an empty room. He closes the

10. Or, as Nell McCafferty put it in an article on the dismissal of pregnant young women or girls from Catholic schools, "Incontrovertible evidence that the Catholic ethos is not being upheld is usually established by referring to babies. Only females can have babies. It is therefore the single pregnant school-attending female of the species who will bear the brunt of punishment should the boom be lowered in Catholic-run schools at a great rate in post-[eighth]amendment Ireland" (McCafferty 1984, 55).

door and kisses her. She pushes him away and tells him firmly to stop. He persists, and Margaret smacks him on the head and tells him to behave himself, pointing out that he is her cousin and asking, "What would your father think?" Margaret defends herself by scolding her cousin, pointing to his impropriety, and invoking the higher authority of his father. Kevin, seemingly humbled by her assertiveness, leaves, closing the door behind him. As Margaret goes to open it, Kevin shoves the door into her face, knocks her onto the floor, puts his hand over her mouth, and rapes her.

In the scene that follows, when Margaret tells a female cousin what Kevin has just done, the film uses selective silence to cut out all dialogue. The sound that remains is diegetic; the music, clapping, and dancing of the wedding's *céilí* continues its raucous pace, callously indifferent to Margaret's anguish. As Smith argues, the music maintains the "illusion of communal harmony through the continuing dance and celebration" (2007, 143). The lack of voices in this sequence corresponds to the cultural silence surrounding incest and other forms of abuse that may fester in families. Through this selective silence, the film calls attention to how the family is fortified by socially enforced silence—a silence carefully constructed and rigorously policed. The lack of dialogue also aligns the spectator with Margaret, leaving us as excluded from the narration of events and therefore as disempowered as she is, a condition that the film enforces by shooting the sequence through Margaret's visual and audio point of view. After a traumatized Margaret tells her cousin what has happened, the cousin marches up to Kevin and confronts him. The film cuts to a shot of Margaret sitting on a bench crying, her eyes anxiously darting back and forth to follow the action offscreen. Her cousin then tells Kevin's father and Margaret's father, who in turn confront Kevin. Margaret's father pulls Father Doyle off stage to notify him about the rape. Each shot of the men learning about Margaret's violation is taken from a low angle that approximates Margaret's position and is intercut with close-ups of her watching the men discuss her case. Finally, her father and Father Doyle decide her fate, and as Margaret looks on, rapidly losing hope for justice, her (and our) fears are confirmed in a close-up of her father. Lit from below, with Father Doyle literally talking in his ear, Margaret's father glares directly into the camera. In the final shot of this sequence, Margaret's eyes are cast down in defeat.[11] The next morning, a car arrives to shuttle Margaret away, as her mother stares blankly out the window, visually trapped behind a pane of glass.

Like Margaret, who broke cultural codes that equate silence with chastity, Bernadette and Rose are also punished for talking: Bernadette's speech is taken as a sign of her loose morality, and Rose speaks up for herself against her father and the local priest. Raised in St. Attracta's industrial school, Bernadette is sent to the laundry after she is spied talking to the local Dublin boys who lean over the schoolyard railing to flirt with her. In the next shot, her bed is rolled up, and the meager possessions she had are left behind for younger girls to scavenge. The third and final vignette, "Rose," opens with Rose imploring her mother to look at her newborn baby. She lies in a hospital bed cradling her child, while her mother sits stiffly upright in an adjacent chair, refusing to acknowledge either Rose or the baby. Rose's soft pleas to "just look at him, Ma" continue as her mother stares straight ahead, stone-faced and silent, in a shot that shatters idealizations of maternal love as unconditional and enduring. Rose's father calls her out to the hallway, where a priest awaits with paperwork. She signs away her baby, after the priest reminds her that with her, the child would grow up a "bastard, a social outcast" paying for his mother's sins for the rest of his life. After her son is pulled from her arms, Rose changes her mind and begins to reach out, shouting that she wants her baby back. But her father blocks her way and wraps his arms around her, not to comfort her but to restrain her. The cruelty of this paternal embrace is heightened by the sound of Rose and her father's clothes rustling as she cries out and struggles against his strength. Rose's father holds her tightly and stares straight ahead; eventually the coat across his broad back fills the screen and blocks out the image.

11. Smith sees this sequence as implicating the viewer in the powerful gaze of the men; he writes of Margaret as the object of their point of view. But I think the entire sequence is focused around Margaret's point of view, fostering spectatorial allegiance with and empathy for her. The final shot of her father, clearly a point-of-view shot, is terrifying and uses expressionistic rather than realist lighting, suggesting Margaret's subjectivity.

If the family is the foundation of the nation, to be without family is to be cast out of the nation. Banishment from the home can thus be understood as including eviction from Ireland, an expulsion that is symbolic but also became material for some, in that women behind convent doors ceased to exist as Irish women for those on the outside. *Sinners* juxtaposes a prayer of spiritual exile with romantic establishing shots of the Irish landscape, thus opening up the possibility of connecting Ireland occupied by British colonialism to Ireland occupied by Catholicism and national patriarchy. After Kitty is abandoned by Patrick and her baby is taken away, she commits suicide by jumping off the roof of one of the buildings on the convent grounds. The women rush to the scene, and the garda sergeant suggests that "the poor girl" has had an accident. Sister Bernadette agrees, and the characters stand around the spectacle of Kitty's broken body while the nun leads them in the "Salve Regina": "Hail Holy Queen, Mother of Mercy! . . . To thee we do cry, poor banished children of Eve. . . ." The prayer continues over a shot of Kitty's corpse dressed in a white habit and laid out in a satin-lined oak coffin, which is covered in a white veil, "to thee do we send up our sighs, mourning and weeping in this valley, of tears. Turn, then, most gracious advocate, thine eyes of mercy toward us; and after this our exile show unto us the blessed fruit of thy womb Jesus. . . ." The prayer ends at her burial, when it is replaced in the soundtrack by the priest's recitation of the "Our Father." Kitty's burial takes place in a cemetery high on a cliff overlooking the sea. Afterward, the women walk back to the laundry on a country road. Nuns march at the head and the rear of the group, their voluminous black habits billowing in the wind. Between them is an orderly line of penitents whose blue-gray dresses contrast with the thick forms of black. This beautifully symmetrical line of women in the Irish countryside is taken from a high angle in a shot that allows the landscape to dwarf the characters.

The "Salve Regina" centers on the theme of exile from Eden, and "banished children of Eve," also the title of Peter Quinn's book on Irish immigrants in New York, is evocative of a diaspora marked by the shocks of colonialism. The themes of exile, displacement, and reluctant emigration are central to how Irish history is understood in national popular culture. But while the condition of statelessness was one historically imposed on

Irish nationalists by the British colonial administration, the postcolonial state perpetuated this exile within its own borders by allowing families to incarcerate daughters who were often legal adults. In this sequence, *Sinners* juxtaposes the condition of spiritual exile in the prayer with gloriously sublime shots of the Irish landscape that evoke representations of romantic Ireland; a mystical land whose brush shelters nationalist insurgents and who mourns the children banished and slain while defending her from foreign exploiters. Like the banished children of Eve, Kitty is brought back from exile despite having committed the mortal sin of suicide (thanks to the quick thinking of the sergeant and Sister Bernadette, she is buried in consecrated ground). Thus after her death, when she is no longer a threat to the security of Ireland's saintly self-image, Kitty is readmitted to the national-religious community. Although the land embraces Kitty in death, it remains otherwise indifferent to the penitents. As they walk back to the laundry through a rural landscape that they could easily disappear in, no one tries to escape. The pastoral appeal of a symmetrical column of pious women walking on a country road is undercut by the string of abuses that have occurred on screen up to this point.

Similarly, *The Magdalene Sisters* subverts the meaning of the Irish countryside, which as Martin McLoone argues, is the "chosen environment for nationalist Ireland's own self-image, the residue of all that is perceived as pure and essential in Irish identity" (2000, 20). McLoone's analysis of landscape in Irish nationalism builds on Gibbons's argument that in romantic images on stage and screen, the Irish countryside functions "not merely as a picturesque backdrop, but as a layer of meaning in its own right, a thematic element which may reinforce or cut across the other levels of meaning in a text" (1988, 210). In cinema, beginning with the Kalem Company's silent-era adaptations of Dion Bouccicault's plays, the landscape's nationalist significance is augmented by its touristic function. The camera casts a loving gaze on fields, cliffs, beaches, lakes, and mountains, marketing the beauty of Ireland to Irish and non-Irish audiences alike. In this respect, regardless of what is happening on-screen, the glorious land serves as a relief and a counterpoint, facilitating a nostalgic view of Ireland in diaspora (Gibbons 1988, 210). This distorted glance back is one that Shane McGowan eloquently summed up in "Thousands

Are Sailing," a Pogues song about reluctant emigration, wherein Irish exiles around the world mourn and toast the nation that turned them into religious "refugees" from the oppressiveness of collection-plate-wielding clergy and guilt-inducing holy statues. For a film set in the Ireland of the past, *The Magdalene Sisters* is strikingly devoid of the usual elements that bring comforting feelings about Ireland. Also absent is a soundtrack by the Chieftains, Bill Whelan, or even Bono. Mullan studiously avoids any cinematic romanticizing of Ireland. In fact, the production avoided Ireland altogether: Mullan shot the film in Scotland.

The one moment when the film offers a spectacular view of "Ireland" occurs when Margaret has a chance to escape. However, any sense of relief through beauty that the glory of cinematic Ireland might offer is contained by the fact that this scene comes at a point when Margaret realizes that there is no safe space for her in Ireland. During a rare day of recreation, Margaret, who has just witnessed Father Fitzroy forcing Crispina to perform oral sex on him, decides to take revenge on the priest on Crispina's behalf. She slips away from the potato-sack races and wanders down to the convent walls, where she plans on picking poison ivy to slip into a dryer with the priest's vestments. As she goes to pick the weed, Margaret sees that the garden's back gate is ajar. She wanders through the open door, and the film cuts to a shot of a sprawling landscape from Margaret's point of view. Waves of vivid green dotted by white sheep fill the screen, and the soundtrack is overrun with the rustle of leaves and the chirping of birds. After over an hour of Mullan's restriction on sights and sounds, the shot becomes a moment of sensory overload, reflecting Margaret's own feelings of being overwhelmed by open space after years of confinement. A car approaches, and she holds out her hand to flag it down. The driver stops and asks if she'd like a lift. Margaret takes in his brown leather jacket and Brylcreemed hair, and shakes her head. The driver expresses annoyance at the inconvenience of stopping and calls her a "loony." He drives off, and Margaret turns her back on the open land and re-enters the confines of the laundry compound, carefully leaving the door exactly as she found it (fig. 9).

In this pivotal scene, Margaret, like Una before her, realizes the extent of her incarceration. *The Magdalene Sisters* poignantly constructs all of

9. Margaret shuts herself back in. From *The Magdalene Sisters* (directed by Peter Mullan, produced by Frances Higson, 2002). Courtesy of Frances Higson.

Ireland as a prison for women like Margaret. The laundry is only the most visible way in which she is incarcerated. Margaret is also confined by her exile from the family, which means she has no community in which to seek refuge. She seems suddenly and forcefully aware of the utter impossibility of her liberation, as well as her precarious safety as a young woman. Given the fact that Margaret was raped by a family member and banished from home by her own father, she has no reason to trust the man in the driver's seat either. This heartrending moment in an already harrowing film conveys the depths of Margaret's institutionalization. Like Una, she is radically alienated from the nation. In her eyes, the laundry is a safer space for her than the open country. All she can do is poison the priest's clothing, which offers a moment of comic relief but is immediately followed by devastating effects.

Film Reflexivity as Critique

The Magdalene Sisters operates on a dynamic tension between realism and anti-realist techniques, and while the former offers a harrowing portrayal of incarceration, the latter complicates the seamless suturing of the spectator into the text. Before making the film, Mullan had worked with one of the principal architects of British realism, Ken Loach, on *My Name Is Joe*, and in interviews he frequently cites Loach as a key influence. Like Loach, Mullan shot the film on location, usually with handheld cameras, in light that often seems to be natural, and on film stock that is frequently grainy. The film uses non-diegetic music sparingly; what little music there is comes in the form of a minimalist piano and cello motif. With the exception of Geraldine McEwan (Sister Bridget), none of his actors could be considered stars at the time of shooting; the four young women who make up the story's backbone are played by relatively new actors, while veteran Irish film actors like Britta Smith (Katie) have more marginal roles. At the same time, the film revels in moments of visual excess, one of which is the shot whereby Sister Bridget appears in Bernadette's bloody eye. After Sister Bridget has violently cut Bernadette's hair as punishment for her first escape attempt, the film cuts to a shot of blood-soaked gauze dropped into a basin of water. The gauze expands with water, Bernadette's blood ebbs from it, and Sister Bridget's voice commands, "Open your eyes, girl." In extreme close-up, Bernadette's eye blinks; her lid and lashes are coated in congealed blood, which the film heightens through a wet sound effect. The camera slowly zooms to an even tighter shot of Bernadette's eye, which contains Sister Bridget's distorted reflection. The nun tells her, "I want you to see yourself as you really are, now that your vanity is gone and your arrogance defeated, you're free. Free to choose between right and wrong, good and evil. So now you must look deep into your soul, find that which is pure and decent, and offer it up to God. Then and only then will you find salvation."

This shot is so deliberately over the top as to call attention to its own excess, which is one reason critics single it out as out of place in a "realist" film, while remaining mute about other moments of cinematic excess—for example, the melodramatic underlighting of Margaret's father, which is the oldest trick in the book of cinematic vilification. The shot of Sister Bridget in Bernadette's eye forcefully conveys the idea that she has penetrated Bernadette's psyche, but it is also a visual quote from Michael Powell's *Peeping Tom* (1960), in which the act of looking takes on epic Freudian proportions as a serial killer hides his murder weapon in a camera tripod and films his victims' dying expressions of terror. While Mullan shares Loach's socialist politics, he is also "not a social realist. I grew up on too many different films. . . . So as we shot the film in sequence, something I did learn from Ken, when it came to cutting the hair, I just couldn't do the social realist shit anymore, I had to do something completely unsubtle" (Chaw 2003). The film's interplay of melodramatic excess and cinematic reflexivity is one of its strengths; it helps Mullan maintain a respectful gap between representation and experience. By consistently pulling his film back to the realm of the artistic, Mullan avoids the arrogance of a film-maker like Paul Greengrass, who uses historical trauma—Bloody Sunday, the Omagh bombing, and 9/11—in conjunction with a relentless direct cinema style in order to resurrect past experience as present reality. Watching *The Magdalene Sisters* is not the same as being in a laundry, and Mullan reminds his audience of that fact in sequences like this one, which is the first of several examples where the film makes specific reference to the medium of cinema.

The shot of Bernadette's eye is followed by another beautifully unsubtle one in which Sister Bridget holds a mirror to Bernadette's face. Sister Bridget's face is framed by the darkness of her habit and shot in medium close-up while Bernadette's reflection appears beside her, framed by the oval mirror. The film cuts to a close-up of Bernadette's face in the mirror. With her hair unevenly cropped, her head bowed, and her eyes looking up in defiance, the shot recalls images of Maria Falconetti in the title role of Carl Theodore Dreyer's *The Passion of Joan of Arc* (1928). Two streams of blood trickle down Bernadette's forehead and past her eyes, also alluding to Christ's own crown of thorns. Here, the film uses images that have become iconic in the history of visual culture in order to reverse the Church's construction of the Magdalenes as evil and their warders as holy. Throughout the film, Bernadette fiercely resists interpellation into the religious ideology that constructs her as an outcast, a sinner, and a temptress. In this shot, the film affirms her self-image through iconography that links her to stories of martyrdom. In the process, Mullan reminds us that the Catholic Church has a history not only of persecuting those it fears but also reworking that very persecution into a narrative of redemption: Joan of Arc was canonized by the same Church that burned her alive as a heretic. Furthermore, like the women in the laundry, Joan's real sin was her transgression of social rules about proper female comportment.

In assuming that the film aspired to strict social realism, critics miss out on how Mullan plays with cinematic reflexivity to discredit the Church's image. *The Magdalene Sisters* avoids a psychological portrayal of the nuns, but it directly engages with the Church's own self-image and with historical representations of Catholic clergy in two scenes involving the medium of film. On the laundry's annual day of recreation, Father Fitzroy brings an 8 millimeter camera to the convent to film the penitents and nuns enjoying the fresh air and sunshine. The low-tech 8 millimeter footage that signifies the priest's point of view is simulated through saturated film stock and the whirring of the camera apparatus. On the one hand, using the finished product—developed film stock—to convey the moment of shooting with a particular camera is standard practice in films that reference technologies of the past. On the other, the switch to the final product while Fitzroy shoots (rather than simply re-creating the viewfinder of an actual 8 millimeter camera) lends a tinge of nostalgia and idealization to the priest's point of view. Visually protected from the reality of the laundries, Father Fitzroy creates a second reality. Sister Clementine and Sister Jude enter the frame of his footage, and they are no longer the sadistic screws who played a "game" of sexual humiliation with the naked inmates; they are two smiling nuns who calmly walk together through the convent garden.

He directs the sisters from offscreen, telling them to point out the flowers. Sister Jude stiffly holds her arm out and murmurs, "Oh, look at the flowers," while Father Fitzroy tells them to "just relax and try to act natural."[12] Upon his direction to act natural, the priest zooms in for a close-up of the nuns' faces. Sisters Jude and Clementine look blankly into the camera, as if they have no idea what the priest means. The insignificance

---

12. Murray characterizes this scene as a "moment of black comedy" and calls attention to Fitzroy's incompetence with the technology as a way to highlight "a contemporary local inability to competently, let alone progressively, appropriate and/or innovate film production technologies and creative approaches *of any kind*" (2004, 159–60).

of "natural" for them becomes painfully apparent as they stand awkwardly still, trying to force smiles, their faces tight and their movements restricted by heavy, starched habits. In the following shots, Father Fitzroy films the nuns clapping as the "girls" (some of whom are in their seventies) shout and cheer during a potato-sack race and play tug-o-war. This special day of games is the only one of its kind in the movie, and it seems to be orchestrated for the benefit of the camera. Therefore, the "documentary" footage that Father Fitzroy shoots to prove the Church's benevolence and generosity regarding the Magdalenes is no closer to the truth of what the inmates experience than the Hollywood production of *The Bells of Saint Mary's* (shown later in the film) is to how the clergy treat their charges. Mullan's film discredits a staple of the traditional archive and a weapon in the arsenal of "reality"—non-fiction footage—by revealing that what passes for the real is only as reliable as the person behind the camera. In this way, the film preemptively questions the Church's response about the reality of the Magdalene laundries by reminding us that their history is also constructed and with a particular agenda in mind, one that has high stakes in the present, given the stream of abuse stories that have emerged since the mid-1990s.

This sequence comes on the heels of a scene of abuse that reveals the utter bankruptcy of the Church's discourses of sin, redemption, and clerical charity. Earlier in the recreation day, Margaret steps out of line to tie her shoe on the way to Mass. As she glances sideways down a hill, she sees Crispina in the sacristy with Father Fitzroy, who is forcing her to perform oral sex on him. In the following sequence, Father Fitzroy begins Mass. The first line of his prayer, "Judge me, O God, and distinguish my cause from the nation that is not holy," is spoken offscreen, over a shot of Margaret, and the second, "Deliver me from the unjust and deceitful man," over a shot of Crispina. The ironic juxtaposition of Fitzroy's prayer for deliverance over his rape victim's face may not be subtle, but it does make clear the gulf between Catholicism in theory and Catholicism as a power structure that denies sexual experience to women while exploiting that very same sexuality for its own hypocritical ends. We are again reminded of Fitzroy's transgression when he administers the Eucharist to a row of kneeling penitents, each facing up to him with her mouth open. The priest's depravity in the preceding oral sex scene reverberates throughout the shot of the women on their knees (whose mouths are at the height of his waist), sexualizing their position and turning the administration of the Eucharist—the Body of Christ—into a menacing act fraught with potential sexual violence.

While the film clearly lays the blame for the laundries at the doorstep of the Church, avoiding an overt criticism of the state, its attack is a politically situated, thematically nuanced, and compassionate expression of historical rage that humanizes the Church in horrifying ways. It is not monsters who incarcerate women, but people, some of whom chose to enter the convent as nuns rather than risk a life as unmarried women, which could leave them vulnerable to national exclusion. Mullan's church is less a spiritual entity that magically caused the laundries to spring into existence than a material institution that sought money and power and, as a result, oppressed those whom it could oppress. Smith writes that in the first half century of postcolonial Ireland's existence, religious orders grew, particularly ones "dedicated to establishing a worldwide network of Catholic missionaries," which became known as "Ireland's spiritual empire" (2007, 157). In this framework, Catholicism becomes almost a manifestation of Irish nationalism. Both *Sinners* and *The Magdalene Sisters* make oblique references to an idea of Catholic imperialism. In both films, the nuns allude to money for "the black babies"—a shorthand for the Church's missions in Africa that conjures images of scores of unbaptized African children—and *Sinners* makes reference to Catholic couples from the United States who "donate" tens of thousands of dollars to "adopt" Irish babies. The alliance between Ireland and the Vatican enabled Irish nationalism to wrap its imperialist aims in a holy cloak of spiritual legitimacy. Ireland's "spiritual empire" promulgated a mutated form of Irish nationalism whereby gains for the Church were simultaneously gains for Ireland. While this empire has largely crumbled, the Church continues to discredit dissenting voices, often denying the extent of abuse in its institutions and minimizing the existence of Magdalene laundries. The histories addressed in *The Magdalene Sisters* and *Sinners* are unresolved, giving these films the potential to effect change in the present. While Smith's hope that *The Magdalene Sisters* function as an impetus for social change leads him to sometimes fault the film for falling short of the aims of activist cinema, he is nonetheless right to question its relationship to the unresolved histories of the laundries and the trauma that engulfs the survivors of these institutions whose stories form the basis of Mullan's own (Smith 2007, 136–58). In this respect, how *The Magdalene Sisters* and *Sinners* handle their 1960s setting is important to understanding the films in relation to political cinema.

Nostalgia and Escape

The Magdalene laundries were still taking in new inmates as late as the 1980s, but *Sinners* and *The Magdalene Sisters* are both set in the 1960s, a decade that has acquired national symbolic significance as Ireland's turning point as a modern nation. During this decade, a new Ireland emerges under the direction of Seán Lemass—who replaced de Valera as Taoiseach—one open to foreign investors and supposedly liberated from its oppressive past. The films share with Moufida Tlatli's *Silences of the Palace* (1994) and Deepa Mehta's *Water* (2005) an analysis of women held captive by forces beyond their control, whose bodies become prisons within the prison, and for whom national liberation was personally meaningless. In *Silences of the Palace* and *Water*, anticolonial movements in Tunisia and India, respectively, remain marginal to the women's lives, either offering no tangible freedom or arriving too late to protect the women from sexual assault and other severe physical harm. In the Magdalene films, liberation from British colonialism is antecedent to the narrative and clearly brought no freedom for these women. In fact, by portraying the brutality of the institutions, both films hint at the sacrilegious notion that Christina Mulcahy had the right idea—a British state of emergency might be preferable to an Irish one. At the same time, the liberation of Ireland from its second, Catholic and nationalist, occupation also brings no release; the films' characters are incarcerated during this symbolic moment.

In their reluctance to celebrate the 1960s as a national turning point, *Sinners* and *The Magdalene Sisters* resist a triumphal trajectory to Irish history where the politics of gender and sexuality are concerned. Such a rejection of the heroic sixties marks a significant departure from prior cinematic portrayals of Ireland's repressive past, many of which are set squarely between the late 1930s and the late 1950s, the bleak years of de Valera's political and ideological dominance. Although 1959 functions in national memory as "the *annus mirabilis* of modern Ireland, [when] God said 'Let Lemass be,' and there was light, dispelling the myths of traditionalism which had obscured the path to progress and industrialization," Luke Gibbons argues, the traditionalism, nationalism, and Catholicism that were blamed for slowing Ireland's progress toward European modernity and that were thought to have been defeated over the course of the 1960s never really went away, as the events of the 1980s attest (1996, 82–83). Pointing to the abortion referendum, chronic unemployment, and a resurgent nationalism in the wake of the 1981 hunger strike, Gibbons is skeptical about the finality of the 1959 break with the old repressive Ireland that de Valera is largely credited with creating. Films that portray conformity and sexual repression in the republic such as *Evelyn*, *Circle of Friends*, and *The Playboys* take place in the last years of the 1950s, forever playing out images of Ireland on the eve of its true national liberation—a fulfillment of the promise of 1921. Such fictional accounts of Ireland's nightmare past function as what Joe Cleary has characterized as a "negative validation of the present" (Cleary 2000, 108, quoted in Smith 2007, 138). "In this sense," Smith claims, "cultural representations of Ireland's enervating past permit present-day detachment from and complacency about the nation's history—responses Cleary argues are tantamount to 'a lucky escape'" from the torments of the past (Smith 2007, 138). In addition to fostering a sense of complacency about Irish history, by drawing a border between the past and the post-EU present, these films encourage a self-congratulatory satisfaction with modern Ireland, treating patriarchal nationalism as something that the internationalization of the Irish economy in the 1960s permanently fixed.

Given the extended life of the laundries and the fact that the real-life women who inspired Mullan's characters Rose, Margaret, and Bernadette were all incarcerated in the 1940s and 1950s, the choice of the 1960s as the timeframe for both films is striking because it brings to the foreground questions of modernization, secularization, and Europeanization—questions that also surrounded the Celtic Tiger years in which both films were made. On the one hand, it is possible to see the choice of the 1960s as a way for the films to affirm the narrative of Irish social progress. Setting their stories in this supposedly transitional decade instead of earlier or later establishes a sense that we are witnessing the laundries in the peak years of Catholic occupation, when the Church had risen to the height of its power over Ireland and was on the verge of an imperial fall. In that respect, the excesses of the clergy's abuses are consistent with the cinematic portrayal of a brutalizing colonial power just before a nationalist movement coalesces to combat it.[13] Seen in this light, the films would harmonize with the notion of a "lucky escape from the past" and would seem to encourage complacency about the politics of sexuality in contemporary Ireland, which included the Irish government's secret negotiations with the rest of the EU to secure assurances that signing the Maastricht treaty would not affect the illegal and unconstitutional status of abortion in Ireland. This interpretation of the timeframe encourages an understanding of the films' portrayal of the incarceration of women for shaming the family and staining the saintly image of Ireland as a singular moment in a larger national history that moves steadily toward liberalization. Setting the films in the 1960s and having the main characters make it out of the laundry—it could be argued—helps to confine Catholic and nationalist patriarchy safely to the past, blocking ways to understand the existence of the laundries within a broader field of continued sexual oppression.

However, Walsh and Mullan deprive their respective audiences of total reassurance or release. Like *Anne Devlin*, both films end with their characters still incarcerated, if not bodily in the laundries then politically

13. For example: *The Legend of Bhagat Singh* (Rajkumar Santoshi, 2002), set in 1920s India; *Mangal Pandey: The Rising* (Ketan Mehta, 2004), set in India in 1857; portrayals of the Black and Tans during the Irish war of independence in *Shake Hands with the Devil, Michael Collins*, and *The Wind that Shakes the Barley*. Because each of these films ends with the promise of deliverance from colonial oppression (even if, as in the case of *Mangal Pandey*, that deliverance took another ninety years), the violence of the occupying powers is presented as the desperate acts of a dying tyrant even when the films acknowledge that colonialist violence preceded and followed the events depicted on-screen.

within the confines of Irish national patriarchy and psychologically by their own traumatic pasts. *The Magdalene Sisters* does indeed contain an "exhilarating escape scene," one in which Rose and Bernadette boldly stand up to Sister Bridget and the other nuns who try to stop them. Margaret also makes it out of the laundry; prior to the final escape scene, her brother comes to rescue her on Christmas, when he is finally old enough to claim her. Likewise, in *Sinners*, Anne-Marie is safely delivered from the institution through marriage to a kindly widower, Frank, who agrees to her terms of what she euphemistically calls "no children." Anne-Marie's release is not total liberation; it is a practical compromise within the restrictions of patriarchy. She is dependent on Frank's benevolence for her place in "respectable" Irish society; her safety and material comfort continue exclusively at his will. Thus, by allowing Anne-Marie to be freed via a traditional marriage, the film qualifies her liberation as at best partial and maintains an image of Ireland as a larger prison for women. Anne-Marie is not exonerated by the Church or Irish society; she is on lifetime probation, remanded into the custody of a respectable man. *Sinners* conveys the character's limited freedom in its final shots, which use the visual tropes of the convict's moment of release in prison narratives. In an office presided over by the mother superior (the prison governor) and Sister Bernadette (the chief screw), Anne-Marie's brother signs a document ensuring her release. She and Frank walk out of the building and across a courtyard. A high-angle shot reveals the main gate within high stone walls that are secured by shards of broken glass embedded in the top layer of cement—the nuns' do-it-yourself alternative to costly razor wire. Anne-Marie reaches the main gate and smiles. However, there is no final shot of the outside world from her point of view, nor is there a shot of her body beyond the prison gate. Instead, *Sinners* dissolves from a close-up of Anne-Marie's face to a high-angle shot of her fellow inmates at the washtubs scrubbing clothes and praying for Jesus and Mary to intercede on their behalf for salvation. Unlike Kitty and Angela, Anne-Marie makes it out into society alive, but the film's closing images temper any celebratory sentiment.

In *The Magdalene Sisters*, the post-laundry shots of Margaret, Bernadette, Rose, and Crispina depict prolonged confinement. Mullan offers an epilogue for each of these women, a device that has been criticized for a break with what some have seen—wrongly, as I argued—as the film's seam-less realism. What I presented as the film's dialectic between realism and anti-realist techniques provides a context for these epilogues to be under-stood not as a cheap wrap-up to the stories, but as a way for the film to pay homage to the fact that women who survived the laundries did so primarily only in body. Each epilogue explains that the trauma of the laundry contin-ued to haunt its victims, shaping their lives in profoundly disruptive ways. The text appears over an image of the character that emphasizes a contin-ued incarceration that is both psychological and physical. The fogged rear window of a bus separates Rose from the other characters and from the spectator; Bernadette is framed by a heavy stone tunnel; and Margaret is shot through a shop window as she gazes at a washing machine and a box of Persil—a reminder of the violent convergence of the traumatic and the everyday that was crucial to breaking the Magdalene women as well as the political prisoners in Northern Ireland (fig. 10).

Each of these closing shots ends in a freeze-frame, a formal device that works as a visual refusal to move on. The freeze-frame in this con-text mimics the dynamics of trauma, which arrests its victims and holds them hostage to the past. This stylistic element also suggests that the issue of women's incarceration in Magdalene laundries is, even eight years after the film's release, still unresolved.[14] Margaret, Rose, and Bernadette escape the laundry, but Mullan leaves them suspended in 1968; they are forever trapped in the decade that saw their incarceration.

14. The importance that public acknowledgment of wrongdoing can have for releas-ing people from historical trauma became apparent when the Saville Inquiry report was read at Derry's Guildhall on June 15, 2010. Currently, the group Justice for Magdalenes is working toward securing apologies and redress from the state and the Church. Although the McAleese Report is a step in the right direction, it is worth noting that the United Nations Committee against Torture has criticized the report for a lack of independence and not investigating complaints of abuse thoroughly enough (McCormaic 2013). Justice for Magdalenes (JFM): http://www.magdalenelaundries.com/. Smith continues to work with JFM. His book is admirable as an outstanding example of how scholarship can also be a form of activism. Although I have disagreed in places with his criticism of Mullan's film from a cinema studies perspective, I also think his argument about *The Magdalene Sisters* in relation to social action and justice is a valid one.

10. Margaret looks through a window at a commercial washer. From *The Magdalene Sisters* (directed by Peter Mullan, produced by Frances Higson, 2002). Courtesy of Frances Higson.

Margaret, Rose, and Bernadette are freed in body, but the final image of *The Magdalene Sisters* is a shot of Crispina, who was removed from the laundry into an insane asylum for publicly confronting Father Fitzroy for sexually abusing her. In the scene where she reveals the priest's crime, Crispina stands in a field at an outdoor Mass that the penitents attend as a way of showing off the good works of the laundry. The poison ivy that Margaret placed in the dryer with his vestments begins to act on the priest's body, and Father Fitzroy eventually strips naked and runs toward the woods, his white, flabby body covered in angry red blotches. However, this slapstick moment is followed immediately by the chilling revelation of the same blotches on the inside of Crispina's thighs. Panicked and confused, she begs Sister Bridget for help. When the nun tells her to calm down, she turns in the direction of the priest and begins firing her verdict over his conduct, "You're not a man of God!" which she exclaims twenty-four times. Although Mullan breaks the sequence into multiple shots, the repetition of this line becomes the sound equivalent of a long take; the scene is appropriately arduous as the film stops all forward momentum in order to focus on Crispina's anguish and rage. In the next scene, Crispina is taken away in the middle of the night and never seen again until the end of the film. In the final shot, she is now ragged and gaunt from her incarceration in the madhouse. Filmed through the observation window of her cell door, Crispina mutters incoherently to herself and probes the inside of her mouth in an attempt to gag herself, a gesture that enables her to end her life without overtly committing the mortal sin of suicide, but that is also a traumatized reenactment of the oral rape she experienced by the laundry's priest—her body's final attempt to speak of the abuse without vocally breaking silence. The epilogue explains that she died from anorexia in 1971.

That Mullan chooses starvation as Crispina's fate raises questions about the political and metaphoric role of hunger in Irish culture and about who even has access to the political power that comes from public images of suffering. The Blanketmen had at their disposal a rich iconography from which to poach, finding a way to give meaning to their pain that cloaked their commitment to armed struggle in the mantle of passive suffering. The Blanketmen concocted the appearance of a penitent form of nationalism, one that evaded the moral issue of violence. Hunger strike films capitalize on the symbolic potential of such images, using the fusion of Christ and the militant republican to explore the dynamics of national martyrdom. *Silent Grace* also constructs a similar visual language for women nationalists. But such allegorical expression is neither possible nor appropriate in *The Magdalene Sisters*. One of the great strengths of Mullan's film is that it foregrounds the ways in which the "penitents" were valuable only as national refuse, while also refusing to reiterate that symbolic figuring. Mullan's characters are utterly excluded from any circuit of affirmative national value. Their national worthlessness is evident in the fact that of the two Marys central to Christ's life, the laundries were named after the childless repentant whore, despite the fact that many of the women inside were themselves mothers. Even in their names, the Magdalene laundries denied Irish women who broke family laws any participation in the nation. Thus, while *The Magdalene Sisters* avoids a direct engagement with the culpability of the Irish state, it does raise questions about the ways that postcolonial Irish nationalism facilitated acceptance and support of the laundries. In so doing, *The Magdalene Sisters* suggests that even if the Church no longer functions as an occupying power, without a significant change in how family, gender, and sexuality are constructed in relation to the nation and nationalism, Ireland will remain unfree.[15]

15. This is the caution that Mullan's film offers, and it has relevance to nationalisms beyond Ireland and timeframes beyond the film's setting. That is not to suggest that Ireland today is somehow more patriarchal and restrictive than, say, the United States or Britain, or that its history of gender oppression is more horrific than in other countries. The states of emergency addressed in relation to Ireland have, in my opinion, significant relevance beyond their immediate national context.

Conclusion

MAYA DERRINGTON'S DOCUMENTARY *Pyjama Girls* (2010) follows the lives of two Irish teenagers, Lauren and Tara, who, like their
peers, choose to wear pajamas as ordinary daytime clothing. The girls
live in a public housing estate in Ballyfermot, an "inner-city" suburb
of Dublin, and the film portrays their friendship as a vital support system amid the addiction, abuse, unemployment, and high dropout rates
that surround them. Throughout Derrington's film, Lauren and Tara
are framed in close and enclosed spaces—in sparsely furnished rooms,
dimly lit stucco stairwells, fenced-in playgrounds, and courtyards surrounded by utilitarian brick buildings—so that Ballyfermot acquires a
sense of the carceral. The exceptional status of the pyjama girls becomes
explicit when Derrington includes audio excerpts from a Dublin radio
call-in show. The callers weigh in on what they see as the "disgraceful"
and menacing spectacle of unemployed, truant, working-class teen girls
dressed in bright cotton pajamas. As Donald Clarke explains in his review
of the film, during the couple of years prior to the release of *Pyjama Girls*,
"the wearing of pyjamas outside the house [became], for too many main-
stream media outlets, . . . synonymous with social exclusion and loss of
self-respect. To listen to the middle-class gripers on the radio, you'd think
the donning of terry cotton nightwear is akin to horse theft or benefit
fraud" (Clarke 2010). Clarke applauds Derrington's choice to portray two
brash, funny, and very human girls rather than offer a grim analysis of
alienated working-class youth.

Derrington's primary concern is with the relationships among working-class girls and women, but that project is accompanied by an analysis
of economic and social exclusion. The bond Tara and Lauren share with

each other as well as with Lauren's grandmother and sister prevents the film from taking a sensationalist, patronizing, or otherwise exploitative tone, but the amount of empty time the girls have to wander through the neighborhood, smoke in stairwells, browse pajama stores, and simply hang out underscores their marginalization. Furthermore, the mere fact that they are wearing pajamas suggests their detachment from school or work, two spaces that have at least minimal dress codes. In *Pyjama Girls*, Ballyfermot becomes another of Ireland's spaces of the exception. The film imparts a sense of Ballyfermot's enclosure and its geographical location away from Dublin's city center. In doing so, *Pyjama Girls* suggests that what really incenses middle-class radio-show callers is the way that pajamas function as a gendered sign of the persistence of poverty in Celtic Tiger Ireland. The pajama phenomenon is a style choice among working-class *girls* and thus could also signify a refusal to conform to cultural standards of femininity as well as expectations that urban poverty and unemployment remain invisible. Standing in stark contrast to popular representations of a wealthy and cosmopolitan Ireland, *Pyjama Girls* resists nationalist amnesia by representing contemporary, non-fictional girls whose economic exclusion is accompanied by a space built specifically to deal with people displaced by urban development projects that eradicated slums but also relocated to the city's outskirts low-income families that had lived in its center for generations.

I mention *Pyjama Girls* en route to a conclusion because it is consistent with the films I have addressed in the preceding chapters in its willingness to confront questions of exceptionality in relation to gender and in its resistance to dominant cultural narratives of forward national progress out of the prison house of Irish history. In these narratives, Ireland's emergence as a modern nation is dependent on a divorce from the past, an embrace of the Euro, and a new European identity. However, the celebration of Ireland's cosmopolitanism and modernity is not the opposite of nationalism, it is merely a mutated form of nationalism, one tailored to accommodate globalization. As a result, narratives of progress away from the specter of Irish history actually help to fuel nationalist amnesia. While life in Ireland on both sides of the border is clearly better for most citizens than it was even a generation ago, the positive changes that have resulted from the Good Friday Agreement in the North and legislative and economic developments grouped together as Celtic Tiger Ireland in the Republic have not permanently eradicated the structures of exclusion that pre-dated their arrival.

Spaces of confinement have provided a valuable framework for thinking through questions of gender, history, and the state of emergency because carceral institutions tend to endure despite changes in government. The prison persists even past the moment of national liberation, and it becomes a necessary institution in the project of regulating the national image. Furthermore, incarceration reveals the state's own role in the construction and maintenance of gender norms. Run by the state, or by private or religious bodies with the government's blessing, prisons segregate prisoners by sex and develop divergent forms of control based on how men and women are expected to behave, thus also assuming an essential link between sex and gender. This conflict takes place on the prisoner's body. The excessive strip searching of women prisoners in Armagh and Maghaberry and the derisive comments guards made about the women's bodies was humiliating precisely because of cultural codes around female modesty and shame about the body. In the H-Blocks, focus on the prisoner's anus as a site of investigation and invasion achieved a similar effect because of cultural taboos against the orifice and the heteronormative notion that male bodies penetrate; they are not penetrated. The fact that Magdalene laundries functioned as an auxiliary prison system suggests an assumption on the part of the state that the female body needed a degree of moral reform and control that secular institutions could not provide. This reasoning is again reinforced by the idealization of motherhood by Irish anti- and postcolonial nationalism as well as legislation in the postcolonial republic.

Throughout the preceding chapters, I have been rethinking the categories of incarceration and occupation in order to complicate Ireland's apparent binary structures and analyze the role of visual representation in advancing and critiquing nationalism's amnesiac and nostalgic histories. Such polarizations include an image of the North as mired in an atavistic Irish nationalism, while the South becomes increasingly European; a construction in troubles films of politics as masculine and destructive and the domestic realm as feminine and creative; and the installation of a clear border between past and future. I have also tried to trouble the borders around the category of "political film," questioning cinema's part in revealing, critiquing, or relegating to the past a given state of emergency, and doing so by studying film's role in visualizing genders. Gender, like incarceration, remains an integral part of how the nation and state imagine and regulate normative Irish identities, thus opening up new avenues to see films that address gendered histories as political cinema regardless of their investment in formal and narrative experimentation. All of the films in this book engage with Irish history and therefore risk imposing a border between past and present, sealing off histories that remain unresolved. While some of them do shut down historical debate in the end, given the audio-visual and narrative complexity of any movie, the question remains as to whether a film's ending is truly enough to restore a comforting sense of normalcy and corral dissenting bodies back into their cells.

Ultimately, I would like to end on an optimistic note, not about Ireland's future as a nation, but about the place of "Irish-themed films"[1] in a history of political filmmaking. This book has (I hope) revealed the extent to which Irish filmmakers are willing to interrogate the sanctity of Irish nationalism and confront the brutalities of Irish history. Alongside the familiar cinematic images of rolling green hills, feisty colleens, morose gunmen, and weeping mothers is another history of films set in Ireland, one that deserves wide recognition and integration into global political film studies. This history is the one I have focused on, and like the best of Irish culture, it concerns itself with the dispossessed, the forgotten, and the excluded. This cinema challenges orthodoxies with wit and innovation, and it opens up a space for a multiplicity of Irish faces, voices, and identities. It speaks eloquently about historical injustice, and by guarding against both colonialist and nationalist amnesia and nostalgia, it provides a blueprint for future Irish political film as Ireland and its cinema continue to transform.

1. The phrase is Michael Patrick Gillespie's (Gillespie 2008).

References

Filmography

Index

References

Adams, Gerry. 1996. *Before the Dawn*. London: Heineman Press.

Agamben, Giorgio. 1998. *Homo Sacer: Sovereign Power and Bare Life*. Translated by Daniel Heller-Roazen. Stanford: Stanford University Press.

Amireh, Amal. 2003. "Between Complicity and Subversion: Body Politics in Palestinian National Narratives." *South Atlantic Quarterly* 102, no. 4: 747–72.

An Phoblacht [Republican News], April 5, 1977.

Aretxaga, Begoña. 1997. *Shattering Silence: Women, Nationalism, and Political Subjectivity in Northern Ireland*. Princeton: Princeton University Press.

Barton, Ruth. 2004. *Irish National Cinema*. London: Routledge.

Benjamin, Walter. 1969. *Illuminations*. Translated by Harry Zohn. Edited by Hannah Arendt. New York: Schoken Books.

Berresford, David. 1989. *Ten Men Dead: The Story of the 1981 Hunger Strike*. New York: Atlantic Monthly Press.

Berlant, Lauren. 1997. *The Queen of America Goes to Washington City: Essays on Sex and Citizenship*. Durham: Duke University Press.

Bunreacht na hÉireann [The Irish Constitution]. 1937. http://www.taoiseach.gov .ie/upload/static/256.htm.

Cahill, Sean. 1995. "Occupied Ireland: Amid Hope of Peace Repression Continues." *Radical America* 25, 51–56.

Campbell, Brian, Lawrence McKeown, and Felim O'Hagan, eds. 1998. *Nor Meekly Serve My Time: The H-Block Struggle, 1976–1981*. Belfast: Beyond the Pale Publications.

Certeau, Michel de. 1984. *The Practice of Everyday Life*. Translated by Steven Rendall. Berkeley and Los Angeles: University of California Press.

Chanan, Michael. 2007. "Outsiders: *The Battle of Algiers* and Political Cinema." *Sight and Sound* 17, no. 6: 38–40.

Chaw, Walter. 2003. "Interview with Peter Mullan." *Film Freak Central*, http://www.filmfreakcentral.net/notes/pmullaninterview.htm.

Clarke, Donald. 2010. "So, What Are Pyjama Girls Really Like?" *Irish Times*, August 14, http://www.irishtimes.com/newspaper/weekend/2010/0814/1224 276780461.html.

Cleary, Joe. 2000. "Modernization and Aesthetic Ideology in Contemporary Irish Culture." In *Writing in the Irish Republic, 1949–1999*, edited by Ray Ryan, 105–29. London: Macmillan.

———. 2002. *Literature, Partition, and the Nation-State: Culture and Conflict in Ireland, Israel, and Palestine*. Cambridge: Cambridge University Press.

Clover, Carol J. 1992. *Men, Women, and Chain Saws: Gender in the Modern Horror Film*. Princeton: Princeton University Press.

Coleman, Karen. 2009. "Interview with Maureen O'Sullivan." *The Wide Angle*, Newstalk Radio, Ireland, July 12, http://www.youtube.com/user/Karen ColemanIE#p/u/42/Gbe4HqgGfB8.

Conrad, Kathryn. 2004. *Locked in the Family Cell: Gender, Sexuality, and Political Agency in Irish National Discourse*. Madison: University of Wisconsin Press.

Coogan, Tim Pat. 1980. *On the Blanket: The H-Block Story*. Dublin: Ward River Press.

Cormac. 1982. "Irish Joke." Cartoon printed in untitled pamphlet published by Manchester Women and Ireland Group. Northern Ireland Political Collection, Linen Hall Library, Belfast.

D'Arcy, Margaretta. 1981. *Tell Them Everything*. London: Pluto Press.

Davies, Lyell. 2001. "Republican Murals, Identity, and Communication in Northern Ireland." *Public Culture* 13, no. 1: 155–58.

de Lauretis, Teresa. 1985. "Aesthetic and Feminist Theory: Rethinking Women's Cinema." *New German Critique*, no. 34 (Winter): 154–75.

Diawara, Manthia. 2006. "Power and Territory: The Emergence of Black British Film Collectives." In *Fires Were Started: British Cinema and Thatcherism*, edited by Lester D. Friedman, 125–35. London: Wallflower Press (revised and updated edition).

Douglas, Mary. 1966. *Purity and Danger: An Analysis of the Concepts of Pollution and Taboo*. New York: Routledge, 1995.

Edkins, Jenny. 2009. "Sovereign Power, Zones of Indistinction, and the Camp." *Alternatives* 25, no. 1: 3–25.

Ellmann, Maud. 1993. *The Hunger Artists: Starving, Writing, and Imprisonment*. Cambridge: Harvard University Press.

Enwezor, Okwui. 1999. "Haptic Visions: The Films of Steve McQueen." In *Steve McQueen*, ICA Exhibition Catalogue, 37–50. Manchester: Cornerhouse Publications.

Farley, Fidelma. 2000. *Anne Devlin*. Wiltshire: Flicks Books.

Feldman, Allen. 1991. *Formations of Violence: The Narrative of the Body and Political Terror in Northern Ireland*. Chicago: The University of Chicago Press.

Finnegan, Frances. 2004. *Do Penance or Perish: Magdalen Asylums in Ireland*. Oxford: Oxford University Press.

Fisher, Jean. 2002. "Intimations of the Real: On *Western Deep* and *Carib's Leap*." In *Steve McQueen: Carib's Leap/Western Deep*, catalogue for traveling exhibition, 117–25. Tielt, Belgium: Lannoo. Exhibited at Documenta XI (June 9–September 15, 2002), 117–25; Artangel, London (October 4–November 10, 2002); Museu de Arte Contemporânea de Porto, Portugal (January 25–April 13, 2003); Mead Gallery, Warwick Arts Centre, Ireland (April 25–May 26, 2003); and Fundació Antoni Tàpies, Barcelona (December 5, 2003–February 16, 2004).

Fitzsimons, Lily. n.d. *Does Anybody Care?: A Personal Journal, 1976–81*. Belfast: Glandore Publishing.

———. 1996. *Women in Ireland: The Unsung Heroes of Conflict in Ireland's Six Northeast Counties*. Community-produced pamphlet, place of publication and publisher unknown.

Foucault, Michel. 1995. *Discipline and Punish: The Birth of the Prison*. Translated by Alan Sheridan. New York: Vintage Books.

———. 2000. *Power: The Essential Works of Foucault, Volume 3*. Translated by Robert Hurly. Edited by James D. Faubion. New York: The New Press.

Fox, Trisha. 1984. "Culture and the Struggle: An Interview with Pat Murphy and Rita Donagh." *IRIS Magazine*, June, 28–31.

Gal, Nissim. 2009. "Bare Life: The Refugee in Contemporary Israeli Art and Critical Discourse." *Art Journal* (Winter): 25–43.

George, Terry, and Jim Sheridan. 1996. *Some Mother's Son: The Screenplay*. New York: Grove Press.

Gibbons, Luke. 1988. "Romanticism, Realism, and Irish Cinema." In Gibbons, Rockett, and Hill, *Cinema and Ireland*, 194–257.

———. 1992. "On the Beach: Luke Gibbons on the Other Ireland." *ArtForum International*, October, 13.

———. 1996. *Transformations in Irish Culture*. Notre Dame: University of Notre Dame Press.

Gibbons, Luke, Kevin Rockett, and John Hill. 1988. *Cinema and Ireland*. Syracuse: Syracuse University Press.

Gillespie, Michael Patrick. 2008. *The Myth of an Irish Cinema: Approaching Irish-Themed Films*. Syracuse: Syracuse University Press.

Gogan, Johnny. 1988–1989a. "The Banning of Mother Ireland." *Film Base News*, December–January, 10.

———. 1988–1989b. "The Legislation." *Film Base News*, December–January, 11.

Gregory, Derek. 2004. *The Colonial Present*. Malden, MA: Blackwell.

———, and Allen Pred, eds. 2007. *Violent Geographies: Fear, Terror, and Political Violence*. New York: Routledge, 2007.

Grosz, Elizabeth. 1994. *Volatile Bodies: Toward a Corporeal Feminism*. Bloomington: Indiana University Press.

Guneratne, Anthony, and Wimal Dissanayake. 2003. *Rethinking Third Cinema*. London: Routledge.

Harris, Helen, and Eileen Healy, eds. 2001. *Strong about It All: Rural and Urban Women's Experiences of the Security Forces in Northern Ireland*. Derry: North West Women's/Human Rights Project Publications.

Hill, John. 1988. "Images of Violence." In Gibbons, Rockett, and Hill, *Cinema and Ireland*, 147–93.

———. 1997. "*Some Mother's Son* Review," *Cineaste* 23, no. 1: 44–45.

———. 2006. *Cinema and Northern Ireland: Film, Culture, and Politics*. London: BFI.

Holledge, Julie, and Joanne Tompkins. 2000. *Women's Intercultural Performance*. New York: Routledge.

Inglis, Tom. 1998. *Moral Monopoly: The Rise and Fall of the Catholic Church in Modern Ireland*. Dublin: University College Dublin Press.

Inter-Departmental Committee to Establish the Facts of State Involvement with the Magdalen Laundries. 2013. Report, Department of Justice and Equality, Republic of Ireland, http://www.justice.ie/en/JELR/Pages/MagdalenRpt 2013.

Johnston, Claire. 1981a. "*Maeve*," *Screen* 22, no. 4: 54–63.

———. 1981b. "Interview with Pat Murphy." *Screen* 22, no. 4: 63–71.

Kearns, Gerry. 2007. "Bare Life, Political Violence, and the Territorial Structure of Britain and Ireland." In Gregory and Pred, *Violent Geographies*, 7–35.

Kelly, Seán. 2005. "This Is Serious: Reflecting on John Byrne's Exhibition at the Fenton Gallery in Cork, June 2005." *Circa Art Magazine*, http://www.recirca.com/reviews/2006/johnbyrne/jb.shtml.

Kiberd, Declan. 1995. *Inventing Ireland: The Literature of the Modern Nation.* Cambridge: Harvard University Press.

Kristeva, Julia. 1982. *Powers of Horror: An Essay on Abjection.* Translated by Leon S. Roudiez. New York: Columbia University Press.

Lehman, Peter. 1993. *Running Scared: Masculinity and the Representation of the Male Body.* Philadelphia: Temple University Press.

Lloyd, David. 1993. *Anomalous States: Irish Writing and the Post-Colonial Moment.* Durham: Duke University Press.

———. 1999. *Ireland after History.* Cork: Cork University Press.

Lyons, Laura E. 1996. "Feminist Articulations of the Nation: The 'Dirty' Women of Armagh and the Discourse of Mother Ireland." In *Genders 24: On Your Left—Historical Materialism in the 1990s,* edited by Ann Kibbey, 110–49. New York: New York University Press.

Mac Giolla Léith, Caoimhín. 2008. "Flesh Becomes Words." *Frieze* 117, http://www.frieze.com/issue/article/flesh_becomes_words.

Maloney, ed. 1978. "Inside H Block." *Magill*, December, 24–25.

Mansour, Camille. 2001. "Israel's Colonial Impasse." *Journal of Palestine Studies* 30, no. 4: 83–87.

McAuley, Chrissie. 1989. *Women in a War Zone: Twenty Years of Resistance.* Dublin: Republican News Print, 1989.

McCafferty, Nell. 1981. *The Armagh Women.* Dublin: Co-op Books.

———. 1984. *The Best of Nell: A Selection of Writings over Fourteen Years.* Dublin: Attic Press.

———. 1985. *A Woman to Blame: The Kerry Babies Case.* Dublin: Attic Press.

McClintock, Anne. 1995. *Imperial Leather: Race, Gender, and Sexuality in the Colonial Contest.* New York: Routledge.

McCormaic, Ruadhan. 2013. "UN Watchdog Criticises Magdalene Report for Lack of Independence." *Irish Times,* June 3, accessed October 2013, http://www.irishtimes.com/news/un-watchdog-criticises-magdalene-report-for-lack-of-independence-1.1415043.

McGarry, Patsy. 2002. "Revisiting the Nightmare." *Irish Times,* October 5, http://web.lexis-nexis.com/universe.

McIlroy, Brian. 2001. *Shooting to Kill: Filmmaking and the "Troubles" in Northern Ireland.* Richmond, British Columbia: Steveston Press.

McKeown, Lawrence. 2001. *Out of Time: Irish Republican Prisoners, Long Kesh, 1972–2000*. Belfast: Beyond the Pale Publications.

McKibben, Sarah. 2010. *Endangered Masculinities in Irish Poetry: 1540–1780*. Dublin: University College Dublin Press.

McLoone, Martin. 2000. *Irish Film: The Emergence of a Contemporary Cinema*. London: British Film Institute.

Murphy, Patsy. 1990. "Hush-A-Bye Baby." *Filmbase News*, 8–10.

Murray, Jonathan. 2004. "Convents or Cowboys?: Millennial Scottish and Irish Film Industries and Imaginaries in *The Magdalene Sisters*." In Rockett and Hill, *National Cinema and Beyond*.

Murray, Raymond. 1998. *Hard Time: Armagh Gaol, 1971–1986*. Dublin: Mercier Press.

Naficy, Hamid. 2001. *An Accented Cinema: Exile and Diasporic Filmmaking*. Princeton: Princeton University Press.

Neale, Steve. 1993. "Masculinity as Spectacle." In *Screening the Male: Exploring Masculinities in Hollywood Cinema*, edited by Steven Cohan and Ina Rae Clark, 9–22. New York: Routledge.

Neti, Leila. 2003. "Blood and Dirt: Politics of Women's Protest in Armagh Prison, Northern Ireland." In *Violence and the Body: Race, Gender, and the State*, edited by Arturo Aldama, 77–93. Bloomington: Indiana University Press.

O'Leary, Deirdre. 2004. "Marketing the North in John Byrne's 'The Border Itself,'" *Irish Studies Review* 12, no. 2.

O'Malley, Padraig. 1990. *Biting at the Grave: The Irish Hunger Strikes and the Politics of Despair*. Boston: Beacon Press.

O'Toole, Fintan. 2003. "The Sisters of No Mercy." *Observer*, February 16, http://film.guardian.co.uk/print/0,,4606672-3181,00.html.

Pettitt, Lance. 2000. *Screening Ireland: Film and Television Representation*. Manchester: Manchester University Press.

Pines, Jim, and Paul Willemen. 1994. *Questions of Third Cinema*. London: British Film Institute (reprint of 1989 edition).

Republican POWs. 1991. "Maghaberry Strip Search Sexual Assault." *An Glór Gafa* [The Captive Voice] 3, no. 4: 10.

Rockett, Kevin, and John Hill, eds. 2004. *National Cinema and Beyond*. Dublin: Four Courts Press.

Rolston, Bill. 1992. *Drawing Support: Murals in the North of Ireland*. Belfast: Beyond the Pale.

Sands, Bobby. 1997. *Writings from Prison*. Boulder: Roberts Rinehart Publishers.

Scarry, Elaine. 1985. *The Body in Pain: The Making and Unmaking of the World*. New York: Oxford University Press.

Shohat, Ella, and Robert Stam. 1994. *Unthinking Eurocentrism: Multiculturalism and the Media*. New York: Routledge, 1994.

Smith, James M. 2007. *Ireland's Magdalen Laundries and the Nation's Architecture of Containment*. Notre Dame: University of Notre Dame Press.

Smyth, Lisa. 2005. *Abortion and Nation: The Politics of Reproduction in Contemporary Ireland*. Burlington, VT: Ashgate Publishing.

Stam, Robert. 2000. *Film Theory: An Introduction*. Oxford: Blackwell Publishers.

Stam, Robert, and Toby Miller, eds. 1999. *A Companion to Film Theory*. Oxford: Blackwell Publishers.

———. 2000. *Film and Theory: An Anthology*. Oxford: Blackwell Publishers.

Sullivan, Megan. 1999. *Women in Northern Ireland: Cultural Studies and Material Conditions*. Gainesville: University Press of Florida.

Wayne, Mike. 2001. *Political Film: The Dialectics of Third Cinema*. London: Pluto Press.

Willemen, Paul. 1994. *Looks and Frictions: Essays in Cultural Studies and Film Theory*. London: British Film Institute.

Williams, Alan, ed. 2002. *Film and Nationalism*. New Brunswick: Rutgers University Press.

Williams, Patrick, and Laura Chrisman, eds. 1994. *Colonial Discourse and Post-Colonial Theory: A Reader*. New York: Columbia University Press.

Women against Imperialism (WAI). 1980. *Women Protest for Political Status in Armagh Gaol: A Report*. Belfast: WAI. (Northern Ireland Political Collection, Linen Hall Library, Belfast.)

Filmography

After 68. Director, Stephen Burke, 1994.

Angel. Director, Neil Jordan, 1982.

Anne Devlin. Director, Pat Murphy, 1984.

Bloody Sunday. Director, Paul Greengrass, 2002.

The Bloody Sunday Murders. Directors, Margo Harkin and Eamonn McCann, 1992.

Bogwoman. Director, Tom Collins, 1997.

Breakfast on Pluto. Director, Neil Jordan, 2005.

Budawanny. Director, Bob Quinn, 1987.

The Butcher Boy. Director, Neil Jordan, 1998.

Cal. Director, Pat O'Connor, 1983.

Caoineadh Airt Uí Laoire [Lament for Art O'Leary]. Director, Bob Quinn, 1975.

Circle of Friends. Director, Pat O'Connor, 1995.

The Crying Game. Director, Neil Jordan, 1992.

December Bride. Director, Thaddeus O'Sullivan, 1991.

Down the Corner. Director, Joe Comerford, 1977.

81. Director, Stephen Burke, 1996.

Evelyn. Director, Bruce Beresford, 2002.

Four Days in July. Director, Mike Leigh, 1984.

High Boot Benny. Director, Joe Comerford, 1994.

H3. Director, Les Blair, 2001.

La hora de los hornos [Hour of the furnaces]. Directors, Fernando Solanas and Octavio Getino, 1968.

Hunger. Director, Steve McQueen, 2008.

Hush-a-Bye Baby. Director, Margo Harkin, 1989. Derry Film and Video Workshop.

In the Name of the Father. Director, Jim Sheridan, 1993.

Korea. Director, Cathal Black, 1995.

Maeve. Director, Pat Murphy, 1981.

The Magdalene Sisters. Director, Peter Mullan, 2002.

Michael Collins. Director, Neil Jordan, 1996.

Mother Ireland. Director, Anne Crilly, 1988. Derry Film and Video Workshop.

Nothing Personal. Director, Thaddeus O'Sullivan, 1996.

Odd Man Out. Director, Carol Reed, 1947.

Omagh. Director, Paul Greengrass, 2004.

Our Boys. Director, Cathal Black, 1981.

Picturing Derry. Director, Dave Fox, 1985.

Pigs. Director, Cathal Black, 1984.

The Playboys. Director, Gillies MacKinnon, 1992.

Poitín. Director, Bob Quinn, 1978.

Pyjama Girls. Director, Maya Derrington, 2010.

Reefer and the Model. Director, Joe Comerford, 1988.

Samt el qusur [The silences of the palace]. Director, Moufida Tlatli, 1994.

Sex in a Cold Climate. Director, Steve Humphries, 1998.

Silent Grace. Director, Maeve Murphy, 2001.

Sinners. Director, Aisling Walsh, 2002.

Some Mother's Son. Director, Terry George, 1996.

Sunday. Director, Jimmy MacGovern, 2002.

Traveller. Director, Joe Comerford, 1981.

Water. Director, Deepa Mehta, 2005.

Index